This book analyses key elements of leadership in Chinese culture with contemporary paradigms. It not only provides Chinese managers with a solid observation framework, but also inspires foreign managers to understand Chinese leadership in depth. In addition, the research results are supported by experiences of 391 expatriate senior managers in leading and managing Chinese employees, which are detailed, reliable and interesting.

Xianglin (Shirley) Ma
Cross-Cultural Management Expert,
Modern Management Center,
Shanghai, China

How employees are managed and led is a perennially important topic. This becomes even more so when leaders are from different nationalities to their 'followers'. That is the focus of this excellent and path-breaking book on cross-cultural leadership. For instance, it is based on the views of not only nearly 400 expatriate senior managers from a wide variety of countries and sectors in China, but also over 350 of their employees. It not only covers much of the relevant literature and theories, but is also practical as it concludes with 12 helpful and useful 'tips' for expats to manage and lead local employees, from the macro, such as understanding indigenous culture to the micro, such as training staff to work on their own. Some of these may well have application for expats in other locales.

Professor Chris Rowley
Kellogg College,
University of Oxford & Bayes Business School,
City, University of London,
London, UK

This insightful and well-researched book provides a welcome addition to the burgeoning literature on leadership across cultural frontiers. Grounded in a solid review of leadership theory, both generically and as it pertains to the social context in China, the author carefully explores the nature and effectiveness of business leadership both from the perspective of the leaders themselves and from those being led, i.e., their employees. This dyadic approach is then further enriched through discussions with expatriate leaders from a multitude of national culture contexts. The wealth of insights generated from their experiences is competently harnessed in the closing chapters which then delineate more practically how to successfully lead Chinese employees. Highly recommended.

Tim G. Andrews
Editor, Cross-cultural Management (Routledge Major Works)
Visiting Research Professor
Chiang Mai University Business School
Chiang Mai, Thailand

EXPATRIATE MANAGERS AND CROSS-CULTURAL LEADERSHIP IN CHINA

RESEARCH AND PRACTICE IN LEADING AND MANAGING CHINESE EMPLOYEES

World Scientific Series in Asian Business and Management Studies

Print ISSN: 2810-9201
Online ISSN: 2810-921X

Series Editor

Chris Rowley
Visiting Fellow, Kellogg College, University of Oxford, UK
Professor Emeritus, Cass Business School, City, University of London, UK
Visiting Fellow, Institute of Asia and Pacific Studies, Nottingham University, UK
Professorial Fellow, Institute of Hallyu Convergence Research,
    Korea University, Seoul, Korea
Adjunct Professor, Griffith Business School and Griffith Asia Institute,
    Griffith University, Australia
Email: C.Rowley@city.ac.uk

This Series covers the spectrum of Asian business and management topics and issues broadly in terms of how its forms and practices developed indigenously and are now conducted within and outside the region and how outsiders interact with them in Asia itself.

We cover all types and forms of organization, from small and medium sized enterprises to large firms and multinational companies in public and private sectors. We also encourage works to cover the context and integrate both theory and practice.

Published:

Vol. 2   *Expatriate Managers and Cross-Cultural Leadership in China:*
        Research and Practice in Leading and Managing Chinese Employees
        by Chin-Ju Tsai (Royal Holloway University of London, UK)

Vol. 1   *Changing Face of E-commerce in Asia*
        edited by Abhishek Behl (O P Jindal Global University, India), Pratima Sheorey
        (Symbiosis International University, India), Pankaj Dutta (Indian Institute of
        Technology, Bombay, India) and Chris Rowley (University of Oxford, UK)

Forthcoming

Sustainable Development in Asia: Policies, Practices and Strategies in Manufacturing and Service Industry
        Chris Rowley (City University of London, UK) and
        Sudhanshu Joshi (Doon University, India)

WORLD SCIENTIFIC SERIES IN ASIAN BUSINESS AND
MANAGEMENT STUDIES: VOL 2

EXPATRIATE MANAGERS AND CROSS-CULTURAL LEADERSHIP IN CHINA

RESEARCH AND PRACTICE IN LEADING AND MANAGING CHINESE EMPLOYEES

CHIN-JU TSAI

Royal Holloway University of London, UK

World Scientific

NEW JERSEY · LONDON · SINGAPORE · BEIJING · SHANGHAI · HONG KONG · TAIPEI · CHENNAI · TOKYO

Published by

World Scientific Publishing Co. Pte. Ltd.

5 Toh Tuck Link, Singapore 596224

USA office: 27 Warren Street, Suite 401-402, Hackensack, NJ 07601

UK office: 57 Shelton Street, Covent Garden, London WC2H 9HE

Library of Congress Control Number: 2023026016

British Library Cataloguing-in-Publication Data
A catalogue record for this book is available from the British Library.

World Scientific Series in Asian Business and Management Studies — Vol. 2
EXPATRIATE MANAGERS AND CROSS-CULTURAL LEADERSHIP IN CHINA
Research and Practice in Leading and Managing Chinese Employees

Copyright © 2024 by World Scientific Publishing Co. Pte. Ltd.

ISBN 978-981-127-878-5 (hardcover)
ISBN 978-981-127-879-2 (ebook for institutions)
ISBN 978-981-127-880-8 (ebook for individuals)

For any available supplementary material, please visit
https://www.worldscientific.com/worldscibooks/10.1142/13482#t=suppl

Desk Editors: Nambirajan Karuppiah/Nicole Ong

Typeset by Stallion Press
Email: enquiries@stallionpress.com

Printed in Singapore

This book is dedicated to Alexis for accompanying me in the research & write up journeys.

About the Author

**Chin-Ju Tsai**, MA, PhD, is Senior Lecturer (Associate Professor) of Human Resource Management at Royal Holloway, University of London. Prior to this, she had held a research position at Warwick Business School, University of Warwick, U.K., and a management position at Standard Chartered Bank, Taiwan. She holds a PhD in Management Studies from the University of Cambridge. She is a Member of the Academy of Management (AoM) and a Senior Fellow of the Higher Education Academy (SFHEA). Her research focusses on cross-cultural leadership, international human resource management, strategic human resource management, organizational performance, workplace emotion, human resource development, and employment relations in small and medium-sized enterprises (SMEs). Her work has appeared in top management journals including *Human Relations, Human Resource Management Journal, Work and Occupations, International Journal of Human Resource Management, Organization,* and *International Small Business Journal.* She was the winner of the 2017 Academy of Management (AoM) annual conference's Best Paper (HR Division) award, the 2015 International Academy of Management and Business (IAMB) conference's Best Overall Paper award, and the 2010 *International Small Business Journal*'s Best Overall Paper award.

Acknowledgments

I would like to thank the 391 expatriate senior managers who shared their views and experiences of leading and managing Chinese employees. Reading and analyzing their responses to the survey questions were both enjoyable and inspiring. Their dedication to their leadership roles to make their Chinese teams and business operations a success, their cultural learning and adjustment journeys, their dealing with the various challenges associated with leading and managing Chinese employees, their strategic considerations for leading them, and the sense of achievement and/or frustration they experienced in the process were vividly revealed in their words. I would also like to thank the Chinese employees who completed the survey and took part in the interviews. They provided valuable perspectives, experiences, assessments, and expectations in relation to the leadership exhibited by their expatriate supervisors.

The participation of the expatriate managers and Chinese employees in my research made it possible to produce this book to help both academics and practitioners to understand cross-cultural leadership issues, particularly in the context of China and of anywhere business leaders face high degrees of novelty in terms of cultural values and the attitudes, behaviors, and expectations of local employees. This book could not have been written without their inputs.

Contents

Part I

Cross-Cultural Business Leadership

Chapter 1

Introduction

As the second largest economy in the world, China is a strategic destination for the international business ventures of many multinational corporations (MNCs). For example, Shanghai, China's largest city, is home to around 857 MNC regional headquarters and 516 research and development (R&D) centers (*SHINE News*, 2022). A large number of expatriates are currently working in China. According to the most recent Chinese National Census, held in 2020, a total of 845,697 foreigners were living in mainland China, with at least 500,000 expats working in cities throughout the country (*China Daily*, 2021; National Bureau of Statistics of China, 2022). Many of them are assigned by their companies to lead and manage their operations in China, where expatriate managers need to work with local employees who hold rather different cultural values, norms, and beliefs from their own and from those held by the employees in their home country and/or other countries in which they have worked. For many expatriate managers, cross-cultural management can be challenging, as their own management and leadership approaches may not always be compatible with local cultures and practices. This makes understanding Chinese culture and practices and employee workplace behaviors and expectations an important item on the agenda of MNCs and expatriate managers in order to effectively lead and manage Chinese employees.

This book covers various aspects directly related to leading and managing Chinese employees. From it, readers will learn the following:

(1) concepts and theories related to cross-cultural leadership;
(2) the traditional and contemporary business leadership in China;

(3) how Chinese cultural values shape the work attitudes and behaviors of Chinese employees;
(4) the leadership behaviors expected by Chinese employees and how these are associated with their satisfaction;
(5) the experiences of 391 expatriate senior managers in leading and managing Chinese employees;
(6) the challenges faced by expatriate senior managers in managing their Chinese employees;
(7) expatriate senior managers' degrees and patterns of cross-cultural leadership adjustment; and
(8) the sample expatriate senior managers' suggestions for effectively leading and managing Chinese employees.

The insights presented in this book were derived from my research conducted on 391 expatriate senior managers and over 350 Chinese employees. The research project had multiple objectives; it was aimed at uncovering the following:

(1) expatriate senior managers' views and experience in leading and managing Chinese subordinates;
(2) the challenges encountered by expatriate managers when leading/ managing Chinese employees and their suggestions for overcoming such challenges;
(3) the extent to which expatriate business leaders adjust their leadership behaviors when exercising cross-cultural leadership, how and why they adjust, and their patterns of adjustment; and
(4) what Chinese workers expect of their leaders and how their expectations are associated with their satisfaction.

In presenting my research findings in this book, I often use the exact words used by the sample expatriates to illustrate their views and experiences. I do so in the hope that this will (a) make the book interesting to read; (b) help readers understand and see for themselves the reasons why the sample expatriate leaders had held their particular views or perspectives, behaved in the way they did, and took particular approaches; (c) help readers understand the work values and behaviors of Chinese employees; and (d) enable readers to formulate their own interpretations, judgments, and people management strategies.

Many of the expatriates participating in the research said that they had found China to be a challenging place in which to lead. That was because they had found that their Chinese employees possessed an array of unique characteristics that differed substantially from those found in their home country and/or in the other countries in which they had worked. For example, they observed that their Chinese employees exhibited the following characteristics: they tended not to speak up, particularly in meetings; they preferred to receive instructions from supervisors, rather than take initiatives; they assigned great importance to saving "face"; and they valued financial rewards much more than non-financial ones. Many of the participating expatriates stated that such characteristics caused unmodified Western leadership approaches to rarely work in China and that they thus had needed to adjust their own.

This book is among the first to address cross-cultural business leadership in the Chinese context from the perspectives of "expatriate" senior managers and Chinese employees. Most other books on leadership in China are based on interviews conducted with "Chinese" business leaders, whose experiences, approaches, and wisdom are invaluable; however, I believe that those of expatriate senior managers, as presented in this book, can be even more useful for MNCs and expatriate managers, as research has shown that the expectations and attitudes held by Chinese employees toward expatriate managers differ from those they hold toward local ones (Templer, 2010; Varma *et al.*, 2011). Thus, expatriate managers would need to take leadership approaches that differ from those of their Chinese counterparts.

This book is written for three groups of readers: (1) expatriate business managers who are currently working or planning to work in China; (2) management consultants who want to gain empirical insights into cross-cultural leadership in China; and (3) researchers who want to learn about the cross-cultural management issues found in Chinese workplaces. I hope that expatriate managers will find this book useful to (a) understand how to respond to the work attitudes and behaviors of Chinese employees, behave in socially acceptable ways, and avoid misunderstandings; and (b) make sense of their own and other leaders' approaches, and come up with even more effective ways to lead/manage Chinese employees. I also hope that the other two groups of readers will find this book to be a good reference guide for the issues related to cross-cultural leadership and leadership behavior adjustment.

Readers should note that the research findings presented in this book may run the risk of being generalized. But generalization, which is usually established on most observed phenomena, is necessary to understand the overall sphere of Chinese cultural characteristics, leadership, management practices, and employee expectations. Readers should be aware of this general sphere as well as of the likelihood of exceptions to it, as there are always situations that deviate from the generally observed ones.

The remainder of this book is structured as follows:

Chapter 2 provides a review of the literature linked to three leadership theories and of the research findings related to cross-cultural leadership, and presents a discussion of the concepts and research findings related to cross-cultural leadership adjustment and to the fit/match between the leadership behaviors expected by followers and those actually demonstrated by leaders.

Chapter 3 provides an explanation of how I conducted my research and how I collected and analyzed the data.

Chapter 4 presents an explanation of the four doctrines of Confucianism that are most relevant to Chinese leadership and of the three key Chinese cultural values that have deeply influenced the social relations and exchange rules in China and the work attitudes and behaviors of Chinese leaders and employees.

Chapter 5 provides a review of the literature on the traditional Chinese leadership approach and a discussion on whether it can be effective for modern businesses. It also presents a discussion of the four key leadership styles adopted in contemporary China: (1) paternalistic, (2) communal, (3) market, and (4) hybrid.

Chapter 6 presents my research findings on the views and experiences of 391 expatriate senior managers in relation to leading Chinese employees, including the challenges they faced.

Chapter 7 reports my research findings on the sample expatriate senior managers' degrees and patterns of adjustment and on the top 10 aspects in relation to which they had adjusted themselves and/or changed (or tried to change) their Chinese employees.

Chapter 8 presents the findings of prior research on the work aspects valued by Chinese workers and on the leadership attributes and behaviors they tend to expect. This chapter also reports the results of my analysis on the expectations held by Chinese employees in relation to the leadership behaviors exhibited by their expatriate supervisors and to how the fit between their expected and observed leadership behaviors was associated with their satisfaction levels.

Chapter 9 reports the key suggestions made by the 391 sample expatriate business leaders for effectively leading/managing Chinese employees.

Chapter 10 concludes this book by presenting the three key themes derived from the research findings reported in it and a discussion of their significance for leading and managing Chinese employees.

References

China Daily. (2021). *China embraces increasing foreign residents*, 12 May. Available from http://www.china.org.cn/china/2021-05/12/content_77489167. htm#:~:text=China%20has%20seen%20an%20increasing,250%2C000%20 from%20a%20decade%20ago (Accessed: 16 May 2022).

National Bureau of Statistics of China. (2022). Available from http://www.stats. gov.cn/english/ (Accessed: 16 May 2022).

SHINE News. (2022). *Shanghai a hotspot for foreign investment*, 8 August. Available from https://www.shine.cn/news/metro/2208088951/ (Accessed: 10 Nov. 2022).

Templer, K. J. (2010). Personal attributes of expatriate managers, subordinate ethnocentrism, and expatriate success: A host-country perspective. *The International Journal of Human Resource Management, 21*(10), 1754–1768.

Varma, A., Budhwar, P., & Pichler, S. (2011). Chinese host country nationals' willingness to help expatriates: The role of social categorization. *Thunderbird International Business Review, 53*(3), 353–364.

Chapter 2

Cross-Cultural Leadership: Concepts, Theories, and Research Findings

The term "leadership" has been defined in various ways, for example, as *the ability of an individual to influence, motivate, and enable others to contribute toward the effectiveness and success of the organizations of which they are members* (House *et al.*, 2002: 5), *the process of influencing activities of an organized group in its efforts toward goal setting and goal achievement* (Stogdill, 1950, cited in Bass & Stogdill, 1990: 13), and *the process of influencing others to understand and agree about what needs to be done and how it can be done effectively, and the process of facilitating individual and collective efforts to accomplish the shared objectives* (Yukl, 2013: 7). Despite the existence of these various definitions, a common theme of leadership pertains to the ability and process of influencing others to achieve certain goals.

Cross-cultural leadership is the ability and process of influencing and leading groups of people or organizations from different cultural or national backgrounds in order to achieve set objectives. In the globalized business world, effective cross-cultural leadership is more important than ever for multinational corporations, the success of which is largely determined by the adaptability of their leadership and by how effectively people are managed across borders (Yukl, 2019).

In this chapter, to help readers understand the concept of and research related to cross-cultural leadership, I first provide a brief review of three leadership theories and research findings related to it. I then discuss the concepts and research findings related to the fit/match between the leadership behaviors expected by followers and those demonstrated by leaders. Following this, I discuss the concepts and research related to cross-cultural leadership adjustment.

Leadership Theories and the Research Findings Related to Cross-Cultural Leadership

Over the past few decades, several leadership theories have been developed, including trait theories, style and behavioral theories, great man theories, situational and contingency theories, leader–member exchange theory, servant leadership theory, and transformational leadership theory. In this section, I provide a brief review of three theories and the research findings that are relevant to cross-cultural leadership: Situational Leadership Theories (SLTs), Implicit Leadership Theory (ILT), and Culturally Endorsed Implicit Theories of Leadership (CLTs).

Situational leadership theories (SLTs)

SLTs (e.g., Hersey and Blanchard's Situational Leadership Theory and House's Path–Goal Theory) have emerged in response to the shortcomings associated with trait and behavioral theories, which neglect the situational factors tied to leadership (Hollander & Offermann, 1990). SLTs propose that the qualities demanded of leaders depend on situations and may thus vary.

Hersey and Blanchard (1972, 1982) developed SLT by building on Reddin's (1967) 3D management style theory. The central proposition of their theory is that leaders should modify their leadership style according to the task-relevant maturity of their followers. It proposes that optimal leadership styles (defined as specific combinations of leader task and relationship behaviors) should match the levels of subordinate maturity (defined as combinations of follower commitment and competence). For example, in the presence of very low-level subordinate maturity, managers are advised to adopt a "telling" style; on the other hand, when dealing with very mature subordinates, a "delegating" style is recommended.

SLT is among the best-known leadership theories; it has been covered in many textbooks and used in leadership training programs. However, it has been criticized for being prescriptive and lacking empirical support (Graeff, 1983; Northouse, 2007; Thompson & Vecchio, 2009; Vecchio,

1987; Yukl, 2019). Although the validity of SLT is yet to be verified, its main contributions include highlighting the importance of flexibility in leadership behavior and considering the level of subordinate maturity as an important situational determinant of appropriate leader behavior (Graeff, 1983; Northouse, 2007).

Another well-known SLT is Path–Goal Theory. It was developed by Robert House (1971, 1996), who proposed that the effectiveness of leadership will be contingent on two main categories of factors: (1) task and environmental characteristics (e.g., task structure and the degree of ambiguity of task demands) and (2) the personal characteristics of subordinates (e.g., their levels of preference for independence and need for achievement). In other words, leader effectiveness is situational and determined by task, environmental, and subordinate characteristics.

A well-supported hypothesis drawn from Path–Goal Theory is that the influence of directive leadership behaviors on subordinate satisfaction will be inversely corresponding to the degree to which a task is structured (i.e., it will be positive when a task is unstructured and negative when it is highly structured) (see, e.g., House & Dessler, 1974; Jermier & Berkes, 1979; Wofford & Liska, 1993). The explanation given for this finding is that, in situations with low degrees of task structure, directive leadership behaviors help clarify any task ambiguity and thus increase subordinate satisfaction; on the other hand, in situations with high degrees of task structure, additional directive leadership behaviors are perceived as redundant and controlling. It is thus suggested that, to be effective, leaders need to provide and compensate for what is missing in a situation in order to enhance subordinate motivation, satisfaction, and performance.

In brief, SLTs state that leader effectiveness is situation-dependent and suggest that leaders need to adapt/change or take different approaches according to situational characteristics, such as task structure, task demands, and personal subordinate features (e.g., their maturity, levels of preference for independence, and need for achievement).

Implicit leadership theory (ILT)

ILT, which was proposed by Robert Lord and his colleagues (see, e.g., Lord & Alliger, 1985; Lord *et al.*, 1986; Lord & Maher, 1993), is seen as a cognitive basis suited to understand how employees interpret managerial behaviors (Poole *et al.*, 1989; Weick, 1995). It contends that, through socialization and past experiences with leaders, individuals develop and hold sets of beliefs—or implicit expectations and assumptions—regarding the traits, characteristics, skills, and behaviors that constitute either effective or ineffective leadership, and that such beliefs affect and guide individuals' attitudes and responses to and influence the extent to which they accept a leader (Lord *et al.*, 1978, 1984, 1986). In other words, individuals' expectations or conceptualizations of what makes the ideal leader influence the extent to which they accept, are willing to work with, and judge the effectiveness of a leader. For instance, individuals who believe a leader should be goal-oriented, intelligent, and inspiring will tend to respond favorably to leaders who possess those characteristics but will evaluate leaders less positively if they don't.

ILT suggests that it is important for leaders to be aware of their followers' implicit expectations and assumptions because these will affect the ways in which their followers will assess, react to, and interact with them. ILT also suggests that leadership adjustment is necessary because good matches between follower implicit expectations and leader characteristics can be conducive to high levels of subordinate satisfaction and performance, whereas any mismatches can lower such levels.

Empirical research has found that the degree of match between an individual's expectations of a leader and such a leader's actual behavior is positively associated with the follower–leader relationship and with the individual's reactions to and evaluation of the leader (Epitropaki & Martin, 2005; Lord *et al.*, 1984; Ehrhart, 2015; Nye and Forsyth, 1991). For example, Epitropaki and Martin (2005), who conducted a longitudinal study of a sample of 439 employees, found that the more closely employees perceive their actual managers' profiles to match their own beliefs about the ideal leader, the better the quality of the manager–employee exchanges.

Culturally endorsed implicit theories of leadership (CLTs)

While SLTs and ILT draw our attention to the importance of matching leadership behaviors to employee and task characteristics, the CLTs (House *et al.*, 2004) go a step further by including cross-cultural contexts and emphasizing the importance of followers' cultural expectations of leaders. CLTs were developed on the basis of ILT by Robert House and his colleagues, who proposed that beliefs about leadership are shared among individuals with a common cultural background and that expectations regarding the best way to lead vary by culture (see, e.g., House &

Aditya, 1997; House *et al.*, 2004; Javidan *et al.*, 2006). It has been asserted that those leaders who behave in ways that conform to their followers' cultural/social norms and expectations are more likely to be accepted by them, while those who deviate from such social norms and expectations are less so, thus giving rise to diminished respect and weaker effectiveness (House *et al.*, 2004; Yukl, 2013).

Evidence from the Global Leadership and Organizational Behavior Effectiveness (GLOBE) research program (House *et al.*, 2004), which examined leadership prototypes and leader effectiveness in 62 different cultures, showed that people from similar cultures tend to agree in their beliefs about leadership. For example, it was found that, in high power distance cultures—such as those of China, Taiwan, Mexico, and Venezuela—subordinates expect their leaders to wield greater authority and prefer paternalistic leadership styles that combine autocratic decisions with supportive behaviors (Adsit *et al.*, 1997; Dickson *et al.*, 2003; Dorfman, *et al.*, 1997; Bond, 1996; Li & Sun, 2015). In contrast, in low power distance cultures—such as those of Western Europe, New Zealand, and the United States—participative and charismatic/value-based leadership styles are viewed more favorably (Dorfman *et al.*, 2004; House *et al.*, 2004; Northouse, 2021). Thus, it is suggested that, in order to be effective and accepted by their host country employees, expatriate business leaders need to meet their cultural expectations in terms of the leadership behaviors they adopt. House *et al.* (2004) also suggested that the greater the cultural differences between expatriate managers and local employees, the greater the need for mutual adjustment.

To summarize, SLTs and ILT underscore the importance of matching leadership style with employee and task characteristics, and CLTs advocate the need for leadership to conform to follower cultural expectations. The theories reviewed above provide some important suggestions for expatriate business leaders, i.e., in order to achieve effective cross-border management and leadership, it is essential to be adaptable/flexible and to behave in ways that match employee and task characteristics and employees' cultural expectations of leaders. In other words, the theories posit the importance for leader effectiveness of the fit between leaders and followers and of leadership adjustment.

The following two sections respectively discuss (1) the importance of the fit/match between the leadership behaviors demonstrated by leaders and those expected by followers and (2) the concept of and research related to cross-cultural leadership behavior adjustment.

The Fit/Match between the Leadership Behaviors Expected by Followers and Those Demonstrated by Leaders

The theories reviewed above emphasize the importance of the fit between leaders and followers and of leadership adjustment. This section discusses the concepts and research findings related to the person–supervisor (PS) fit, while the next one presents the concepts and research related to cross-cultural leadership adjustment.

The PS fit is one of the five core types of person–environment (PE) fit—the other four being person–organization (PO), person–job (PJ), person–vocation (PV), and person–group (PG). The PE fit concept is based on the notion that people exhibit varying degrees of compatibility with different jobs, supervisors, organizations, vocations, etc., and that individuals and their work environments are compatible when their respective characteristics are well matched (Kristof-Brown *et al.*, 2005; Edwards & Billsberry, 2010). It is generally argued that a good fit or match between individuals and the various aspects of their work environments (e.g., jobs, supervisors, and/or organizations) can lead to positive work and/or employee outcomes; whereas a low degree of fit has a negative effect on employee outcomes.

PS fit addresses the compatibility between employees and their supervisors (Kristof-Brown *et al.*, 2005), which is considered to be a key determinant of the extent to which employees are satisfied with their supervisors and their jobs. A high degree of fit between the leadership behaviors expected by subordinates and those demonstrated by their supervisors is likely to lead to high degrees of supervisor and job satisfaction. The ways in which managers behave when carrying out their duties can significantly influence the degree of satisfaction employees feel toward both them and their jobs (Lord & Brown, 2001; Henderson *et al.*, 2008; Marstand *et al.*, 2017; Yukl, 2019). This is because managers' duties encompass various tasks (e.g., allocating resources, setting work targets, conducting performance appraisals, and authorizing raises and benefits) that can directly affect their employees' daily work experiences. Further, interacting with a supervisor who represents and is compatible with the traits and skills a subordinate expects in relation to a leadership position can lead to the fulfillment of a desired state (Wanous & Lawler, 1972; Meglino *et al.*, 1992) and can thus elicit feelings of satisfaction with both the supervisor and the job. The ILT reviewed above provides theoretical foundations for these arguments.

A substantial volume of research conducted on the topic has focused on PS fit in *values* (e.g., ethical values and/or social responsibility), *goals* (e.g., manager–employee goals), and *personalities* (e.g., proactive personalities), and found leader–follower fit/congruence affects various employee outcome variables (e.g., performance, commitment, and job satisfaction) (see, e.g., Brown & Treviño, 2009; Zhang *et al.*, 2012; Jordan *et al.*, 2013; Lee *et al.*, 2017; Audenaert *et al.*, 2018; Xu *et al.*, 2019). Only a small number of empirical studies has examined the fit/congruence between expected and observed "leadership behaviors" (see, e.g., Epitropaki & Martin, 2005; Subramaniam *et al.*, 2010; Lambert *et al.*, 2012) and found that the greater the agreement between the expected and observed leadership behaviors, the higher the employee outcomes in terms of—among other aspects—performance, commitment, and job satisfaction. For example, Epitropaki and Martin (2005), who conducted a longitudinal study of 439 British employees, found that the more closely employees perceive the actual profiles of their manager to match the one they expect, the better the quality of leader–member exchanges and employee organizational commitment, job satisfaction, and well-being. As a result of their survey of 137 Malaysian managers, Subramaniam *et al.* (2010) found that the smaller the gap between employee expectations and actual leader behaviors, the better the leader–member relationship quality. Other empirical research has found that any non-adapted and inappropriate leadership styles adopted by expatriates are associated with negative consequences, such as high employee turnover, low employee morale, high absenteeism, and even riots. These findings indicate the importance of adapting leadership behaviors to meet employee expectations.

The positive association between expected and observed leadership behaviors found by the small number of extant studies, however, has been mainly the result of research conducted in *mono-cultural* settings, with only limited research having examined such a relationship in *cross-cultural* ones. The question this raises is as follows: How is any (in)congruence in the expatriate leadership behaviors expected and observed by host country employees associated with their work-related attitudes? I addressed this research gap and investigated how the fit between the *leadership behaviors* expected and observed by Chinese employees is associated with their job and supervisor satisfaction. My statistical analysis shows that Chinese employee satisfaction with their expatriate managers is higher in the presence of high degrees of match between the leadership behaviors they expect of the latter and those demonstrated by them. The details of this research finding are reported in Chapter 8.

Leadership behaviors

Leadership behaviors pertain to the actions undertaken by managers in carrying out their roles, which can significantly influence employees' daily work experience, attitudes, and behaviors. Leadership research has mostly focused upon task- and relations-oriented leadership behaviors. The former, which are mainly aimed at the efficient improvement or accomplishment of tasks (Vroom & Jago, 2007; Yukl, 2013), include behaviors such as organizing and planning work activities, assigning tasks, setting priorities, and monitoring operations and performance to improve efficiency. Conversely, relations-oriented behaviors, which are mainly concerned with the establishment of mutual trust, cooperation, commitment, and job satisfaction (Stogdill, 1974; Yukl, 2013), include behaviors such as providing support and encouragement, showing trust and respect, consulting with subordinates, empowering people, and providing coaching and mentoring (Fleishman, 1953; Vroom & Jago, 2007).

Much of the early research conducted in the field of leadership, which examined the "direct" relationship between leadership behaviors and leader effectiveness (see, e.g., House, 1971; Zaccaro *et al.*, 1991; Yukl, 2019), supports the key proposition that leaders can influence individuals and groups by adopting the two types of behaviors reviewed above. The most commonly used leader effectiveness indicators are subordinate satisfaction, commitment, and performance (see, e.g., House, 1971, 1996; Bushra *et al.*, 2011). Survey research has shown that high task- and high relations-oriented leadership behaviors are associated with the highest degrees of subordinate satisfaction and performance (Fleishman & Simmons, 1970; Yukl, 2019); however, a number of exceptions to this association have also been found (Yukl, 2019). The results obtained through other research methods—such as critical incidents, experiments, and interviews—are more consistent and show that effective leaders engage in both task-oriented and relations-oriented behaviors, adopting certain types based on situational specificity (Yukl, 2013). In the light of these mixed results, SLTs were developed and various studies were conducted to examine the effects of situational variables (e.g., task characteristics, employee personal characteristics, and employee cultural expectations of a leader) on the relationship between leadership behaviors and leader effectiveness (see section "Situational Leadership Theories").

As mentioned above, I examined how the fit between expected and observed leadership behaviors is associated with employee job and supervisor satisfaction; this is a step further in the study of the direct relationship between leadership behavior and leader effectiveness and is consistent with the key argument proposed by situational theories. My research findings are reported in Chapter 8.

Cross-Cultural Leadership Behavior Adjustment

Can Western leadership approaches be applied in China without modification? Based on the leadership theories reviewed above, the answer is a clear "no". The findings of my research project show that most of the participating expatriate senior managers perceived the need for an adaptation or adjustment of leadership when working in China; only a small number of them expressed the belief that their leadership approaches could be used anywhere in the world (see Chapter 7 for the research findings).

This section first presents a discussion of two scholarly perspectives related to leadership across cultures and then the concepts and research related to leadership behavior adjustment in cross-cultural contexts. Following this, I explain how I developed four patterns of cross-cultural leadership behavior adjustment.

Leadership across cultures: Universalistic and cultural congruency perspectives

The universalistic and cultural congruency perspectives are the two main scholarly perspectives relating to leadership across cultures (Arvey *et al.*, 2015). The universalistic perspective argues that many leadership behaviors are universally effective and accepted. This view is based on the grounds that leaders face common issues and tasks wherever they are; for instance, they need to influence, motivate, and manage others to achieve organizational goals. As an example of this perspective, transformational leadership is strongly viewed as universally effective, i.e., it is argued to be effective irrespective of the cultures and nations within which leaders operate. The research conducted on this perspective, however, has yielded mixed findings. Some empirical studies have found that transformational leadership is more effective than transactional leadership in cultural contexts that include Canada, India, Japan, the Netherlands, Singapore, and the United States (Arvey *et al.*, 2015). Nevertheless, the emphasis placed by transformational leadership on encouraging subordinates to be independent and to use their initiative has been found to go against the prevalent norms of dependency and conformity of China's collectivist culture.

The second perspective, the cultural congruency view, which is mainly based on House *et al.*'s CLTs (reviewed above), proposes that cultural factors affect expectations of leadership, that effective and accepted leadership thus varies by culture, and that the behaviors related to such leadership are those that conform to cultural/social norms and expectations. Scholars who support this perspective thus argue that leadership is a culture-specific construct. For instance, the concept of *Guanxi* (see Chapter 4 for its meaning and functions) and a paternalistic leadership style, both typical of China, have been argued to be rarely found in the West. Conversely, empowerment and delegation, which are relatively common in the West, are rarely used by Chinese leaders. For Americans, leading means *finding a parade and getting in front of it* (Naisbitt,1982: 162, cited in Arvey *et al.*, 2015); in contrast, for Singaporeans, good leaders are those who get *behind* the group so as to watch over it and protect it from threats and failures (Menon *et al.*, 2010). The GLOBE Project found that societal leadership expectations strongly predict the leadership styles of the CEOs of companies in different countries and that the closer the match between societal expectations and CEO leadership behaviors, the stronger the performance of companies (Arvey *et al.*, 2015).

The cultural congruency perspective and the empirical findings discussed above suggest that, when working in unfamiliar cultural settings, expatriate business leaders need to adjust their leadership behaviors and behave in ways that are expected and accepted by local employees. The following section discusses the concepts and research related to cross-cultural leadership behavior adjustment.

Leadership behavior adjustment in cross-cultural contexts

Adjustment in a cross-cultural setting is commonly regarded as the process by which an individual achieves an *increased fit and reduced conflict between the environmental demands and the individual's behavioral and attitudinal inclinations* (Zimmermann & Sparrow, 2007: 66). In expatriate adjustment research, adjustment to cross-cultural settings refers to an acculturation process and is conceptualized as the degree of fit between the expatriate manager and the environment (Black *et al.*, 1991; Aycan, 1997).

In their theoretical paper, Festing and Maletzky (2011) defined cross-cultural leadership adjustment as *the process of synchronization of incompatible work-related interaction routines* (p. 186). They argued that, to be successful in foreign assignments, expatriate leaders need to find a way of bringing together the apparently incompatible routines (e.g., work patterns and leadership approaches) of expatriates and local employees in order to overcome any differences and guarantee effective collaboration. The focus here is on the fit between leadership approaches and follower characteristics, as leading and managing subordinates are central to the leadership role.

Consistent with Festing and Maletzky's (2011) argument and to provide a clearer definition of leadership behavior adjustment in cross-cultural contexts, in my study, the concept of cross-cultural leadership behavior adjustment refers to the process by which expatriate business leaders change their own leadership behaviors and/or those of their host country subordinates. This definition was developed based on Nicholson's (1984) theory of work role transitions (WRTs) which has been praised as an exemplary theoretical framework for explaining work roles and adjustment (Black *et al.*, 1991). Drawing on the WRTs' perspective, I also developed four patterns of cross-cultural leadership behavior adjustment, which can help in gaining a better understanding of the patterns by which expatriate business leaders adjust their leadership behaviors. In the following, I explain how those four patterns were developed.

Patterns of cross-cultural leadership behavior adjustment

WRTs theory proposes that, when individuals encounter role transitions (e.g., international transfers, job relocations, and new jobs), they are likely to demonstrate two dimensions of adjustment: personal development and role development (Nicholson, 1984). Personal development involves any "reactive" changes that see individuals adjusting their own attributes— such as their values, skills, attitudes, and behaviors—with the aim of meeting environmental requirements (Nicholson & West, 1988).

Role development, on the other hand, involves any "active" changes that involve individuals actively altering role requirements to better suit their needs, abilities, and identities (Nicholson, 1984); this may include changing task objectives, subordinates, work methods, and interpersonal relationships.

In applying the two dimensions to leadership behavior adjustment, I posited that, when working in unfamiliar cultural settings, expatriate business leaders are likely to demonstrate two dimensions of behavior adjustment: (1) leadership behavior change, by which they change their leadership behaviors in order to meet local conditions, and (2) subordinate behavior change, by which they change the behaviors of their host country subordinates in order to match their own personal requirements.

Combining these two dimensions of behavior adjustment and adapting the four modes of adjustment to transition proposed by Nicholson (1984), I developed four patterns of leadership behavior adjustment: determination, exploration, replication, and absorption. These patterns, which are summarized in the following (see also Figure 1), reflect the different degrees to which expatriate leaders change the two dimensions of (1) their leadership behaviors and/or (2) the behaviors of their subordinates. For example, those expatriate leaders who significantly change their own leadership behaviors but make little change to the behaviors of their subordinates show an *absorption* adjustment pattern.

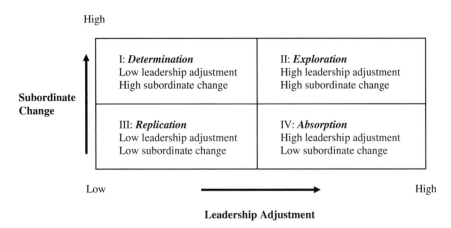

Figure 1. Patterns of cross-cultural leadership behavior adjustment, developed on the basis of Nicholson's (1984) theory of work role transitions.

***Determination* (quadrant I; low leadership adjustment, high subordinate change):** This pattern represents those adjustments whereby subordinate behaviors are altered while leadership ones are left almost unchanged. The leaders determine the behaviors that they believe should ideally be demonstrated by their subordinates and actively try to get the latter to conform to them while maintaining their own existing leadership behaviors in the new cultural setting. In other words, this pattern emerges when expatriate leaders actively change their subordinates' behaviors but make little change to their own leadership behaviors.

***Exploration* (quadrant II; high leadership adjustment, high subordinate change):** This pattern pertains to those adjustments that produce changes in both the leadership and subordinate behaviors. The leaders simultaneously make changes to their own leadership behaviors to meet local requirements and to the subordinates' behaviors to match their own requirements. In brief, this pattern transpires when expatriate leaders significantly change both their leadership behaviors and the behaviors of their subordinates.

***Replication* (quadrant III; low leadership adjustment, low subordinate change):** This pattern represents those adjustments that generate minimal changes to both the leaders' and subordinates' behaviors. The leaders make few adjustments to their own and their subordinates' behaviors—they perform in much the same manner they did in their previous leadership roles and leave their subordinates' behaviors almost undisturbed. In brief, this pattern occurs when expatriate leaders make few changes to their leadership behaviors and impose little change upon their subordinates' behaviors.

***Absorption* (quadrant IV; high leadership adjustment, low subordinate change):** This pattern represents those adjustments in which only leadership behaviors are changed while little is done to modify the subordinates' behaviors. Role learning is the central characteristic of this pattern, whereby leaders dedicate themselves to changing their own leadership behaviors in order to meet the requirements of their new cultural context. In brief, this pattern emerges when expatriate leaders significantly change their leadership behaviors but impose little change to their subordinates' behaviors.

These four patterns of adjustment provide a taxonomy of expatriate business leader behavior adjustment; they indicate not only the degree to which leaders change their own leadership behaviors but also the degree to which they change the behaviors of their local subordinates.

Although cross-cultural *leadership behavior* adjustment is viewed as essential to effectively manage foreign subsidiaries and to motivate host country employees (Ralston *et al.*, 1997; Hofstede, 2001; House *et al.*, 2004; Yukl, 2019), most research on expatriate adjustment has focused on exploring the factors that influence the degree to which expatriate managers adjust to the host countries along three dimensions: general, social interaction, and work/role (see, e.g., Shaffer *et al.*, 1999; Shay & Baack, 2004; Ravasi *et al.*, 2015; Davies *et al.*, 2019). No detailed account has been provided for *leadership behavior* adjustment, with only a very small number of studies having examined how expatriate managers react to unfamiliar cultures and why and how they adjust their *leadership behaviors*.

In their review of research on expatriate adjustment, Festing and Maletzky (2011) pointed out that cross-cultural leadership adjustment has been neglected and that the [r]*esults of current conceptual and empirical research do not allow one to draw adequate conclusions regarding the adjustment of leadership behavior* (p. 190). Although the authors called for more research to be conducted on cross-cultural leadership adjustment, to date, very few studies have empirically examined the extent to which expatriate business leaders adjust their *leadership behaviors*. As a result, little is known about whether, to what degree, and how expatriate business leaders do so.

I contributed to closing this gap by investigating whether, to what degree, and how expatriate business leaders working in China adjust their leadership behaviors. I found that most of the expatriate business leaders participating in my study had adjusted their leadership behaviors when working in China and that to varying degrees and with varying frequencies, they had demonstrated the four patterns of adjustment presented above. The research methods I used to analyze the degrees and patterns of adjustment are explained in Chapter 3, while the related research findings are presented in Chapter 7.

Summary

- Cross-cultural leadership refers to the abilities and processes whereby groups of people or organizations in different cultures or nations are influenced and led in order to achieve set objectives.

- The three leadership theories reviewed in this chapter (i.e., SLTs, ILT, and CLTs) emphasize the importance of fit between leaders and followers and of adjusting leadership approaches. They provide important suggestions for expatriate business leaders: in order to effectively manage and lead people across borders, it is essential to be adaptable/flexible and to demonstrate leadership in ways that match employee and task characteristics and employee cultural expectations of leaders.

- High degrees of fit/match between the leadership behaviors demonstrated by expatriate managers and those expected by Chinese employees are likely to lead to high degrees of supervisor and job satisfaction. This is because the ways in which expatriate managers behave can significantly influence employees' daily work experience and the degree of satisfaction they feel in relation to their managers and their jobs.

- Leadership across cultures is mainly viewed by scholars from the universalistic and cultural congruency perspectives. The former argues that many leadership behaviors are universally effective and accepted regardless of cultural or national context, while the latter asserts that effective and accepted leadership varies by culture, as cultural factors affect leadership expectations.

- In my research, cross-cultural leadership behavior adjustment is defined as the process by which expatriate business leaders change their own leadership behaviors and/or the behaviors of their host country subordinates. Building on this, I developed four patterns of cross-cultural leadership behavior adjustment (i.e., determination, exploration, replication, and absorption) to examine how expatriate business leaders adjust their leadership behaviors and/or the behaviors of their subordinates when working in China.

- Cross-cultural leadership behavior adjustment has not received enough attention from researchers. Indeed, empirical research examining whether leaders adjust their leadership approaches and the ways in which they do so, particularly in a cross-cultural setting, is virtually non-existent. My research explored the extent to which and the patterns whereby expatriate business leaders working in China had adjusted their leadership behaviors, thus closing a gap in the extant research.

References

Adsit, D. J., London, M., Crom, S., & Jones, D. (1997). Cross-cultural differences in upward ratings in a multinational company. *International Journal of Human Resource Management, 8*(4), 385–401.

Arvey, R., Dhanaraj, C., Javidan, M., & Zhang, Z. X. (2015). Are there unique leadership models in Asia? Exploring uncharted territory. *Leadership Quarterly, 26*(1), 1–6.

Audenaert, M., Carette, P., Shore, L. M., Lange, T., Van Waeyenberg, T., & Decramer, A. (2018). Leader-employee congruence of expected contributions in the employee-organization relationship. *The Leadership Quarterly, 29*(3), 414–422.

Aycan, Z. (1997). Acculturation of expatriate managers: A process model of adjustment and performance. In Z. Aycan (Ed.), *New Approaches to Employee Management, Vol. 4. Expatriate Management: Theory and Research* (pp. 1–40). US: Elsevier Science/JAI Press.

Black, J. S., Mendenhall, M., & Oddou, G. (1991). Toward a comprehensive model of international adjustment: An integration of multiple theoretical perspectives. *Academy of Management Review, 16*(2), 291–317.

Bond, M. H. (1996). Chinese values. In M. H. Bond (Ed.), *The Handbook of Chinese Psychology* (pp. 208–226). Hong Kong: Oxford University Press.

Brown, M. E., & Treviño, L. K. (2009). Leader–follower values congruence: Are socialized charismatic leaders better able to achieve it? *Journal of Applied Psychology, 94*(2), 478.

Bushra, F., Ahmad, U., & Naveed, A. (2011). Effect of transformational leadership on employees' job satisfaction and organizational commitment in banking sector of Lahore (Pakistan). *International Journal of Business and Social Science, 2*(18), 261–267.

Davies, S. E., Stoermer, S., & Froese, F. J. (2019). When the going gets tough: The influence of expatriate resilience and perceived organizational inclusion climate on work adjustment and turnover intentions. *The International Journal of Human Resource Management, 30*(8), 1393–1417.

Dickson, M. W., Den Hartog, D. N., & Mitchelson, J. K. (2003). Research on leadership in a cross-cultural context: Making progress, and raising new questions. *The Leadership Quarterly, 14*(6), 729–768.

Dorfman, P. W., Hanges, P. J., & Brodbeck, F. C. (2004). Leadership and culture variation: The identification of culturally endorsed leadership profiles. In R. J. House, P. J. Hanges, M. Javidan, P. W. Dorfman, & V. Gupta (Eds.), *Leadership, Culture, and Organizations: The GLOBE Study of 62 Societies* (pp. 669–719). Thousand Oaks, CA: Sage.

Dorfman, P. W., Howell, J. P., Hibino, S., Lee, J. K., Tate, U., & Bautista, A. (1997). Leadership in Western and Asian countries: Commonalities and differences in effective leadership processes across cultures. *The Leadership Quarterly, 8*(3), 233–274.

Edwards, J. A., & Billsberry, J. (2010). Testing a multidimensional theory of person-environment fit. *Journal of Managerial Issues, 22*(4), 476–493.

Ehrhart, M. G. (2015). Self-concept, implicit leadership theories, and follower preferences for leadership. *Zeitschrift für Psychologie, 220*(4), 231–240.

Epitropaki, O., & Martin, R. (2005). From ideal to real: A longitudinal study of the role of implicit leadership theories on leader-member exchanges and employee outcomes. *The Journal of Applied Psychology, 90*, 659–676.

Festing, M., & Maletzky, M. (2011). Cross-cultural leadership adjustment—A multilevel framework based on the theory of structuration. *Human Resource Management Review, 21*(3), 186–200.

Fleishman, E. A. (1953). The description of supervisory behavior. *Journal of Applied Psychology, 37*(1), 1–6.

Fleishman, E. A., & Simmons, J. (1970). Relationship between leadership patterns and effectiveness ratings among Israeli foremen. *Personnel Psychology, 23*(2), 169–172.

Graeff, C. L. (1983). The situational leadership theory: A critical view. *Academy of Management Review, 8*, 285–291.

Henderson, D. J., Wayne, S. J., Shore, L. M., Bommer, W. H., & Tetrick, L. E. (2008). Leader-member exchange, differentiation, and psychological contract fulfillment: A multilevel examination. *Journal of Applied Psychology, 93*, 1208–1219.

Hersey, P., & Blanchard, K. (1972). *Management of Organizational Behavior* (2nd ed.). Englewood Cliffs, NJ: Prentice-Hall.

Hersey, P., & Blanchard, K. (1982). *Management of Organizational Behavior: Utilizing Human Resources* (4th ed.). Englewood Cliffs, NJ: Prentice-Hall.

Hofstede, G. (2001). *Culture's Consequences: Comparing Values, Behaviors, Institutions and Organizations across Nations.* Thousand Oaks, CA: Sage Publications.

Hollander, E. P., & Offermann, L. R. (1990). Power and leadership in organizations: Relationships in transition. *American Psychologist, 45*, 179–189.

House, R. (1996). Path-goal theory of leadership: Lessons, legacy, and a reformulated theory. *The Leadership Quarterly, 7*(3), 323–352.

House, R. J. (1971). A path-goal theory of leader effectiveness. *Administrative Science Quarterly, 16*, 321–338.

House, R., & Aditya, R. N. (1997). The social scientific study of leadership: Quo vadis? *Journal of Management, 23*(3), 409–473.

House, R., & Dessler, G. (1974). The path-goal theory of leadership: Some post hoc and a priori tests. In J. G. Hunt, & L. L. Larson (Eds.), *Contingency Approaches to Leadership.* Carbondale: Southern Illinois University Press.

House, R. J., Hanges, P. J., Javidan, M., Dorfman, P. W., & Gupta, V. (Eds.) (2004). *Culture, Leadership, and Organizations: The GLOBE Study of 62 Societies.* Thousand Oaks, CA: Sage Publications.

House, R., Javidan, M., Hanges, P., & Dorfman, P. (2002). Understanding cultures and implicit leadership theories across the globe: An introduction to project GLOBE. *Journal of World Business, 37*, 3–11.

Javidan, M., Dorfman, P., De Luque, M. S., & House, R. (2006). In the eye of the beholder: Cross cultural lessons in leadership from project GLOBE. *Academy of Management Perspectives, 20*(1), 67–90.

Jermier, J. M., & Berkes, L. J. (1979). Leader behavior in a police command bureaucracy: A closer look at the quasi-military model. *Administrative Science Quarterly, 24*(1), 1–23.

Jordan, J., Brown, M. E., Treviño, L. K., & Finkelstein, S. (2013). Someone to look up to: Executive–follower ethical reasoning and perceptions of ethical leadership. *Journal of Management, 39*(3), 660–683.

Kristof-Brown, A. L., Zimmerman, R. D., & Johnson, E. C. (2005). Consequences of individuals' fit at work: A meta-analysis OF person–job, person–organization, person–group, and person–supervisor fit. *Personnel Psychology, 58*(2), 281–342.

Lambert, L. S., Tepper, B. J., Carr, J. C., Holt, D. T., & Barelka, A. J. (2012). Forgotten but not gone: An examination of fit between leader consideration and initiating structure needed and received. *Journal of Applied Psychology, 97*(5), 913.

Lee, D., Choi, Y., Youn, S., & Chun, J. U. (2017). Ethical leadership and employee moral voice: The mediating role of moral efficacy and the moderating role of leader–follower value congruence. *Journal of Business Ethics, 141*(1), 47–57.

Li, Y., & Sun, J. M. (2015). Traditional Chinese leadership and employee voice behavior: A cross-level examination. *The Leadership Quarterly, 26*(2), 172–189.

Lord, R. G., & Alliger, G. M. (1985), A comparison of four information processing models of leadership and social perceptions. *Human Relations, 38*(1), 47–65.

Lord, R. G., Binning, J. F., Rush, M. C., & Thomas, J. C. (1978). The effect of performance cues and leader behavior on questionnaire ratings of leadership behavior. *Organizational Behavior and Human Performance, 21*(1), 27–39.

Lord, R. G., & Brown, D. J. (2001). Leadership, values, and subordinate self-concepts. *The Leadership Quarterly, 12*, 133–152.

Lord, R. G., De Vader, C. L., & Alliger, G. M. (1986). A meta-analysis of the relation between personality traits and leadership perceptions: An application of validity generalization procedures. *Journal of Applied Psychology, 71*(3), 402.

Lord, R. G., Foti, R., & De Vader, C. (1984). A test of leadership categorization theory: Internal structure, informational processing, and leadership perceptions. *Organizational Behavior and Human Performance, 34*, 343–378.

Lord, R. G., & Maher, K. J. (1993). *Information Processing. Linking Perceptions and Performance.* London: Routledge.

Marstand, A. F., Martin, R., & Epitropaki, O. (2017). Complementary person-supervisor fit: An investigation of supplies-values (SV) fit, leader-member exchange (LMX) and work outcomes. *The Leadership Quarterly, 28*(3), 418–437.

Meglino, B. M., Ravlin, E. C., & Adkins, C. L. (1992). The measurement of work value congruence: A field study comparison. *Journal of Management, 18*(1), 33–43.

Menon, T., Sim, J., Fu, J. H. Y., Chiu, C. Y., & Hong, Y. Y. (2010). Blazing the trail versus trailing the group: Culture and perceptions of the leader's position. *Organizational Behavior and Human Decision Processes, 113*(1), 51–61.

Nicholson, N. (1984). A theory of work role transitions. *Administrative Science Quarterly, 29*(2), 172–191.

Nicholson, N., & West, M. A. (1988). *Managerial Job Change: Men and Women in Transition*. Cambridge: Cambridge University Press.

Northouse, P. G. (2007). *Leadership: Theory and Practice*. Thousand Oaks, CA: Sage Publications.

Northouse, P. G. (2021). *Leadership: Theory and Practice*. Thousand Oaks, CA: Sage Publications.

Nye, J. L., & Forsyth, D. R. (1991). The effects of prototype-based biases on leadership appraisals: A test of leadership categorization theory. *Small Group Research, 22*, 360–375.

Poole, P. P., Gioia, D. A., & Gray, B. (1989). Influence modes, schema change, and organizational transformation. *The Journal of Applied Behavioral Science, 25*(3), 271–289.

Ralston, D. A., Holt, D. H., Terpstra, R. H., & Yu, K.-C. (1997). The impact of national culture and economic ideology on managerial work values: A study of the United States, Russia, Japan, and China. *Journal of International Business Studies, 28*(1), 177–207.

Ravasi, C., Salamin, X., & Davoine, E. (2015). Cross-cultural adjustment of skilled migrants in a multicultural and multilingual environment: An explorative study of foreign employees and their spouses in the Swiss context. *The International Journal of Human Resource Management, 26*(10), 1335–1359.

Reddin, W. J. (1967). The 3-D management style theory. *Training & Development Journal, 21*, 8.

Shaffer, M. A., Harrison, D. A., & Gilley, K. M. (1999). Dimensions, determinants, and differences in the expatriate adjustment process. *Journal of International Business Studies, 30*(3), 557–581.

Shay, J. P., & Baack, S. A. (2004). Expatriate assignments adjustment and effectiveness: An empirical examination of the big picture. *Journal of International Business Studies, 35*(3), 216–232.

Stogdill, R. M. (1950). Leadership, membership and organization. *Psychological Bulletin, 47*, 1–14.

Stogdill, R. M. (1974). *Handbook of Leadership: A Survey of Theory and Research*. New York: Free Press.

Subramaniam, A., Othman, R., & Sambasivan, M. (2010). Implicit leadership theory among Malaysian managers: Impact of the leadership expectation gap on leader-member exchange quality. *Leadership & Organization Development Journal, 31*(4), 351–371.

Thompson, G., & Vecchio, R. P. (2009). Situational leadership theory: A test of three versions. *Leadership Quarterly, 20*, 837–848.

Vecchio, R. P. (1987). Situational leadership theory: An examination of a prescriptive theory. *Journal of Applied Psychology, 72*, 444–451.

Vroom, H., & Jago, G. (2007). The role of the situation in leadership. *American Psychologist, 62*(1), 17–24.

Wanous, J. P., & Lawler, E. E. (1972). Measurement and meaning of job satisfaction. *Journal of Applied Psychology, 56*(2), 95–105.

Weick, K. E. (1995). *Sensemaking in Organizations*. Thousand Oaks, CA: Sage.

Wofford, J. C., & Liska, L. Z. (1993). Path-goal theories of leadership: A meta-analysis. *Journal of Management, 19*(4), 857–876.

Xu, M., Qin, X., Dust, S. B., & DiRenzo, M. S. (2019). Supervisor-subordinate proactive personality congruence and psychological safety: A signaling theory approach to employee voice behavior. *The Leadership Quarterly, 30*(4), 440–453.

Yukl, G. (2013). *Leadership in Organizations* (8th ed.). Harlow: Pearson.

Yukl, G. (2019). *Leadership in Organizations* (9th ed.). Harlow: Pearson.

Zaccaro, S. J., Gilbert, J. A., Thor, K. K., & Mumford, M. D. (1991). Leadership and social intelligence: Linking social perspectiveness and behavioral flexibility to leader effectiveness. *The Leadership Quarterly, 2*(4), 317–342.

Zhang, Z., Wang, M. O., & Shi, J. (2012). Leader-follower congruence in proactive personality and work outcomes: The mediating role of leader-member exchange. *Academy of Management Journal, 55*(1), 111–130.

Zimmermann, A., & Sparrow, P. (2007). Mutual adjustment processes in international teams: Lessons for the study of expatriation. *International Studies of Management & Organization, 37*(3), 65–88.

Chapter 3

The Study Methodology

This chapter explains how I conducted my research and how I collected and analyzed the data. It includes three sections: the first pertains to the mixed methods methodology adopted for the research and to the data/ information collected from both expatriate managers and Chinese employees in three stages through online surveys and semi-structured interviews. The second section presents the data collection procedures, how the variables were measured, the response rate, and the profiles of the research participants. The third section provides an explanation of how the collected qualitative and quantitative data were analyzed.

Research Design and Stages

My research was intended to explore the perspectives and experiences of both expatriate senior managers and their Chinese employees. To achieve my research objectives (stated in Chapter 1), I adopted a mixed methods methodology and collected data/information from both expatriate managers and Chinese employees in three stages: first, I distributed an online survey questionnaire containing both qualitative and quantitative questions to a sample of expatriate senior managers working in China; second, I sent another online quantitative survey questionnaire to those expatriate managers who left their contact information in the aforementioned survey and asked them to forward the survey link to their directly reporting Chinese subordinates; and third, I conducted semi-structured interviews with Chinese employees who were working or had worked under the supervision of expatriate managers. The data collected provided rich and

31

balanced explanations for the research issues under study and avoided any biases associated with single-source data.

The Research Participants and the Data Collection Procedures

My research survey was completed by 391 expatriate senior managers working in China. Among them, 71 expatriate senior managers also helped collect data from their directly reporting Chinese subordinates (356 in total). The expatriates were contacted through LinkedIn, an online professional social network that was used to build the sampling frame, given the unavailability of a readily compiled contact list of expatriate managers. LinkedIn is the largest business-oriented professional networking platform on the Internet, with over 830 million users from more than 200 countries as of May 2022. As LinkedIn enables its users to create professional profiles, I was able to view their professional information (e.g., occupations, job roles, job levels, countries in which they worked, industry sectors, and years of service) and to select my research sample.

When contacting expatriate senior manager, I used two sampling criteria. First, they had to hold senior-level jobs—with titles, such as CEO, CFO, director, chairman, managing director, president, senior vice president, and general manager. Senior managers were selected because, being commonly regarded as leadership figures, they are critically important to the success of their organizations, and their experiences could greatly contribute to the knowledge of leadership and of organizational practices. The second sampling criterion involved the exclusion of Chinese nationals—this was effected by checking the names and photos shown on the LinkedIn profiles and the nationality information provided in the completed questionnaires.

Starting from my initial connections with three expatriates working in China, I expanded my LinkedIn network to over 5,000 connections through a three-step procedure. First, I searched the connections of each of my existing contacts using China as the search location criterion. Second, I checked the work profiles of my existing contacts' connections and asked those who matched my sampling criteria to add me to their LinkedIn networks. Third, I sent a research invitation to all the expatriates who had accepted me in their networks. The invitation introduced my research project; provided a web link to the survey, assured respondent anonymity, included my contact information; and offered the research respondents a report on the findings on completion of the project. I performed these tasks with the help of two research assistants.

Online surveys

This section provides details of the two online survey questionnaires respectively sent to the expatriate senior managers and to their directly reporting Chinese subordinates.

The Expatriate Leader Survey (ELS) questionnaire

The research invite I sent to the expatriate leaders contained a web link to the Expatriate Leader Survey (ELS) questionnaire, which consisted of both qualitative and quantitative questions. The *qualitative questions* were aimed at exploring the expatriate leaders' experiences and views in leading Chinese subordinates and to gain a deep understanding of their leadership adjustment, if any, when working in an unfamiliar cultural setting. These open-ended questions were organized in three sets (see Table 1). The first was designed to explore the expatriate managers' leadership approaches in leading their Chinese subordinates and the challenges they had encountered. The second was intended to investigate whether the expatriates had adjusted their leadership approaches and, if so, what they had adjusted, why, and how. The third was aimed at exploring whether they had changed (or had tried to change) their subordinates' and/or the subsidiaries' work practices. These questions had been developed and refined based on a pilot study/interview—conducted with 178 expatriate

Table 1. Qualitative survey questions used in the Expatriate Leader Survey (ELS).

1. Is leading Chinese employees different from leading employees in your home country? What are the similarities and differences? What are the challenges?

2. Have you had to adjust your leadership approach while working in China at all? If so, what have you had to adjust? What led to the need for adjustment? How have you adjusted?

3. Have you changed (or tried to change) your Chinese employees and/or the subsidiary's work practices? If so, what have you changed (or tried to change)? What led to the need for change? How did you go about changing it? What challenges have you faced?

business leaders working in Thailand—that had involved face-to-face semi-structured interviews and a qualitative survey.

The *quantitative questions* in the ELS questionnaire were intended to examine the respondents' degree of leadership behavior adjustment and whether or not the fit between observed and expected leadership behaviors is associated with employee satisfaction. The questions were related to the expatriates' perceptions of the cultural distance between China and their home countries, their *current* leadership behaviors (task- and relations-oriented), and those they had adopted *prior to* entering into China.

At the end of the ELS questionnaire, the expatriates were asked to leave their names and email addresses if they were interested in the viewpoints of their directly reporting Chinese employees on their leadership behaviors. They were told that, should they have opted to leave their contact information, they would be sent (1) an online link to the Chinese Manager Survey (CMS) questionnaire to be forwarded to their directly reporting Chinese subordinates and (2) an anonymous statistical report of their subordinates' responses on completion of the CMS questionnaire.

The full ELS questionnaire can be found in Appendix A.

Chinese Manager Survey (CMS)

Similar to the ELS, the CMS also included measures of the expatriate managers' current and past leadership behaviors. In addition, the Chinese subordinates were asked to express their opinions on the leadership behavior they expected their supervisor to demonstrate as well as the degree of their satisfaction towards their jobs and their expatriate supervisors.

The leaders' names were shown on both the introduction and second pages of the CMS so that their subordinates would be informed about who they were being asked to assess. The confidentiality of the completed survey was assured in the introduction page.

The CMS questionnaire can be found in Appendix B.

Both survey questionnaires, the ELS and CMS, were in English and administered through Qualtrics, an online survey platform. The CMS was in English as the Chinese subordinates reported directly to expatriates and were thus expected to have had a good understanding of the language.

The data collection phase of the two online surveys involved various time-consuming tasks, including the following: searching for expatriate senior managers on LinkedIn; sending out LinkedIn connection invitations, research invitations, and survey links; replying to queries; and soliciting responses.

Measures
This section explains how the variables used in the quantitative survey questions were measured.

Leadership behaviors: In my study, I measured two categories of leadership behaviors that are commonly used in leadership research: task-oriented (four items) and relations-oriented (five items). The question items used in this study were derived from the taxonomy of leadership behaviors developed by Yukl *et al.* (2002: 17), who had selected each behavior using criteria that included the following: directly observable, potentially applicable to all types of leaders, and grounded in prior theory and research on effective leadership. A sample item for task-oriented behaviors was *Clarify what results are expected for a task*; and a sample item for relations-oriented behaviors was *Consult with people on decisions affecting them.*

Both the expatriate managers and their directly reporting Chinese subordinates were asked to provide assessments of leadership behaviors. The managers were asked to answer the nine question items *twice*—once to indicate the extent to which they were *currently* adopting each of the behaviors (*current*) and once to reveal the extent to which they had adopted each behavior *prior to entering China* (*past*)—on a 7-point Likert scale (1 = to an extremely small extent; 7 = to an extremely large extent). The information obtained on the expatriate managers' current and past behaviors was used to assess their degree of leadership behavior adjustment. Cronbach's alpha values I obtained for the two *current* behavior categories (task-oriented and relations-oriented) were 0.70 and 0.84, respectively; and those for the two *past* ones were 0.88 and 0.94, respectively.

The Chinese subordinates were asked to describe their expatriate supervisors' leadership behaviors *three* times on the same 7-point Likert scale. They were asked to indicate the following: the extent to which (a) their leaders were *currently* adopting each behavior (*current*); (b) their leaders had adopted each behavior *during their first three months* of working in the subsidiaries (*first three-month*) (an additional optional answer "0 = don't know" was included in this set of questions to indicate lack of knowledge); and (c) they felt that their leaders *should have adopted* each behavior (*expected*). The subordinates' views on their expatriate leaders' *current* and *first three-month* behaviors were used to examine the latter's degree of behavior adjustment, while the views they expressed on their leaders' *current* and *expected* behaviors were used to examine the effect of the fit between observed (i.e., current) and expected leadership behaviors on employee satisfaction. The Cronbach alpha values I obtained for the two *current* behavior categories (task-oriented and relations-oriented) were 0.83 and 0.92, respectively; those for the two *first three-month* ones were 0.93 and 0.94, respectively; and those for the two *expected* ones were 0.98 and 0.98, respectively.

***Employee satisfaction*:** I measured two outcome variables: subordinate satisfaction with expatriate supervisor (supervisor satisfaction) and job satisfaction.

***Satisfaction with expatriate supervisor (supervisor satisfaction)*:** To measure the sample Chinese employees' satisfaction with their expatriate supervisors, I adapted Hackman and Oldham's (1980) three-item scale. I used a 7-point Likert scale (1 = very dissatisfied; 7 = very satisfied). Example items were *The amount of support and guidance I receive from him/her* and *The overall quality of the supervision I receive from him/her*. The α I obtained was 0.89.

***Job satisfaction*:** To measure the sample employees' overall job satisfaction, I used Hackman and Lawler's (1971) scale (three items). Example items were *I am very satisfied with the kind of work I have to do on my job* and *Generally speaking, I am very satisfied with my job*. I measured this variable on a 7-point Likert scale ranging from 1 (strongly disagree) to 7 (strongly agree) (α = 0.86).

***Controls*:** Prior research suggests a correlation between demographic characteristics and employee satisfaction (see, e.g., Lee & Wilbur, 1985; Clark, 1997; Audenaert *et al.*, 2018). Therefore, in the analyses, I controlled for the employees' genders, ages, educational levels, and organizational tenures. I measured gender as a dichotomous variable, age using nine age ranges (1 = 20–24; 2 = 25–29; 3 = 30–34; 4 = 35–39; 5 = 40–44; 6 = 45–49; 7 = 50–54; 8 = 55–59; 9 = 60 and above), and tenure using five ranges (1 = less than one year; 2 = between one and two years; 3 =

between two and five years; 4 = between five and ten years; 5 = ten years or more).

Semi-structured interviews

Using semi-structured questions, I interviewed 11 Chinese employees who were working or had worked under the supervision of expatriate managers (see Table 2). I conducted the interviews using WeChat—the most widely used social media in China—in September and October 2022, after I had analyzed the data collected from the aforementioned two surveys. The purpose of the interviews was to get employees' perspectives on some issues brought up by the expatriates. For example, many expatriates had stated that the opportunity to earn better salaries elsewhere was the key reason for the high employee turnover rate and that Chinese employees were more loyal to people than to the company. I thus asked the Chinese employees about what would prompt them to seek

Table 2. Questions used in the semi-structured interviews with Chinese employees

1. Many of the expatriate managers who took part in my research said that employee turnover rate is higher in China than in other countries in which they had worked. What are the key reasons for Chinese employees wanting to change their jobs? The expatriate managers said that the opportunity for better pay/salary elsewhere was the key reason. Do you agree?

2. Some of the expatriate managers said that Chinese employees tend to be loyal to "people" (e.g., their line managers), rather than to the company/organization. Do you agree with this view and, if so, why?

3. Many of the expatriate managers said that Chinese employees prefer to wait for detailed instructions on how to complete a task from their supervisors, rather than being given a goal and then work their way to achieve it. Do you agree with what they said and, if so, why?

4. Some expatriate managers suggested that, to cater to their Chinese employees' expectations, expatriate leaders should ideally adopt a paternalistic leadership style (i.e., use a combination of strong authority and fatherly benevolence). Do you agree that a paternalistic leadership is an appropriate approach to adopt for managing and leading Chinese employees?

5. Some expatriate managers said that the level of trust among Chinese people was low and that it took longer to build it up with them. Do you agree with that statement? If so, what are the main reasons for that state of affairs?

employment in a different company and about issues related to loyalty. I used the data collected from the interviews to clarify some of the challenging employee characteristics mentioned by the expatriate senior managers.

The response rate and profiles of the research participants

In total, the ELS was completed by 391 expatriates, 250 of whom left their contact information. The latter were then sent a LinkedIn message thanking them for completing the survey and asking them to forward to all of their directly reporting Chinese subordinates the embedded survey link to the CMS.

The expatriates later received two reminders via LinkedIn messages—respectively three and six weeks after the CMS link had been sent out. Around two-thirds of them either did not reply to the messages or did not forward the CMS link to their subordinates. Some informed us that they had not forwarded the link for reasons that included the following: (i) the headquarters would have needed to approve the survey, (ii) they had since joined other companies, and (iii) they had since returned to their home countries. Eventually, I received 356 valid CMS responses completed by the subordinates of 71 expatriate managers, with a mean of five subordinates per leader (range: 3–17).

Table 3 presents the profiles of the 391 expatriate managers. Most of them were male (86.4%), which is in line with the low ratio of females holding senior positions reported in the business press. Around three-quarters (74.7%) were aged between 35 and 59 and over half (57.3%) had worked in China for more than five years. The sample group covered over 40 different nationalities.

Table 4 presents the profiles of the matched sets of data with 71 expatriates and 356 of their Chinese subordinates. Of the leaders, 93% were male, over 70% were aged between 40 and 59 years old, and about two-thirds (64.8%) had worked in China for more than five years. The sample group covered over 20 different nationalities and 30 industries. Of the Chinese subordinates, 52.1% were female, nearly four-fifths (79.4%) were aged between 25 and 44, and over half (55.3%) had worked in the organization for more than two years.

Table 3. Profiles of the 391 expatriate senior managers

No. of expatriates		(%)	No. of expatriates		(%)
Gender			**Nationality**		
Male	338	(86.4)	Bulgarian	1	(0.3)
Female	26	(6.6)	Canadian	4	(1.0)
No information	27	(6.9)	Canadian & Swedish	1	(0.3)
			Chilean	1	(0.3)
Age			Colombian	1	(0.3)
25–29	15	(3.8)	Czech	1	(0.3)
30–34	39	(10.0)	Danish	8	(2.0)
35–39	58	(14.8)	Dutch	21	(5.4)
40–44	55	(14.1)	Filipino	1	(0.3)
45–49	69	(17.6)	Finnish	9	(2.3)
50–54	66	(16.9)	French	38	(9.7)
55–59	44	(11.3)	French & Congolese	1	(0.3)
60 and above	25	(6.4)	French and Canadian	1	(0.3)
No information	20	(5.1)	German	38	(9.7)
			Greek	1	(0.3)
No. of years worked in China			Indian	1	(0.3)
Less than 1	9	(2.3)	Indo-Canadian	1	(0.3)
Between 1 and 2	41	(10.5)	Irish	1	(0.3)
Between 2.1 and 5	89	(22.8)	Irish and German	1	(0.3)
Between 5.1 and 10	140	(35.8)	Israeli	5	(1.3)
Between 10.1 and 15	49	(12.5)	Italian	27	(6.9)
More than 15	35	(9.0)	Kenyan	1	(0.3)
No information	28	(7.2)	Lebanese	2	(0.5)
			Luxembourger	1	(0.3)
Nationality			Malaysian	1	(0.3)
American	61	(15.6)	Mauritian	1	(0.3)
American & Irish	1	(0.3)	Mexican	2	(0.5)
American & Spanish	1	(0.3)	Nepali	1	(0.3)
Argentinean & French	1	(0.3)	New Zealander	5	(1.3)
Australian	24	(6.1)	Norwegian	2	(0.5)
Australian & Italian	1	(0.3)	Polish	1	(0.3)

(*Continued*)

Table 3. (*Continued*)

No. of expatriates		(%)	No. of expatriates		(%)
Australian & British	1	(0.3)	Russian	2	(0.5)
Austrian	10	(2.6)	Slovak	1	(0.3)
Belgian	9	(2.3)	South African	2	(0.5)
Brazilian	1	(0.3)	Spanish	6	(1.5)
Brazilian & Swiss	1	(0.3)	Swedish	6	(1.5)
British	40	(10.2)	Swiss	10	(2.6)
British & American	2	(0.5)	Swiss & Italian	1	(0.3)
British & Canadian	1	(0.3)	Turkish	1	(0.3)
British & Australian	1	(0.3)	Venezuelan	2	(0.5)
			No information	25	(6.4)
			Total:	**391**	

Table 4. Profiles of the 71 expatriate senior managers and of 356 of their Chinese subordinates

Expatriate senior managers (*n* = 71)			Chinese subordinates (*n* = 356)		
No. of expatriates		(%)	No. of subordinates		(%)
Gender			**Gender**		
Male	66	(93)	Male	143	(40.2)
Female	5	(7)	Female	185	(52.1)
			No information	28	(7.9)
Age					
20–24	0	0	**Age**		
25–29	0	0	20–24	22	(6.2)
30–34	8	(11.3)	25–29	69	(19.4)
35–39	11	(15.5)	30–34	93	(26.1)
40–44	12	(16.9)	35–39	76	(21.3)
45–49	15	(21.1)	40–44	45	(12.6)
50–54	15	(21.1)	45–49	15	(4.2)
55–59	8	(11.3)	50–54	8	(2.2)
60 and above	2	(2.8)	55–59	2	(0.6)
			60 and above	1	(0.3)

Table 4. *(Continued)*

Expatriate senior managers (n = 71)			Chinese subordinates (n = 356)		
No. of expatriates		**(%)**	**No. of subordinates**		**(%)**
Job title			No information	25	(7.0)
Director	18	(25.3)			
President and vice president	8	(11.3)	**Job function area***		
Managing Partner	3	(4.2)	Finance or accounting	33	(9.3)
Chairman	3	(4.2)	Sales and Marketing	59	(16.6)
General Manager	15	(21.1)	Production	47	(13.2)
Chief Officer	24	(33.8)	Human Resources	41	(11.5)
(e.g., CEO, CFO, COO)			IT	21	(5.9)
			Operations	68	(19.1)
			R&D	60	(16.9)
No. of years worked in China			Administration	45	(12.6)
Less than 1	1	(1.4)	Other	78	(21.9)
Between 1 and 2	2	(2.8)	No information	35	(9.8)
Between 2.1 and 5	20	(28.2)			
Between 5.1 and 10	18	(25.4)			
Between 10.1 and 15	24	(33.8)	**Length of service**		
More than 15	4	(5.6)	Less than 1	63	(17.7)
No information	2	(2.8)	Between 1 and 2	70	(19.7)
			Between 2.1 and 5	100	(28.1)
Nationality			Between 5.1 and 10	71	(19.9)
American	6	(8.5)	Between 10.1 and 15	26	(7.3)
American & Spanish	1	(1.4)	No information	26	(7.3)
Australian	10	(14.1)			
Australian & British	1	(1.4)			
Australian & Italian	1	(1.4)			
Austrian	4	(5.6)			
Belgian	1	(1.4)			
British	11	(15.5)			
Canadian	1	(1.4)			
Danish	1	(1.4)			
Dutch	1	(1.4)			
Finnish	2	(2.8)			

(Continued)

Table 4.   (*Continued*)

Expatriate senior managers (n = 71)			Chinese subordinates (n = 356)	
No. of expatriates		(%)	No. of subordinates	(%)
French	5	(7.0)		
German	7	(9.9)		
Indo-Canadian	1	(1.4)		
Irish	1	(1.4)		
Israeli	1	(1.4)		
Italian	8	(11.3)		
Luxembourger	1	(1.4)		
Spanish	1	(1.4)		
Swiss	4	(5.6)		
Thai	1	(1.4)		
Venezuelan	1	(1.4)		

Note: *Some subordinates ticked more than one function area.

Data Analysis

This section explains how I analyzed the qualitative and quantitative data. Table 5 shows a summary of the purposes of the data analysis, data types, data sources and sample sizes, methods of data analysis, and the chapters reporting the research findings.

Analysis of the qualitative data

I analyzed the qualitative data collected from the expatriate senior managers by following two separate data analysis processes according to the objectives of my research. The first process was aimed at exploring the expatriate managers' experiences and views in relation to leading Chinese subordinates—their views on the similarities and differences between leading their Chinese subordinates and those in their home country, and the challenges they had encountered when leading the former. The second process was intended to explore the expatriate managers' patterns of leadership behavior adjustment, which I analyzed by recording the extent to which the expatriate managers had adjusted their own behavior and that to which they had changed (or tried to change) their

Table 5. Summary of the data analysis purposes and methods

Purpose of data analysis	Data type	Data source and sample size	Methods of data analysis	Chapters reporting the research findings
Expatriate managers' experience and perspectives in leading Chinese employees	Qualitative data	Data source: the Expatriate Leader Survey (ELS) I analyzed the expatriate managers' responses to the following questions: *Is leading Chinese subordinates different from leading those in your home country?*, *What are the similarities and differences?*, and *What are the challenges?* Sample size: 391 expatriates.	Thematic analysis.	Chapter 6
Pattern of leadership behavior adjustment	Qualitative data	Data source: the Expatriate Leader Survey (ELS) Procedure 1: to rate the expatriate managers' degrees of adjustment/ change, I used their responses to the following questions: *Have you had to adjust your leadership approach while working in China at all?* and *Have you changed (or tried to change) your Chinese employees and/or the subsidiary's work practices?* Procedure 2: to analyze how and why expatriate managers adjust their leadership behavior and/or change their subordinates, I used their responses to the following questions: *Have you had to adjust your leadership approach while working in China at all?*, *If so, what have you had to adjust?*, *What led to the need for adjustment?*, *How did you adjust?*, *Have you changed (or tried to change) your Chinese employees and/or the subsidiary's work practices?*, *If so, what have you changed (tried to change)?*, *What led to the need for change?*, *How did you go about changing it?*, and *What challenges have you faced?* Sample size: 391 expatriates.	To rate each expatriate manager's degree of leadership adjustment and subordinate change, I used a 7-point Likert scale, which I then allocated to a 2 × 2 matrix to glean each expatriate's adjustment pattern. I performed a thematic analysis to explore the reasons for each pattern of adjustment demonstrated and the key aspects that had been adjusted or changed.	The second part of Chapter 7

(Continued)

Table 5. (*Continued*)

Purpose of data analysis	Data type	Data source and sample size	Methods of data analysis	Chapters reporting the research findings
Degree of leadership behavior adjustment	Quantitative data	Data source: I used the responses of both the expatriate leaders and their directly reporting Chinese subordinates. The Expatriate Leader Survey (ELS) The expatriate managers' responses to their *current* leadership behaviors (task- and relations-oriented) and to those *prior to* entering into China. The Chinese Manager Survey (CMS) The Chinese employees' responses to their expatriate leaders' *current* leadership behaviors and the those of their *first three-month* working in the company. Sample size: 391 expatriates and 356 Chinese employees.	I undertook paired-sample t tests to examine the degrees to which the expatriate managers had adjusted their leadership behaviors by comparing current and past leadership ones.	The first part of Chapter 7
The leadership behaviors expected by Chinese employees	Quantitative data	Data source: the Chinese Manager Survey (CMS) The Chinese employees' responses in relation to the leadership behaviors they expected of their expatriate managers. Sample size: 237 Chinese employees who reported directly to 40 expatriate senior managers.	Descriptive analysis; I calculated the means of the responses.	The third part of Chapter 8
The effect on employee satisfaction of the fit between observed and expected leadership behaviors	Quantitative data	Data source: the Chinese Manager Survey (CMS) The Chinese employees' responses in relation to their satisfaction with their expatriate supervisors (supervisor satisfaction) and their job satisfaction. The Chinese employees' responses in relation to their expatriate leaders' *current* leadership behaviors and those they *expected*. Sample size: 237 Chinese employees who reported directly to 40 expatriate senior managers.	Polynomial regression analyses and response surface modeling.	The fourth part of Chapter 8

Chinese subordinates. These two processes are described separately in the following.

Expatriate managers' experiences and views in relation to leading their Chinese subordinates

To explore the expatriate leaders' experiences and views in relation to leading their Chinese employees, I analyzed their responses to the following questions: *Is leading Chinese subordinates different from leading those in your home country?*, *What are the similarities and differences?*, and *What are the challenges?*.

I performed a thematic analysis that involved six main steps (Braun & Clarke, 2006; Guest, MacQueen, & Namey, 2012). First, I read the survey responses several times in order to familiarize myself with the data. Second, I grouped together any similar topics. Third, I coded the data, generating codes or sub-themes. Fourth, through repeated theme reviews, I counted instances, looked at how all themes were related to each other, and sought key themes suited to explain the expatriate managers' experiences and perspectives in leading their Chinese subordinates. Fifth, I verified whether the themes and patterns corroborated the data. Finally, I identified and summarized the key themes and the leaders' experiences and perspectives.

Figure 1 illustrates part of the data analysis progression. The bottom row in the figure shows the sample qualitative survey questions; the next row displays the codes used to categorize the responses; the next lists the sub-themes emerging from the responses; and the last (top) row shows the key themes.

The results of the analyses are presented in Chapter 6.

Patterns of leadership behavior adjustment

To explore the expatriate business leaders' patterns of adjustment, I undertook two procedures. In the first procedure, to rate the expatriate managers' degree of adjustment/change, I used their responses to the following questions: *Have you had to adjust your leadership approach while working in China at all?* and *Have you changed (or tried to change) your Chinese employees and/or the subsidiary's work practices?*. The analysis of the responses given to the former question enabled me to examine the degrees of "leadership adjustment", while that of those given to the latter

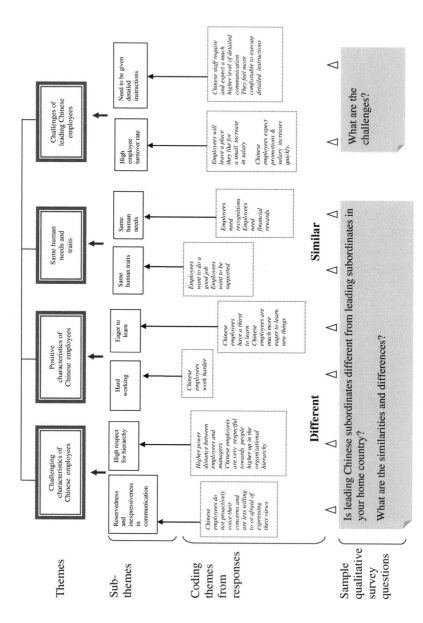

Figure 1. An illustration of the qualitative data analysis progression.

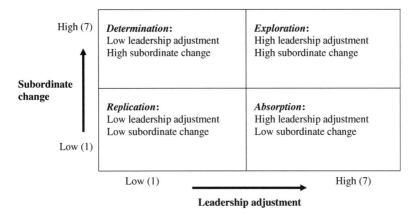

Figure 2. Patterns of cross-cultural leadership behavior adjustment, derived from Nicholson (1984).

enabled me to explore the degrees of "subordinate change". I carefully read each expatriate's responses to the two questions and then rated their degrees of adjustment/change on a 7-point Likert scale (1 = very little support; 7 = very strong support). Any ratings of 1 to 3 represented low degrees of adjustment/change, and any of 5 to 7 implied high ones. I then placed each pair of ratings (e.g., leadership adjustment and subordinate change) into a 2 × 2 matrix, like that shown in Figure 2, according to the points rated. For example, I allocated those expatriates who had received ratings of 6 in both dimensions in the "exploration" pattern of adjustment; and those who had scored 6 in the leadership adjustment dimension and 2 in the subordinate change one in the "absorption" mode. This process helped me identify the expatriates' patterns of adjustment based on the four proposed ones (see Chapter 2).

In the second procedure, to analyze the "whether, what, how, and why" in relation to the degrees to which the sample expatriate managers had adjusted their leadership behavior and/or changed their subordinates, and the key aspects they had adjusted or changed, I used the expatriate senior managers' responses to the following questions: *Have you had to adjust your leadership approach while working in China at all?, If so, what have you had to adjust?, What led to the need for adjustment?, How have you adjusted?, Have you changed (or tried to change) Chinese employees and/or the subsidiary's work practices?, If so, what have you*

*changed (tried to change)?, What led to the need for change?, How did
you go about changing it?,* and *What challenges have you faced?.* To do
so, I performed a thematic analysis similar to that presented in Figure 1.

The results of my analyses are reported in the second to fifth parts of
Chapter 7.

Analysis of the quantitative data

I analyzed the quantitative data collected from the expatriate senior managers and their directly reporting Chinese subordinates to explore (1) the
degree to which the sample expatriate business leaders had adjusted their
leadership behaviors while engaging in cross-cultural leadership and
(2) the effect on employee satisfaction of the fit between the observed and
expected leadership behaviors. In the following sections, I explain how I
analyzed the data.

The degree of leadership behavior adjustment

In order to gain a balanced view of the degree to which the sample expatriate business leaders had adjusted their leadership behaviors while working in China, I analyzed the responses of both the expatriate leaders and
their directly reporting Chinese subordinates. I performed paired-sample
t tests to examine whether the mean scores pertaining to the *current* and
past leadership behavior variables differed from a statistical standpoint. In
regard to the data provided by the expatriates, I compared the mean scores
for the two categories of leadership behaviors (task- and relations-
oriented) they were *currently* adopting and had adopted *prior to* entering
into China. For the data collected from the Chinese subordinates, I also
compared the mean scores for the two leadership behavior categories they
perceived their leaders were *currently* adopting and had adopted during
the *first three months* of working in the subsidiaries. The results of the
analyses are presented in the first part of Chapter 7.

*The effect on employee satisfaction of the fit between observed
and expected leadership behaviors*

To examine whether or not the fit between observed and expected leadership behaviors is associated with employee satisfaction, I analyzed the

hypothesized relationship by performing polynomial regression analyses and three-dimensional response surface modeling (Edwards & Parry, 1993; Edwards & Van Harrison, 1993). The use of polynomial regressions is suited to avoid the numerous methodological problems associated with the difference scores method (e.g., confounded effects, difficulties in distinguishing the independent effect of each component measure) and is more accurate in relation to assessing how the outcome variables are affected by any congruence or incongruence between their component measures. The coefficients drawn from the results of polynomial regression analyses can be interpreted with aid of the shape and direction of a response surface along the (in)congruence line.

I regressed the outcome variables (supervisor and job satisfaction) on the control variables and on the five polynomial terms for task- and relations-oriented leadership behaviors. For the former, the five polynomial terms were as follows: observed task-oriented leadership behaviors (OT), expected task-oriented leadership behaviors (ET), observed task-oriented leadership behaviors squared (OT^2), observed task-oriented leadership behaviors multiplied by expected task-oriented leadership behaviors ($OT \times ET$), and expected task-oriented leadership behaviors squared (ET^2). I computed A similar set of five polynomial terms (OR, ER, OR^2, $OR \times ER$, ER^2) for relations-oriented leadership behaviors. The polynomial (quadratic) regression equations I used were as follows:

$$Y1 \text{ (Supervisor satisfaction)} = b0 + b1OT + b2ET + b3OT^2 + b4OT \times ET + b5ET^2$$

$$Y2 \text{ (Supervisor satisfaction)} = b0 + b1OR + b2ER + b3OR^2 + b4OR \times ER + b5ER^2$$

$$Y3 \text{ (Job satisfaction)} = b0 + b1OT + b2ET + b3OT^2 + b4OT \times ET + b5ET^2$$

$$Y4 \text{ (Job satisfaction)} = b0 + b1OR + b2ER + b3OR^2 + b4OR \times ER + b5ER^2$$

I used the first two equations to test the effects of the fit between observed and expected leadership behaviors (Y1: task-oriented behavior; Y2: relations-oriented behavior) on the first outcome variable—supervisor satisfaction—and the other two equations to test the effects of said fit (Y3: task-oriented behavior; Y4: relations-oriented behavior) on the second—job satisfaction. I then used the coefficients of the five polynomial terms drawn from the four regression analyses to generate the four three-dimensional surface plots. The results of the analyses are presented in the 4th part of Chapter 8.

Summary

- I adopted a mixed methods methodology for the research and collected the data/information from both expatriate managers and Chinese employees in three stages using online surveys and semi-structured interviews.

- The analysis and research findings presented in this book were based on data and information collected by surveying 391 expatriate senior managers working in China and 356 of their directly reporting Chinese subordinates and by interviewing 11 Chinese employees who were working or had worked under the supervision of expatriate managers.

- The Expatriate Leader Survey (ELS), which I sent to the expatriate managers, consisted of both qualitative and quantitative questions and was aimed at exploring the sample expatriate managers' experiences and views in relation to leading their Chinese subordinates and at investigating their degrees and patterns of leadership behavior adjustment.

- The Chinese Manager Survey (CMS), which I sent to the Chinese employees, was aimed at collecting their views on the leadership behaviors of their expatriate supervisors and their own degrees of satisfaction towards their jobs and their expatriate supervisors.

- I used the data collected by interviewing 11 Chinese employees to clarify some of the challenging employee characteristics mentioned by the expatriate senior managers.

- I subjected the qualitative data to a thematic analysis and the quantitative data to paired-sample t tests, polynomial regression analyses, and response surface modeling.

References

Audenaert, M., Carette, P., Shore, L. M., Lange, T., Van Waeyenberg, T., & Decramer, A. (2018). Leader-employee congruence of expected contributions in the employee-organization relationship. *The Leadership Quarterly*, *29*(3), 414–422.

Braun, V., & Clarke, V. (2006). Using thematic analysis in psychology. *Qualitative Research in Psychology*, *3*(2), 77–101.

Clark, A. E. (1997). Job satisfaction and gender: Why are women so happy at work? *Labour Economics*, *4*(4), 341–372.

Edwards, J. R., & Van Harrison, R. (1993). Job demands and worker health: Three-dimensional reexamination of the relationship between person-environment fit and strain. *Journal of Applied Psychology*, *78*(4), 628.

Edwards, J. R., & Parry, M. E. (1993). On the use of polynomial regression equations as an alternative to difference scores in organizational research. *Academy of Management Journal*, *36*(6), 1577–1613.

Guest, G., MacQueen, K. M., & Namey, E. E. (2012). Introduction to applied thematic analysis. *Applied Thematic Analysis*, *3*(20), 1–21.

Hackman, J. R., & Oldham, G. R. (1980). *Work Redesign*. Reading, MA: Addison-Wesley.

Hackman, J. R., & Lawler, E. E. (1971). Employee reactions to job characteristics. *Journal of Applied Psychology*, *55*(3), 259.

Lee, R., & Wilbur, E. R. (1985). Age, education, job tenure, salary, job characteristics, and job satisfaction: A multivariate analysis. *Human Relations*, *38*(8), 781–791.

Yukl, G., Gordon, A., & Taber, T. (2002). A hierarchical taxonomy of leadership behavior: Integrating a half century of behavior research. *Journal of Leadership & Organizational Studies*, *9*(1), 15–32.

Part II

Leadership in China

Chapter 4

Confucianism, Chinese Cultural Values, Social Relations, and Exchange Rules

Cultural values can profoundly influence the attitudes, behaviors, and performance of both leaders and employees. Traditional Chinese philosophies and cultural values have affected both past and current Chinese leadership and worker expectations. To understand leadership in China and develop an effective strategy for leading and managing Chinese employees, it is necessary to understand the traditional Chinese philosophies and cultural values/attributes, which are reflected in and influence the work attitudes and behaviors of Chinese leaders and employees.

In this chapter, I first explain the dominating and most influential ideology in China—Confucianism—and its four doctrines that are most relevant to Chinese leadership. I then explain three key Chinese cultural values that have deeply influenced the social relations and exchange rules in China.

Confucianism

For over 2,000 years, the ideology of Confucianism has dominated and has had the strongest impact on China and on the fundamentals of Asian business leadership. It has exerted a deep influence on the philosophy and moral values of China and other East and South Asian countries. The virtues advocated by Confucianism shape the foundations of all ethics and morality in the Chinese people's personal and social lives and deeply influence their values, thinking, and behaviors. This section first briefly describes the origin of Confucianism and then explains its four key doctrines that are most relevant to Chinese leadership.

Confucianism, also known as Ruism, is mainly concerned with the establishment and maintenance of a harmonious hierarchical social order, humanity, and personal and governmental morality. As a system of social and ethical philosophy or ideology, rather than a religion, Confucianism is based on the teachings and philosophy of K'ung Ch'iu (551–479 BCE). He was later called K'ung-fu-tzu (孔夫子, meaning "Master Kǒng"), is known in the West as "Confucius", and is considered as the greatest Chinese sage and teacher.

Confucius's teaching and philosophy were mainly recorded in the Analects and in two volumes known as the *Four Books* and the *Five Classics*. The Analects contain conversations and discussions held by Confucius with his disciples. It was compiled and documented not by Confucius himself, but by his disciples many years after his death. The Analects are an essential text of Confucianism and are required reading for Chinese schoolchildren. In the following, I explain the four doctrines of Confucianism that are most relevant to Chinese leadership: *xiao* (filial piety), *wu lun, ren,* and *li.*

Xiao (filial piety)

Xiao (孝, in Chinese; pronounced *xiào*) is considered to be the most fundamental of all Confucian values and the root of all other virtues. It is not only about respecting one's parents, elders, and ancestors; it is also about obeying one's parents', observing and realizing their wishes, honoring one's parents and ancestors by preserving their good name (e.g., by honoring them through one's personal career achievements or contributions to society), taking good care of one's body/health (so to not cause one's parents to worry), refraining from causing one's parents to be insulted, and, importantly, repaying and caring for one's aging parents and elderly family members.

From Confucius's point of view, the practice of filial piety is the starting point of all virtues and all positive social relationships, and is the cornerstone of the stability of the social order. His viewpoint can be seen from an excerpt from the Analects, in which he is reported to have said,

Few of those who are filial sons and respectful brothers will show disre-
spect to superiors, and there has never been a man who is respectful to
superiors and yet creates disorder. A superior man is devoted to the
fundamental. When the root is firmly established, the moral law will
grow. Filial piety and brotherly respect are the root of humanity.

(Analects of Confucius I: 2)

Confucius believed that a leader or a ruler needs to practice and demonstrate correct moral and ethical behaviors, such as filial piety, because

If the ruler acts properly, the common people will obey him without
being ordered to; if the ruler does not act properly, the common people
will not obey him even after repeated injunctions.

(Analects of Confucius XIII: 6)

In his discussion of ideological differences and social order, Fung
Yu-lan, a scholar in Chinese philosophy, commented that filial piety is the
foundation of Chinese society, stating that *filial piety is the organizing*
principle of a society based on a family system (Fung, 1949: 25).

Confucius's emphasis on filial piety and his ideal of a righteous leader
have shaped the traditional Chinese paternalistic leadership and employee
expectations of a leader. In Chinese organizations, senior managers/lead-
ers (especially the most senior ones) are often regarded as the father figures of organizations. Leaders are expected to exhibit good moral and
ethical behaviors, practice filial piety, and act with benevolence toward
their subordinates, who, in turn, are expected to respect their leaders
and to follow their orders.

Wu lun (five cardinal human relationships)

Wu lun (五伦, in Chinese; pronounced *wǔ lún*) refers to five cardinal
human relationships: emperor–minister, father–son, husband–wife, older–
younger brother, and friend–friend. Among the various kinds of human
relationships, Confucius saw these five dyadic ones as the most fundamental and believed that social order and stability can be achieved when
all individuals know their places in society and play their roles well.

The five dyadic relationships are subject to the following prescriptions. In the emperor–minister relationship, the ruler should be benevolent in the treatment of his subordinates, who, in turn, should be loyal to him. In the father–son relationship, a father should be kind to his children, who, in turn, should behave respectfully and with filial piety toward him. In the husband–wife relationship, the husband should be righteous and the wife submissive to him. In the older–younger brother relationship, the elder brother should be gentle to his younger brother, who, in turn, should obey him. Finally, in the friend–friend relationship, friends should respect and be faithful to each other.

All these five relationships emphasize the reciprocity and mutual obligations of the parties, highlighting their respective duties and responsibilities. The first four dyadic relationships, however, are unequal, with one party (i.e., the emperor, father, husband, and older brother) assuming a superior role that entails power and authority over the other, albeit owing the other protection and consideration. Those who occupy the subordinate roles (i.e., the minister, wife, son, and younger brother) are expected to be obedient and loyal to their superiors. Only the fifth relationship, friend–friend, is one of equality.

The five cardinal relationships of Confucianism have long shaped the hierarchical relationships found in Chinese families, organizations, and society at large. In terms of the relationship between leaders and subordinates in a business context, under the influence of Confucius's *wu lun*, Chinese leaders are expected to show authority and benevolence to their subordinates, who, in turn, are expected to be loyal and obedient and to comply with their leaders' requests. This leader–subordinate relationship expectation explains why many senior Chinese business leaders often exhibit authoritative and benevolent behaviors and are perceived by Chinese employees as the "fathers" of their organizations. It also explains why many of the expatriate managers who took part in my research observed that their Chinese subordinates were very compliant and rarely expressed objections or different opinions. More details on the expatriate managers' experiences of this hierarchical relationship are reported in Chapter 6.

It is worth providing a detailed explanation of the concept of "obedience", a "virtue" related to Confucius's *wu lun*, as it significantly influences the work attitudes and behaviors of Chinese employees. "Obedience" was considered by Confucius to be the core value for ensuring the observance of the relationships in *wu lun*, which would thus make a stable social order possible. As mentioned above, the first four dyadic relationships are unequal, with those occupying the subordinate roles being expected to "obey" their superiors. Confucius believed that the order and stability of the five relationships could be maintained by embedding obedience and requiring compliance.

This ideology has long influenced the thinking and behaviors of Chinese people. From a very young age, Chinese children are taught to obey their parents, schoolchildren are taught to abide by the rules and instructions set out by their teachers, and young people are told to comply with and respect the authorities. As a result, in past and current Chinese society, those who obey the orders or requests of parents, seniors, and authorities have been seen as worthy of praise, while any disobedience is seen as violating social rules and deserving of condemnation.

"Obedience" has helped in maintaining not only the social order in Chinese society but also the hierarchical relationship between managers and employees in Chinese organizations, which was widely observed by the expatriate managers who participated in my research. Chapter 6 details this observance and its effects on the behaviors of Chinese employees.

Ren (benevolence or humaneness)

Ren (仁, in Chinese; pronounced *rén*), often translated as benevolence or humaneness, is the virtue of being caring, concerned, and altruistic toward other human beings. It was considered by Confucius as the essence of the human being and as the source of all virtues and of the highest morality (Western and Garcia, 2018). This can be illustrated by an excerpt from the *Analects*, in which Confucius said,

> ...*The humane man, desiring to be established himself, seeks to establish others; desiring himself to succeed, he helps others to succeed. To judge others by what one knows of oneself is the method of achieving humanity...*

(Analects of Confucius VI: 28)

Benevolence and humaneness are often connected to the role of the good ruler in Confucian teaching. An ideal Confucian leader is one who demonstrates kind-heartedness, benevolence, and moral courage, which are passed on to those he leads (Linehan, 2017). In China, good leaders are expected to guide and care for their followers, not only within the work domain but also in the personal one. An example is helping those subordinates that are experiencing personal difficulties and showing concern for their familial well-being (Farh *et al.*, 2008). The followers, in turn, are expected to be loyal and deferential toward their leaders.

Confucius's teachings in regard to humane leadership have helped establish in China a system of leadership that supports harmony, conformity, and respect (Linehan, 2017). *Ren,* or benevolence, remains a major characteristic underpinning the practice of leadership in China, as shown in traditional Chinese paternalistic attitudes. Chapter 5 provides more details on paternalistic leadership.

Li (right and appropriate behaviors)

Li (礼, in Chinese; pronounced *lǐ*) is a system of ritual norms and proprieties (i.e., right, appropriate behaviors) that set out how people should properly behave in their everyday lives. The norms and proprieties covered in *Li* are comprehensive and far-reaching, involve all interactions between people, with nature, and even with material objects, and go beyond formal religious ceremonies to include social rituals (i.e., accepted social norms and behaviors; what we now call "social mores"). Examples of *Li* that are required to be observed under Confucianism are as follows: filial piety, brotherliness, righteousness, good faith, obedience, loyalty, and rules and rituals for learning, worship, mourning, and governance.

Confucius believed that rituals could help establish a stable social order and emphasized how, through *Li*, people could learn how to properly behave and relate to others, and understand the underlying order of nature. Confucius saw *Li* as fundamental to proper governmental leadership and believed that rulers should place more emphasis on *Li* and rely less on punishment. For example, *Li* involves leaders treating their subordinates with propriety and respect; and subordinates serving their leaders with loyalty.

An excerpt from the Analects illustrates this:

a prince should employ his minister according to the rules of propriety (Li); ministers should serve their prince with loyalty.

(Analects of Confucius, 3: 19)

The Confucian virtue of *Li* also helped shape traditional Chinese paternalistic leadership.

Chinese Cultural Values, Social Relations, and Exchange Rules

Understanding Chinese cultural values, social relations, and exchange rules is crucial to live and work in Chinese society, do business with the Chinese, and lead and manage Chinese employees. In this section, I explain three important and interrelated Chinese cultural values that profoundly influence Chinese social relations and exchange rules: *guanxi, mianzi* (face), and *renqing*. These values are closely related to each other, with *guanxi* being the central one, supported by the other two. In the following, I explain each of them in turn.

Guanxi (relationships, connections)

The concept and practice of *guanxi* play a very important role in Chinese people's social and work lives and guide their minds and behaviors; it is thus essential to understand it in order to understand and interpret Chinese social behaviors. A common saying and tongue twister humorously depicts the importance of *guanxi* in China: "有关系, 就没关系; 没关系, 就有关系" (pronounced as *yǒu guān xi, jiù méi guān xi; méi guān xi, jiù yǒu guān xi*). It says that, as long as you have *guanxi*, everything will be all right; however, if you don't have *guanxi*, you will be in trouble. In Chinese societies, *guanxi* is highly valued and widely used to get things done or access opportunities. For example, in Chinese workplaces, it is not uncommon to hear that someone has obtained a position, a promotion, or higher financial rewards because he/she has *guanxi* with senior or key people in the organization. In contrast, people who have skills, ability, knowledge, and experience, but no *guanxi*, may not be able to obtain the same advantages, benefits, or treatment. *Guanxi* is used for various situations and activities in Chinese people's lives. For example, to get a placement in a sought-after school, to get quick official approval for a project, to get a hospital bed, to get lucrative information, to be selected as a sponsor for an event, to gain access to a scarce commodity and powerful contacts, etc.

As a widespread phenomenon in China, *Guanxi* is crucial in personal relationships, employee relations, business to business relations, and business to government relations. It is no secret that the Chinese prefer to do business with people they know, trust, and respect. In China, business opportunities and deals are mostly given to and made with people in the *guanxi* network. As a Chinese saying goes: 多一个关系多一条路 (pronounced as *duō yī gé guān xì duō yī tiáo lù*). This literally translates to *To add a relationship is to add another road,* meaning that the more *guanxi* you have, the more solutions or opportunities will come your way.

Building and maintaining good *guanxi* with employees, business contacts, and other stakeholders in business are crucial for doing and operating a business in China. In terms of business dealings and operations, *guanxi* can affect market expansion and sales growth. In terms of employee relations, *guanxi* between managers and workers can affect worker engagement, commitment, and job satisfaction. Maintaining good *guanxi* with Chinese subordinates and obtaining their trust and respect can greatly help in establishing a more cooperative working relationship.

So, what is *guanxi* and how does it operate in practice? How do Chinese people build and maintain *guanxi*? How does it differ from Western "social networking"? The following sub-sections answer these questions.

What is guanxi and how does it operate in practice? *Guanxi* (关系, in Chinese, pronounced *guān xi*) literally means "relationships" and is often translated as "connections", "relationships", or "networks". In China, *guanxi* is generally used to describe "dyadic social exchange relationships" (Yang, 2002) that involve personal connections between two people and the exchange of mutually beneficial favors that can be used for personal and/or business purposes. In practice, however, the exchange relationship is not limited to two people; it can be extended to each other's *guanxi* networks when a favor needs to be sourced from a connection in it. In other words, the social exchange relationship in *guanxi* starts from a dyadic exchange relationship, but it can be extended to the connections of the two people's *guanxi* networks. For example, person A and person B have *guanxi*, and person B and person C have *guanxi*. Person A needs some help that person C can offer. Person A can get such help from person C through his connection with person B.

Guanxi was developed as a result of the influence of Confucian values and a lack of legal protection. Until recently, China did not have a strong rule of law that could enforce agreements or protect individuals and businesses from loss in social and business dealings/exchanges. *Guanxi*'s focus on mutual obligation and reciprocity grew out of the Confucian emphasis on the obligations and reciprocal duties assigned to the various familial and social roles and relationships, and on the etiquettes of gift relations. It was developed as a means of ensuring that favor exchanges would be mutually beneficial.

How do Chinese people build and maintain guanxi? In China, the use of *guanxi* can be a quick—and, in some cases, the only—way to get things done for personal or business purposes. Building and maintaining *guanxi*, however, can be a complex and time-consuming task and may require significant investments in time, efforts, and money. Nevertheless, once *guanxi* is built, it can go much deeper than Western social relationships and the exchanges of favors can move very quickly.

The ways in which Chinese people build *guanxi* may include greeting and chatting, dining together, gift giving, participating in social events, offering help in times of need or personal difficulties, helping with job seeking and promotion, hosting holidays for acquaintances' relatives, etc.; i.e., anything that a person can do as a personal favor to another to reciprocate or in the hope that the other person will do something in return in the future. It is important to note that *guanxi*'s principle of reciprocity and mutual obligation always leads to a never-ending cycle of returning favors as the receiver is obligated to repay the giver.

Chinese people usually develop and maintain *guanxi* in the following ways, which expatriate managers may consider:

Gift giving—The giving of gifts is an important aspect of building *guanxi* in China. Gifts can take the form of money and presents that would honor or be appreciated by the receivers. There are many occasions suited for giving gifts, such as national festivals (e.g., the mid-autumn festival), personal celebrations (e.g., a wedding or a birthday), and condolences (e.g., a funeral).

Offering help in personal events—A helping hand, a gift, and caring words in relation to a wedding, a funeral, an illness, and other personal events can deepen *guanxi* between people. The most meaningful favors occur in times of need.

Protecting and maintaining others' face—For Chinese people, "face", or *mianzi*, is one's esteem, honor, reputation, and social prestige, which needs to be protected and maintained. To develop and maintain good *guanxi*, a person must avoid causing others within one's own *guanxi* network to "lose face", as such a loss would make *guanxi* impossible. The concept of "face" is explained in detail in the following section.

Giving and repaying renqing—*Renqing*, usually interpreted as "favor", is an important medium of social exchange and a precondition for establishing and maintaining *guanxi*. Chinese people build *guanxi* by giving and receiving *renqing* or favors. The concept of *renqing* is explained in the section after the next one.

Joining and/or hosting dinners and entertainment—Food brings Chinese people together and close. By dining together, Chinese people get to know each other better, exchange information, and build trust. Various other social activities, such as karaoke, clubbing, and golf can also serve the same purpose.

Formal and informal introductions—Introducing two connections in one's *guanxi* network is an effective way to build new *guanxi* as Chinese people trust those with whom they are connected.

The differences between guanxi and social networking—In some aspects, the concept of *guanxi* is similar to the Western idea of social networking—both can be seen as ways to accumulate "social capital" suited to open doors and access opportunities. While social connections and networking are important in Western societies, the use of *guanxi* in China is much more prevalent (i.e., it is used in various spheres of personal, professional, and business life) and plays a far more important role. Chinese *guanxi* differs from Western social networking in several ways. In the following, I explain three key differences between guanxi and social networking and their implications for leading and managing Chinese employees.

Built from and on a personal level and based on trust—Western social relationships are relatively formal, mostly built from and on a professional level. Chinese *guanxi*, on the other hand, is always built from and on an intimate personal level. The Chinese's *guanxi* networks often include people they trust and have known personally for a long time, for example, extended family members, schoolmates, close friends, and others with whom they regularly come into contact. Through these personal and trusted relationships, they exchange favors, gifts, and benefits for commercial, social, work, and interpersonal purposes in a long-term process that, in turn, strengthens trust and these personal relationships.

Reciprocity with unequitable return—Both Western social relations and Chinese *guanxi* are established on the basis of a reciprocity process that maintains or strengthens relations, while failure to reciprocate can weaken or damage them. Western social exchanges emphasize an "equitable" reciprocity, in that the values exchanged should be equivalent, while Chinese *guanxi* exchanges are often unequitable. Chinese people tend to return a favor with something worth more than what they had received. An old Chinese saying goes "受人点 滴当 湧泉以报" (pronounced *shòu rén diǎn dī dāng yǒng quán yǐ bào*) which means that, if one receives a drop of kindness from other people, one should reciprocate with a fountain of it. It advises Chinese people to be appreciative, to remember other people's help, charity, and kindness, and to reciprocate with more than what was received.

Unspecified timing for repaying a favor, usually long term—In Western reciprocity, the repayment of a favor is usually expected to take place immediately. In Chinese *guanxi*, a favor can be reciprocated after a while, when the original receiver is able to do so or when the original giver needs or asks for it. This practice of an unspecified timeframe, usually a long one, for the repayment of a favor is largely still in existence in rural areas in China where harmonious and affective social relations are emphasized. In urban areas, however, expectations for the return of a favor are more short term and the attention has shifted from cultivating affective social bonds to gaining desirable exchanges. It has been argued that this instrumental change started in post-Mao era, when commercial activities and profit-making were highly encouraged.

Implications—From the features of Chinese *guanxi* presented above, we can draw at least four implications for the leading and managing of Chinese employees. First, to establish *guanxi* with them, efforts should be made on a "personal" level, rather than on a group or company one.

Second, in the workplace, most Chinese employees will appreciate any personal favors done and/or help given to them by their supervisors and will return these favors with more than what was given, usually in the form of hard work and loyalty.

Third, quick and short-term rewards will work better than long-term ones in motivating employees in large Chinese cities—such as Beijing,

Shanghai, Guangzhou, and Shenzhen—who look for quick monetary returns for the time and effort they put into their work; thus, quick reciprocation is desirable.

Fourth, it will take longer and be more difficult for expatriates to build *guanxi* with Chinese people, as the latter's *guanxi* networks often include people they trust and have known personally for a long time. Chinese people often categorize people into in-group and out-group members; the former usually include their family and extended family members, schoolmates, close friends, and others with whom they regularly come into contact, while the latter include everyone else. Chinese people like to work with/for people they trust and respect, and they are generally nice to their in-group members but may behave uncooperatively towards out-group members. It will thus take longer for outsiders to build trust. Nevertheless, relationships with new Chinese contacts can be built and/or enhanced by showing some knowledge of China and appreciation of its culture. See the suggestions made by the expatriate senior managers in Chapter 9.

Mianzi (face)

The concept of "face" or *mianzi* may not be unfamiliar to expatriates who have worked in Asian countries but could be alien to those coming to Asia for the first time. In Asian societies, "face" is seen as a key variable that has a pervasive and significant influence on social interactions and human behaviors, from individual decision-making to national policy setting (Kim & Nam, 1998). It is thus important for expatriate managers from non-Asian countries to have a good knowledge of this concept in order to understand much of their Asian employees' behavior.

Mianzi is an abstract and intangible concept that has no universal definition. It has been conceptualized in many ways; for example, it is variously seen as *a reputation achieved through getting on in life, through success and ostentation* (Hu, 1944: 45), *a social esteem accorded by others* (Yang, 1945: 167), *an image of self delineated in terms of approved social attributes* (Goffman, 1955: 213), and *the respectability and/or deference which a person can claim for himself from others, by virtue of the relative position he occupies in his social network and the degree to which he is judged to have functioned adequately in that position as well as acceptably in his general conduct* (Ho, 1976: 883).

From the above, we can see that *Mianzi* can represent one's reputation, esteem, pride, social status or prestige, image, and respectability. It is earned or obtained through achievements, taking on certain recognized social role(s), and/or meeting social expectations. To obtain and maintain face, one must fulfill one's obligations and behave in socially acceptable ways. Given its importance, the yearning of and efforts made by Chinese people to preserve face have, in fact, become a means of maintaining social order, often proving to be a more effective tool than laws and legislations.

Face is highly valued by the Chinese and is thus carefully protected and maintained, with most people being ready to go to any length to avoid losing it. Efforts to save or maintain face can be seen in every type of Chinese relationship, from friendships to familial ties and from work relationships to political ones. For example, in the workplace, some Chinese employees may withhold information or hide mistakes in order to preserve their esteem and reputation or those of others. A number of situations may cause a Chinese employee to feel that he or she has lost face; for instance, being publicly rejected, questioned, or criticized; being exposed as lacking in knowledge or ability; failing to fulfill one's social duties; and being the object of a dismissive gesture from a supervisor or of mockery from a colleague.

Face is deeply entwined with *guanxi*—a good *guanxi* can be built with someone by bolstering that person's face (e.g., by publicly appraising his or her achievements and good deeds) while it can be made impossible, soured, or lost by causing someone to lose "face" or the respect of others (e.g., by revealing his or her shortcomings).

The Chinese people's fear of losing face can cause many of them to exhibit certain behaviors, such as not taking any initiative in order to avoid making mistakes and not speaking up in public to avoid saying the wrong things and embarrassing themselves. Many of the expatriates who participated in my research regarded the issue of "saving face" as one of the major challenges for leading/managing Chinese employees. In Chapter 6, I report how issues related to "face" influence the ways in which expatriate managers lead/manage Chinese employees. The suggestions made by the expatriate senior managers on how to avoid making Chinese employees feel that they are losing face are presented in Chapter 9.

Renqing (favor, human emotions)

Renqing is another commonly accepted norm that regulates Chinese social relations and exchanges. It is an important medium of social exchange and a precondition for the establishment and maintenance of *guanxi*. It is based on the Confucian concepts of reciprocity and behavioral propriety *Li* (see a section above entitled "*Li* (right and appropriate behaviors)").

In Chinese society, *Renqing* has two common meanings: one is "human emotions" and the other "favor". First, as "human emotions", as found in the *Li-Ji* (the Book of Rites, an ancient Chinese book), it refers to the personal and emotional responses (e.g., happiness, anger, sadness, fear, love, hatred, and desire) elicited in an individual faced with different situations. A person will be judged as being well aware of *renqing*—and thus as capable of handling social relationship or to have equipped himself or herself with the necessary social knowledge—if he/she is empathic, capable of appreciating other people's emotional responses and of catering to the tastes of others and avoiding their dislikes, and prepared to do them favors when they are in desperate need of them.

The second, and most common, interpretation of *renqing* is as a "favor" that can be done, received, or owed in the social exchange process (Hwang, 1987). It can also be seen as a form of social capital or resource in interpersonal exchange relations (King 1991). For instance, when a person receives a favor from another, the latter can be seen as the owner of social exchange capital—which may be made up of both sentimental and material elements—that ought to be returned. For example, a person has spent two days in hospital helping a sick friend. The friend appreciated the help and later, to express their gratitude, returned the favor in the form of funding and business advice. This may later be reciprocated with something even more valuable. This *renqing* exchange relationship is likely to continue with both sentimental and material exchanges. Thus, *renqing*, which can consist of both abstract sentimental expressions (e.g., gratitude and appreciation) and actual material ones (e.g., money and gifts), can be hard to gauge and reciprocate.

The norm of giving and receiving *renqing* is in line with the operational rules of *guanxi* and has been shaped by it. The reciprocity of *renqing* is essential for the building and maintaining of *guanxi*. A good *guanxi* between two people can only be maintained when each reciprocates the other's favors. For example, a good working relationship between a manager and an employee can be built and maintained through the manager's continued care for the employee's personal life and, reciprocally, through the employee's continued contributions to the work and company goals. A *guanxi* can dissolve or turn into a hostile relationship if one party neglects his/her obligations of reciprocity.

Renqing can be a double-edged sword—on the one hand, it is a form of *guanxi* social capital that can be used and from which benefits can be derived; on the other hand, it is a debt or obligation that is "owed". Most Chinese people are in various *renqing* entanglements and are beholden to the other people in them. They give or owe someone *renqing*, which keeps these entanglements active. Although this can be a source of support in times of celebration or condolence, it can also be a psychological and financial burden, as it is almost impossible to get out of these entangled social relationships.

Several of the expatriate managers who took part in my research observed that Chinese employees tend to be loyal to individuals (e.g., to their supervisors/managers and customers), rather than to the company; and that they will often work harder under a supervisor who had provided them with personal assistance. These employee behaviors can be explained by two key reasons: one, that Chinese social relationships are always built from and on a personal level; and, two, that Chinese employees feel obliged to repay any *renqing* given to them.

Summary

- To understand leadership in China and develop an effective strategy for leading and managing Chinese employees, it is necessary to understand Confucianism and Chinese cultural values, which have deeply shaped Chinese social relation and exchange rules and influence the work attitudes and behaviors of Chinese leaders and employees.

- Confucianism, also known as Ruism, is mainly concerned with ways to establish and maintain a harmonious hierarchical social order, humanity, and personal and governmental morality. It is the dominating and most influential ideology in China; it shapes the foundations of all ethics and morality in Chinese people's personal and social lives, and deeply influences their values, thinking, and behaviors.

- The four doctrines of Confucianism that are most relevant to Chinese leadership are as follows: *xiao* (filial piety), *wu lun, ren,* and *li.*

  o *Xiao* (filial piety) relates to respecting and honoring one's parents and ancestors, taking good care of one's body/health, and repaying and caring for one's aging parents and elderly family members. Filial piety is considered to be the most fundamental Confucian value. Confucius viewed filial piety as the source of all virtues and the cornerstone of the stability of social order. Confucius's emphasis on filial piety and on the righteousness of the ideal leader has shaped the traditional Chinese paternalistic leadership style and employee expectations of a leader. In Chinese organizations, senior managers/ leaders (especially the most senior ones) are often regarded as the father figures of their organizations. Leaders are expected to exhibit good moral and ethical behaviors, practice filial piety, and act with benevolence towards their subordinates, who, in turn, are expected to respect their leaders and to follow their orders.

  o *Wu lun* refers to five cardinal human relationships: emperor–minister, father–son, husband–wife, older–younger brother, and friend–friend. In all these, reciprocity and mutual obligations are emphasized. The first four dyadic relationships, however, are unequal, with the person who holds the superior role (i.e., the emperor, father, husband, and older brother) holding power and authority over the other, to which protection and consideration are owed. Those who are in the subordinate roles (i.e., the minister, wife, son, and younger brother) are expected to be obedient and loyal to their superiors. Confucius believed that social order and stability can be achieved when all individuals know their places in society and play their roles well. The ideology of *Wu lun* has long shaped the hierarchical relationships in Chinese families, organizations, and society at large. In Chinese organizations, leaders are expected to behave with authority and benevolence toward their subordinates, who, in turn, are expected to show loyalty and to comply with their leaders' requests.

o *Ren* refers to the virtue of being caring, concerned, and altruistic toward other human beings. It was considered by Confucius as the essence of the human being and as the source of all virtues and of the highest morality. The ideal Confucian leader demonstrates kindheartedness, benevolence, and moral courage, which are passed on to those he leads. *Ren,* or benevolence, remains a major characteristic underpinning the practice of leadership in China.

o *Li* is a system of ritual norms and proprieties (i.e., right and appropriate behaviors) that governs how a person should properly behave in everyday life. The norms and proprieties covered in *Li* are wide ranging and comprehensive, involving all human interactions and those with nature and even material objects, and go beyond formal religious ceremonies to include social rituals. Confucius saw *Li* as fundamental to proper governmental leadership and believed that rulers should place greater emphasis on *Li* and rely less on punishment.

• The three key Chinese cultural values that most deeply influence the social relations and exchange rules in China and the work attitudes and behaviors of Chinese leaders and employees are as follows: *guanxi, mianzi* (face), and *renqing.* They are closely related to each other, with *guanxi* being the central one, supported by the other two.

o *Guanxi* is a Chinese concept that, in some respects, is similar to the Western idea of social networking—both can be seen as ways to accumulate "social capital" suited to open doors and opportunities. Chinese *guanxi,* however, differs from Western social networking in several ways. For example, its use is more prevalent (i.e., it encompasses various spheres of personal, professional, and business life) and plays a far more important role than that played by social networking in the West. It is always built from and on a personal level and features inequitable reciprocity and unspecified timing for the repayment of a favor. The implications of these features for leading and managing Chinese employees are as follows: (1) any efforts aimed at establishing *guanxi* with Chinese employees should be made on a "personal" level, rather than on the group or company ones; (2) doing personal favors for or helping Chinese employees is worthwhile, as they tend to pay back more than they receive, usually in the form of hard work and loyalty toward the supervisor; (3) quick and short-term rewards will work better than long-term ones in motivating employees in large Chinese cities; and (4) it will take longer and be more difficult for expatriates to build *guanxi* with Chinese people as the latter's *guanxi* networks often include people they trust and have known personally for a long time.

o *Mianzi* (face) is an abstract and intangible concept that has no universal definition. It can represent one's reputation, esteem, pride, social status or prestige, image, and respectability. It is earned or obtained through achievements, by taking on certain recognized social role(s), and/or by meeting social expectations. Face is highly valued by the Chinese and is carefully protected and maintained, with most people being willing to go to any length to avoid losing face. Because of their fear of losing face, many Chinese people will engage in certain workplace behaviors (e.g., withholding information and hiding mistakes) that many of the expatriates who took part in my research regarded as one of the major challenges for leading/managing Chinese employees.

o In Chinese society, *Renqing* has two common meanings: "human emotions" and "favor". It is more commonly interpreted as a "favor" that one can do or receive in the social exchange process. It is based on the Confucian concept of reciprocity and is an important medium of social exchange. The reciprocity of *renqing* is essential for building and maintaining *guanxi*. A good *guanxi* between two people can only be maintained when each reciprocates the other's favors. *Renqing* can be a double-edged sword—on the one hand, it is a form of *guanxi* social capital that can be used and form which benefits can be accrued; on the other hand, it is a debt or obligation "owed" to the original giver of *renqing*. Chinese employees tend to be loyal to individuals (e.g., their supervisors/managers and customers), rather than to the company; as such, they often work harder when working with a supervisor who had provided them with personal assistance. These employee behaviors can be explained by two key reasons: one, Chinese social relationships are always built from and on personal level; and two, Chinese employees feel obligated to repay any *renqing* given to them.

References

Farh, J. L., Liang, J., Chou, L. F., & Cheng, B. S. (2008). Paternalistic leadership in Chinese organizations: Research progress and future research directions. In *Leadership and Management in China: Philosophies, Theories, and Practices* (pp. 171–205). London: Cambridge University Press.

Fung, Y. L. (1949). The philosophy at the basis of traditional Chinese society. In F. S. C. Northrop (Ed.), *Ideological Differences and World Order* (pp. 18–34). New Haven: Yale University Press.

Goffman, E. (1955). On face-work: An analysis of ritual elements in social interaction. *Psychiatry, 18*(3), 213–231.

Ho, D. Y. F. (1976). On the concept of face. *American Journal of Sociology, 81*(4), 867–884.

Hu, H. C. (1944). The Chinese concepts of "face". *American Anthropologist, 46*(1), 45–64.

Hwang, K. K. (1987). Face and favor: The Chinese power game. *American Journal of Sociology, 92*(4), 944–974.

Kim, J. Y., & Nam, S. H. (1998). The concept and dynamics of face: Implications for organizational behavior in Asia. *Organization Science, 9*(4), 522–534.

King, A. Y. C. (1991). Kuan-hsi and network building: A sociological interpretation. *Daedalus, 120*(2), 63–84.

Linehan, P. M. (2017). *The Culture of Leadership in Contemporary China: Conflict, Values, and Perspectives for a New Generation.* London: Lexington Books.

Yang, M. (1945). *A Chinese Village.* New York: Columbia University Press.

Yang, M. M. H. (2002). The resilience of guanxi and its new deployments: A critique of some new guanxi scholarship. *The China Quarterly, 170,* 459–476.

Bibliography

Asia Society. (2020). *Confucianism.* Available from https://asiasociety.org/education/confucianism (Access: 22 May 2020).

Cheng, B. S., Chou, L. F., Wu, T. Y., Huang, M. P., & Farh, J. L. (2004). Paternalistic leadership and subordinate responses: Establishing a leadership model in Chinese organizations. *Asian Journal of Social Psychology, 7*(1), 89–117.

Farh, J. L., & Cheng, B. S. (2000). A cultural analysis of paternalistic leadership in Chinese organizations. In *Management and Organizations in the Chinese Context* (pp. 84–127). London: Palgrave Macmillan.

Fu, P. P., & Tsui, A. S. (2003). Utilizing printed media to understand desired leadership attributes in the People's Republic of China. *Asia Pacific Journal of Management, 20*(4), 423–446.

Hamilton, G. G. (1990). Patriarchy, patrimonialism, and filial piety: A comparison of China and Western Europe. *The British Journal of Sociology, 41*(1), 77–104.

Li, Y., & Sun, J. M. (2015). Traditional Chinese leadership and employee voice behavior: A cross-level examination. *The Leadership Quarterly, 26*(2), 172–189.

Ma, L., & Tsui, A. S. (2015). Traditional Chinese philosophies and contemporary leadership. *The Leadership Quarterly, 26*(1), 13–24.

Oxnam, R., & Bloom, I. (n.d.). The three Confucian value. Columbia University Available from: http://pascal.iseg.utl.pt/~cesa/Three%20Confucian%20 Values.pdf (Accessed: 1 June, 2020).

Western, S., & Garcia, É. J. (2018). *Global Leadership Perspectives: Insights and Analysis*. London: Sage.

World History Encyclopaedia. (2022). *Confucianism*. Available from: https:// www.worldhistory.org/Confucianism/ (Accessed: 18 May 2022)

Yang, B. (2012). Confucianism, socialism, and capitalism: A comparison of cultural ideologies and implied managerial philosophies and practices in the PR China. *Human Resource Management Review, 22*(3), 165–178.

Yan, Y. (1996). *The Flow of Gifts: Reciprocity and Social Networks in a Chinese Village*. Stanford, CA: Stanford University Press.

Chapter 5

Traditional and Contemporary Leadership in China

This chapter is divided into two parts: one dedicated to explaining traditional Chinese leadership and the second its contemporary equivalent. In the first, I start by explaining the traditional leadership style adopted in China—i.e., paternalistic leadership—covering its definitions, dimensions, and roots. I then discuss why paternalistic leadership has long been accepted and practiced in China, and also why it tends to receive negative criticisms from Western scholars, despite its ideology being increasingly adopted by Western organizations. Finally, I present the findings of the existing research on the effects of paternalistic leadership on employee outcomes and discuss whether it can be an effective leadership approach for modern businesses. In the second part of the chapter, I discuss the four key contemporary leadership styles found in China, how they are influenced by different ideologies, and the types of organizations commonly found to have adopted each.

Part 1. Traditional Chinese Leadership

Paternalistic leadership

Despite being a salient characteristic in Pacific Asian (e.g., Chinese, Japanese, Korean, Taiwanese, and Indian), Middle-Eastern, and Latin American cultures, paternalism is treated as a complex and controversial concept in the management literature (Aycan, 2006). What does paternalistic leadership mean in the context of China? This section presents its definitions, dimensions, and roots.

Definitions and dimensions

Webster's dictionary (1975, cited in Aycan, 2006) defines paternalism as *the principle or system of governing or controlling a country, group of employees, etc. in a manner suggesting a father's relationship with his children.* This definition suggests that, in the organizational context, paternalism occurs in dyadic and hierarchical relationships between supervisors and subordinates and that it involves top-down controlling mechanisms. Researchers studying paternalistic leadership in China, however, oppose Webster's sole focus on the controlling aspect and argue that paternalistic managers show not only strong control/authority but also care and support toward their subordinates (Redding *et al.*, 1994; Farh & Cheng, 2000).

Based on research conducted in China, Farh and Cheng (2000: 94) defined paternalistic leadership as *a style that combines strong discipline and authority with fatherly benevolence and moral integrity couched in a personalistic atmosphere*—a definition widely used and cited by Chinese researchers. The authors identified three dimensions or constructs of paternalism: **authoritarianism, benevolence, and morality**. Authoritarianism refers to leader behaviors that involve exerting power and control over subordinates and demanding their obedience and submission. Benevolence refers to those leader behaviors that exhibit personalized and thorough concern for the subordinates' well-being in both work and non-work domains. Morality portrays those leader behaviors that demonstrate high levels of integrity, morality, and selflessness. This dimension is analogous to the "integrity" one (consisting of the attributes of fairness, honesty, and trustworthiness) in the GLOBE research (House *et al.*, 2004), a pioneering large-scale research project on global leadership in 62 societies.

In brief, Chinese scholars view paternalistic leadership as a style in which a leader exercises strong authority over subordinates, shows concern for their personal and family well-being, and demonstrates high moral standards. The subordinates under such leadership are expected to comply with their leaders' orders and reciprocate their benevolence with loyalty, respect, and conformality.

The duality of paternalistic leadership (i.e., its combination of authoritarianism and benevolence) can be viewed as analogous to that involved in the relationship between parents and children within a family, in which the former commonly take on a dual role of both control and care, being strict disciplinarians and yet caring and loving (Aycan, 2006). This duality actually reflects the two seemingly conflicting and yet often coexisting leadership behavior styles most examined in leadership research in Western contexts: task- and relations-oriented (Tsui *et al.*, 2004).

Task-oriented behaviors are mainly aimed at the efficient improvement or accomplishment of tasks (Vroom & Jago, 2007; Yukl, 2013), and include behaviors such as organizing and planning work activities, assigning tasks, setting priorities, and monitoring operations and performance to improve efficiency. Strictly task-oriented managers can be portrayed as authoritarian (Aycan, 2006). Relations-oriented behaviors, on the other hand, are mainly concerned with the establishment of mutual trust, cooperation, commitment, and job satisfaction (Stogdill, 1974; Yukl, 2013), and include behaviors such as providing support and encouragement, showing trust and respect, consulting with subordinates, empowering people, and providing coaching and mentoring (Fleishman, 1953; Vroom & Jago, 2007). Candidly relations-oriented managers can be portrayed as caring and participative (Aycan, 2006).

Aycan's (2006: 449) outline of paternalistic leadership behaviors, listed in the following, is helpful to understand how paternalistic leaders operate in practice:

- *Creating a family atmosphere in the workplace*: Engaging in fatherly behaviors toward subordinates and giving them fatherly advice in both their professional and personal lives.
- *Establishing close and individualized relationships with subordinates*: Establishing close individual relationships with all subordinates, getting to know them in person (personal problems, family life, etc.), being genuinely concerned with their welfare, and taking a close interest in their professional and personal lives.
- *Getting involved in the non-work domain*: Attending the events (e.g., wedding and funeral ceremonies, and graduations) that are important to subordinates and to their immediate family members, providing help and assistance (e.g., financial) to subordinates in need, acting as a mediator between employees and their spouses in the event of marital problems.

- *Expecting loyalty*: Expecting loyalty and commitment from subordinates, expecting them to immediately attend to any company emergency even if this will require them to do so at the expense of their private lives.
- *Maintaining authority/status*: Assigning importance to status differences (positions and ranks), and expecting employees to behave accordingly; assuming to know what is good for subordinates and their careers; not wanting anyone to doubt their authority.

The roots of paternalistic leadership: Confucian ideology

As mentioned in Chapter 4, Confucianism is the dominating and most influential ideology in China. As such, it deeply influences the values, thinking, and behaviors of the Chinese people. It may thus be unsurprising that Chinese scholars regard Confucian ideology to be the root of paternalistic leadership. In this section, I explain the roots of the three dimensions of paternalistic leadership: *authoritarianism, benevolence, and morality.*

- **Authoritarianism:** It is considered to reflect Confucius's *wu lun* (i.e., the five cardinal relations, see Chapter 4 for details). In dyadic relationships, individuals are expected to play their roles, with those holding subordinate ones being expected to be obedient and loyal to their superiors (Li & Sun, 2015; Farh & Cheng, 2000; Tsui *et al.*, 2004).
- **Benevolence:** It is seen as reflecting a foundation element of Confucianism—*ren*, the virtue of being caring, concerned, and altruistic toward other human beings (see Chapter 4 for details). An ideal Confucian leader is one who demonstrates kindness and genuine concern toward those he leads.
- **Morality:** It is considered to be rooted in Confucius's teachings on leadership. Confucius advised that leaders should hold and demonstrate high moral character in order to gain the trust, support, and confidence of their followers (Farh & Cheng, 2000; Wah, 2010). He believed that leaders should rule by moral virtue rather than by laws, as leaders who are morally upright will cultivate followers who adhere to moral and ethical standards (McDonald, 2012), thus being more effective than those who threaten them with punishments and negative consequences. Confucius saw righteousness as the most important character in both

leaders and followers. To him, intelligent and knowledgeable people with low morality are harmful. He once said,

Noble leaders consider righteousness to be of the highest importance. A noble leader who has courage but is not righteous becomes a rebel; a common person who has courage but is not righteous becomes a thief.

(Analects of Confucius 17: 23)

Why is paternalistic leadership accepted and practiced in China?

Influenced by Confucian ideas, paternalistic leadership is still practiced in modern Chinese organizations. It has long been accepted and practiced in China for two key reasons. First, it is in line with China's collectivistic and high power distance culture (Aycan, 2006; Pellegrini & Scandura, 2008), which causes it to be considered positively because, in such cultures, people are more interdependent, more conformist, and more accepting of power inequality (Aycan, 2006). Paternalistic leadership, which involves strict and caring fatherly behaviors that encompass the employees' personal lives, is thus accepted and even expected. This is in contrast to individualistic cultures, in which people value autonomy, self-reliance, and self-determination, and thus view paternalism as an undesirable practice that restricts or violates the rights of individuals to exercise autonomy and choice (Blokland, 1997 cited in Aycan, 2006).

The second reason for the acceptance of paternalistic leadership in Chinese organizations is related to the Chinese cultural characteristic of valuing strong family bonds, whereby both employers and employees tend to see their organization as a family. Thus, employers feel responsible for looking after their employees, who, in turn, expect to be looked after in both their professional and personal lives. For example, Chinese employees commonly perceive their employers as being responsible for providing training for their professional development and expect them to participate in their personal lives, by visiting them when they are ill, attending their families' weddings and funerals, and helping them when they encounter personal difficulties.

In brief, the Chinese cultural characteristics of collectivism, strong family bonds, and acceptance of hierarchy and of power inequalities between managers and employees have made paternalistic leadership an enduring approach in China.

Why does paternalistic leadership receive negative criticism from western scholars, despite the increasing use of its ideology in western organizations?

Despite the longstanding and present use of paternalistic leadership in Chinese society and other non-Western countries and regions (e.g., Japan, Korea, Taiwan, India, the Middle East, and Latin America), it is generally perceived negatively in the Western management literature. Western scholars, in general, perceive it as authoritative and manipulative, and use various negative metaphors and descriptions for it, such as *benevolent dictatorship* (Northouse, 1997: 39), *a hidden and insidious form of discrimination* (Colella *et al.*, 2005: 26, cited in Pellegrini & Scandura, 2008), *an anachronism* (Padavic & Earnest, 1994: 389) *discrimination without the expression of hostility* (Jackman, 1994: 10), and *non-coercive exploitation* (Goodell, 1985: 252).

The core criticism leveled at paternalistic leadership by Western scholars largely lies on three aspects: *control, the intent of benevolence,* and *inequality in the power relationship.* In terms of *control,* paternalistic leadership has been criticized for the control it exercises over subordinates. Nevertheless, control of employees can be ascribed to various motivations linked to the differences between the authoritarian and authoritative management styles. In the former, control mechanisms such as rewards and punishments are used to ensure employee compliance (Aycan, 2006). On the other hand, in authoritative management styles, control is used to ensure that employees follow company rules in order to achieve organizational goals.

In terms of the *intent of benevolence,* some Western scholars argue that paternalistic leaders show benevolence (care, concern, and altruism) toward their subordinates because they want to be repaid with loyalty and obligations—rather than for selfless reasons—and that the loyalty and obligations stemming from the leaders' benevolence cause subordinates to become indebted and oppressed (Uhl-Bien & Maslyn, 2005, cited in Pellegrini & Scandura, 2008). The issue of the intent that underpins benevolent leadership behaviors has been discussed using the concepts of benevolent vs. exploitative paternalism (Aycan, 2006). In the former, leaders are genuinely concerned about the welfare of their followers', who, in turn, reciprocate by exhibiting loyalty out of respect and appreciation (Aycan, 2006). In contrast, in exploitative paternalism, leaders engage in benevolent behaviors only to elicit employee compliance in order to achieve organizational goals, and employees show loyalty and deference mainly because they know that the fulfillment of their needs is in the hands of their leaders (Aycan, 2006).

Some may ask whether Chinese leaders engage in benevolent behaviors out of genuine care for their subordinates or do so merely in order to protect their personal interests. I would aver that both scenarios could be true. Many Chinese leaders do care about their employees and their families while at the same time, under the social norm of reciprocity, expect their employees to repay them with things such as respect and loyalty. Some scholars have ruled out malicious intentions as the motive for Chinese leaders' benevolent behaviors toward their subordinates and their families (see, e.g., Aycan, 2006; Tsui *et al.*, 2004), arguing that such behavior is embedded in Chinese culture and is not necessarily aimed at achieving instrumental or immediate objectives.

In terms of the *inequality in the power relationship*, paternalistic leadership has been criticized for the superior position assumed by leaders in terms of skills, knowledge, experience, authority, and moral standards, while employees take an inferior one, being obliged to follow the leaders' instructions (Aycan, 2006). Western scholars consider paternalistic leaders' expectations for their employees to show compliance and conformity to be coercive and non-voluntary, and thus oppressive. But the assumption that employees are always forced to be compliant would not hold in the case of those employees who wish to show their loyalty in order to repay their leaders' benevolence by voluntarily complying and conforming with their wishes.

Although paternalism is under attack from many Western scholars on ideological and philosophical grounds (Aycan, 2006), ironically, Western organizations seem to be increasingly adopting the paternalistic ideology and taking paternalistic management approaches. For example, many large Western organizations are helping themselves by helping their employees deal with their personal and family responsibilities through various work-life balance related HR policies and practices such as child care, flexible and remote working programs, health cash plans, fitness perks, and paid family leave, thus enhancing employee productivity and reducing sick leave and absenteeism. A more recent practice involves employee financial well-being programs whereby organizations provide their employees with financial consultations, free debt management advice, and information about the benefits they offer. Some organizations even offer financial education courses and give employees access to loans. All these HR programs, which show the characteristics of the paternalistic management approach, are intended to promote the commitment and performance of employees by helping them to manage their personal responsibilities. Some have argued that the increasing adoption of paternalistic approaches in business settings is likely due to their potential beneficial outcomes for organizations, and others have argued that such approaches are used as an alternative middle way to humanity and labor exploitation (Aycan, 2006).

Can paternalistic leadership produce employee outcomes beneficial for organizations? Can paternalistic leadership be an effective approach for modern businesses? To answer these questions, we need to take a closer look at what research has found in regard to the effects of paternalistic leadership on employee work outcomes. The following section provides a review of some such findings.

Existing research findings on the effects of paternalistic leadership on employee work outcomes

In this section, I provide a review of the research findings on the effects of paternalistic leadership on employee work outcomes. Much of the early research had treated and examined paternalistic leadership as a unidimensional (or unified) construct, while more recent work has examined it as a multidimensional one (i.e., has investigated the differential impacts of its three dimensions on employee outcomes). The empirical research that has examined paternalistic leadership as a unidimensional construct generally found that it is *positively* related to numerous employee work outcomes regardless of cultural context; while those scholars who have examined it as a multidimensional construct have shown that its three dimensions have different effects on subordinate attitudinal and behavioral outcomes. In the following, I first present a summary of the findings yielded by the examination of paternalism as a unidimensional construct and then those produced by considering it a multidimensional one.

The unidimensional approach

Most of the early research on the effects of paternalistic leadership on employee work outcomes treated and examined paternalistic leadership as a unidimensional construct. This line of research was conducted in various cultural settings and generally found paternalistic leadership to be associated with positive employee work outcomes, such as job satisfaction, leader–member relationship, obligation, goal setting, job performance, and organizational commitment. For example, Uhl-Bien *et al.* (1990), who studied a sample of 1,075 Japanese line managers working in five leading Japanese organizations, found that the degree to which the managers believed in company paternalism was positively and significantly associated with career investments, quality of leader–member relationships, and job satisfaction. Aycan *et al.*'s (2000) empirical study of 1,954 employees from 10 countries found that India, Pakistan, China, and Turkey scored highest on paternalism, whereas Israel and Germany scored lowest, and Romania, Russia, Canada, and the USA recorded mid-range scores. They also found that high paternalism predicated greater obligation toward others. Pellegrini *et al.* (2010) compared the attitudes of 207 Indian and 215 American employees with respect to paternalistic leadership and found it to be positively related to leader–member exchange and organizational commitment. The above research findings suggest that paternalistic leadership may foster various positive employee work outcomes across cultures.

The multidimensional approach

Most recent studies on the effects of paternalistic leadership on employee work outcomes, particularly those conducted in China and Taiwan, used Farh and Cheng's (2000) three dimensions of paternalism (i.e., authoritarianism, benevolence, and morality) to examine whether they have different effects on employee attitudinal and behavioral outcomes. Overall, their findings indicate a negative relationship between authoritarianism and employee outcomes but a positive relationship for the benevolence and morality dimensions.

Authoritarianism: Authoritarianism has been found to be *negatively* related to subordinate attitudes and behaviors, such as employee satisfaction with their leaders (Cheng *et al.*, 2002a), organizational commitment (Farh *et al.*, 2006), organizational citizenship behavior (Cheng *et al.*, 2002b), and team interaction (Cheng *et al.*, 2002a). Research has also shown that authoritarian leadership evokes employee obedience, dependence, and compliance (Farh & Cheng, 2000; Cheng *et al.*, 2004), fear of supervisors (Cheng *et al.*, 2004; Farh *et al.*, 2006), and angry emotions (Wu *et al.*, 2002). Nevertheless, the various negative relationships were found to be weakened or to disappear and become positive in the presence of high subordinate respect for hierarchy and dependence on their leaders. For example, some researchers found that authority-oriented subordinates (i.e., those holding strong traditional values and high respect for, or the will to respect, social hierarchies) exhibit high identification and compliance with leader authoritarianism and high satisfaction with supervision (Cheng *et al.*, 2004; Farh *et al.*, 2006). Researchers have also found that subordinates who are highly dependent on their supervisors for the work resources needed for job completion and performance rewards tend to display better job performance and more positive organizational citizenship behaviors, be more loyal toward their supervisors, and respond more favorably to authoritarianism (Farh *et al.*, 2006; Pellegrini & Scandura, 2008; Farh & Cheng, 2000).

To summarize, the findings of research on authoritarian leadership reviewed above indicate that it is *negatively* related to various employee outcomes and evokes employee obedience, dependence, and fear of supervisors. However, such a negative relationship is weakened or disappears and turns positive when subordinates hold a high respect for hierarchy and are highly dependent on their leaders.

Benevolence and morality: Contrary to the negative employee work outcomes found to be associated with authoritarianism, benevolence and morality have consistently been found to be related to positive ones. For example, benevolent paternalism has been found to be positively related to organizational commitment (Pellegrini & Scandura, 2008), gratitude and repayment for leaders' care (Cheng *et al.*, 2004; Farh & Cheng, 2000), and better work performance (Wu *et al.*, 2012; Zhang *et al.*, 2015). Moral leadership has been found to result in high levels of respect for and strong identification with leaders (Farh & Cheng, 2000). Both benevolent and moral leadership have been found to be positively associated with satisfaction with team leaders, commitment to the team (Cheng *et al.*, 2002a), organizational commitment (Farh *et al.*, 2006), loyalty toward and trust in leaders, organizational citizenship behavior (Cheng *et al.*, 2002b), identification with leaders, gratitude, and compliance without dissent (Cheng *et al.*, 2004).

In brief, the above research findings suggest that those leaders who are benevolent and behave morally can expect to earn the commitment, respect, gratitude, identification, and loyalty of their subordinates.

Can paternalistic leadership be an effective approach for modern businesses?

The research findings reviewed in the previous section indicate that, when examined as a unidimensional construct, paternalistic leadership is associated with various positive employee outcomes. When the differential effects on employee outcomes of its three dimensions are examined separately, benevolence and morality are found to be associated with positive employee work outcomes, while authoritarianism is related to positive outcomes only when employees have high respect for hierarchy and high job dependence on their leaders. Overall, it can be concluded that paternalistic leadership has been found to be positively associated with employee attitudes and behaviors, particularly when employees have a high respect for hierarchy and high reliance on leaders for resources.

What do these research findings tell us? What are their implications for expatriate business leaders working in China? Can paternalistic leadership be an effective leadership approach for modern businesses? The research findings suggest that it would be appropriate and advantageous for expatriate business leaders to adopt it when managing Chinese employees because of the collectivism and acceptance of hierarchy that characterize the local culture and due to the greater interdependence exhibited by Chinese people, who tend to see the organization for which they work as a family. In this cultural context, a paternalistic leadership approach—which involves playing a dual role as a strict and a caring father who is involved in his employees' personal lives—will be accepted and even expected.

In recent years, many leadership researchers have focused their attention on leadership related to interpersonal and relational skills. They found that leaders endowed with high levels of interpersonal and relational skills are associated with employee loyalty and commitment (Pellegrini & Scandura, 2008). Paternalistic leadership, as one such relational leadership approach, has also been found to be associated with various positive employee outcomes, as discussed in the previous section.

My research findings, drawn from the study of 391 expatriate senior managers, show that many of them had chosen to take a paternalistic leadership approach in order to more effectively lead/manage their Chinese employees (see Chapter 9 for the expatriates' suggestions). My view is that paternalistic leadership would be a viable leadership strategy for contemporary businesses if the three key criticisms leveled at it (i.e., control, the intent of benevolence, and inequality in the power relationship) were to be addressed correctly. First, control should be used to promote employee welfare and to ensure that company policies are followed, rather than as a mechanism for employee compliance. Researchers have found that forced employee compliance can influence the relationship between subordinates' attitudes and organizational behaviors and that compliance to authority is no longer a value common to all Chinese, especially in regard to the younger generations (Cheng *et al.*, 2004: 97). Second, engagement in benevolent behaviors should be motivated by genuine concern for employee welfare, rather than by instrumental objectives. Third, the power relationships between leaders and their subordinates should be based on skill, knowledge, and experience levels, rather than on hierarchy and expectations of unconditional compliance. After all, leadership is about leading and managing "people", most of whom will want to be treated with respect and fairness and will want leaders who genuinely care about their welfare and possess high moral standards.

Part 2. Contemporary Business Leadership in China

Some readers may think that "Chinese leadership" is homogenous and monolithic. However, the vastness of mainland China is punctuated by various ideologies and sub-cultures that influence leaders' thought patterns and behaviors; therefore, no single version of leadership can encompass the underlying complexity. Moreover, due to China's rapid economic development, its leadership is changing and exhibiting multiple facets.

Contemporary Chinese business leadership is shaped by various ideologies and political and economic systems. After reviewing a large volume of relevant literature, I observed that contemporary Chinese leadership can be categorized into four key styles: (1) paternalistic, (2) communal, (3) market, and (4) hybrid. The first three are respectively shaped by the three ideological systems of Confucianism, socialism, and capitalism. The fourth is the result of combinations of the other three. These four types of leadership co-exist in China and are prevalent in different organizational contexts.

First of all, the paternalistic leadership style—which, as discussed previously, is based on the ideology of Confucianism—is commonly found in family-owned and private businesses. Second, the communal leadership style, which is built on socialist ideology, is mostly found in state-owned enterprises (SOEs). Third, the market leadership style, which is largely influenced by capitalist values and beliefs, is more likely to be found in joint ventures and foreign-owned enterprises. Last, the hybrid leadership style is taking hold in many Chinese organizations because of the combined influences from the three previously mentioned ideologies.

The following sections present the four leadership styles in greater detail and illustrate how they are influenced by different ideologies.

Paternalistic leadership

As explained in the first part of this chapter, paternalistic leadership is a style that combines strong discipline and authority with fatherly benevolence and moral integrity. It has traditionally been used in China and can still be found in contemporary Chinese organizations, particularly family-owned and private ones (Cheng *et al.*, 2004).

Chinese researchers have observed that, despite China's economic development, certain underlying Confucian values and beliefs (e.g., obedience, *wu lun, ren, li*, and the class system) have remained unchanged and continue to influence the work attitudes and behaviors of Chinese people, including business leaders (Fu & Tsui, 2003). Some Chinese researchers have suggested that paternalistic leadership is commonly used in Chinese family-owned businesses due to its effectiveness in maintaining control over employees and family wealth (Farh *et al.*, 2006). Many owners and senior managers of family-owned and private businesses still exhibit authoritative and benevolent fatherly behaviors, and are perceived by their employees as the "fathers" of their organizations.

Communal leadership

Another key influencer of the leadership practices enacted in China is the ideology associated with its political and economic systems. The country is ruled by the Communist Party of China (CPC) and its socialist ideologies are explicitly and implicitly reflected on the management practices and leadership approaches of Chinese companies, particularly SOEs. The CPC's ideologies are derived from Marxism–Leninism, Maoism, Deng Xiaoping Theory, and the theory of Three Represents.

Party members are expected to work hard, be loyal and honest to the Party, abide by Party policies and state laws, and promote communist moral codes. Further, they are expected to resist corruption, to put the collectivity's interests before their own, to serve the people unreservedly even at their own expense, and to be ready to sacrifice their lives during times of difficulties and danger.

Party leaders of all levels are expected to show concern for their followers and to sacrifice themselves for them; they are also expected to be devoted, determined, hardworking, collectivistic, principled, self-sacrificing, service-oriented, value-driven, corruption-resistant, and vision-driven. Using its privileged ruling position, the CPC urges its members to devote themselves to communist causes and to follow and personify the aforementioned leadership attributes. As, in China, all the leaders of Chinese SOEs and many other business leaders are Party members, some studies have found that many Chinese business leaders "wear two hats"—those of business leader and of Party member, and work toward the achievement of the party's goals.

Communal leadership has much in common with the traditional paternalistic leadership in terms of its emphasis on authority and hierarchical power. Although the CPC is theoretically committed to communism, it is actually hierarchical. Its overall strategy is based on a central planning system, with low-level managerial staff having little or no decision-making power and being obligated to passively follow the instructions emanated from the top. Communication is primarily top-down, people occupying lower-level positions being required to follow the commands of the party's central committee. Mao's leadership principle recites that the *minorities must obey the majorities, subordinates must obey supervisors, and all party members must obey the central committee* (Yang, 2012: 173). The feature of leaders holding high authority and hierarchical power, which is shared by the paternalistic and communal leadership style, is likely to be the key reason for the submissiveness of many Chinese employees to any orders given by people in authority or higher positions. This characteristic of Chinese employees is described in detail in Chapter 6.

Market leadership

Capitalism has influenced almost all developed countries. It has also exerted a strong influence on the development of China since late 1978, when China initiated its economic reform and open-door policy. Since then, certain capitalist elements, such as the free market and financial incentives, have been considered to be a necessity for economic growth. It has also been considered necessary to draw upon Western managerial theories and practices to help more effectively manage business processes and personnel. Furthermore, the unprecedented level of international trade and the influx of foreign direct investment that has entered China in recent decades has also fostered the adoption of Western management and leadership ideas. The management knowledge learned and brought home by Western-educated Chinese managers has also promoted the use of Western leadership approaches. A market leadership style has thus emerged in contemporary China as a result of the influence of Western values, beliefs, norms, and practices.

Two key features of the capitalist management philosophy are technical rationality and profit maximization. For instance, in capitalist economies, most organizations are geared to maximize profits; decisions are largely made through rational processes (i.e., linear, step-by-step, maximizing outcomes); innovation, system, structure, and progression are emphasized as viable means to maximize profits; communication takes place via formal channels; and the key roles of leaders are to develop a clear vision, to clarify organizational objectives, and to be accountable for outcomes. Thus, under the influence of the capitalist ideology, market leadership in China tends to emphasize technical competencies and skills in order to maximize profits.

Most joint ventures and wholly foreign-owned enterprises (WFOEs) operating in China are run mostly based on capitalist ideology. Although China styles itself as a non-capitalist country, research has shown that many Chinese businesses and organizations have been borrowing managerial ideas and approaches from capitalist economies. For example, some researchers have found that certain Western values—such as aggressiveness, ambitiousness, competency, and entrepreneurship—are held by Chinese managers. Western management practices—such as 360-degree feedback, information sharing with the frontline workforce, and ability-based promotions (as opposed to seniority-based ones)—have been adopted to varying degrees by Chinese organizations. It has been stated that, in the Chinese private sector, capitalism *has gone from pariah to member of the elite* (Redding, 2002: 237). Despite the fact that many Chinese organizations have been adopting capitalist ideas and employing Western management practices, the word "capitalism" is carefully avoided in the media and in official documents for political and ideological reasons.

Hybrid leadership

The hybrid leadership style has emerged in China as a result of the combined influence of the aforementioned three ideologies, i.e., the continuing prevalence of Confucian values, the socialist ideologies held by the ruling political party, and the technical rationality and profit maximization featured in the capitalist management philosophy. These three seemingly different ideologies co-exist and have been adopted, to varying degrees, in different business settings, evolving into a hybrid model of Chinese management. On the one hand, traditional Chinese values (such as social harmony, hierarchy, control, and family collectivism) and traditional social practices (such as *guanxi* and face-saving) endure and still influence management style and leadership in China. On the other hand, the government continues to advocate communist ideologies and promote the country's technological and economic development through technical rationality. At the same time, capitalism and Western management approaches are continuing to influence Chinese management and leadership as a result of business interactions between China and Western countries and through the approaches taken by Western-educated Chinese managers.

Several empirical studies have found evidence of the existence in China of a hybrid model of management practices that reflects a confluence of traditional and Western practices and socialism. For example, a hybrid HR management model has been found in Chinese organizations that combine traditional management practices with those used by foreign MNCs. Some prominent Chinese CEOs have been found to exhibit leadership attributes that feature ideologies based upon Confucian, communist, and modern Western values. It has been noted that Chinese private businesses can be seen to practice "network capitalism", wherein *guanxi* is intensively used to achieve business goals and gain profits (Yang, 2012: 176). It has been observed that Chinese leadership remains Sino-centric and that Chinese leaders have succeeded in adopting some modern Western practices without losing their "Chineseness" (Littrell, 2002).

To summarize, the three ideologies discussed above and China's political and economic systems all significantly influence contemporary Chinese leadership. Consequently, when considering the most suitable leadership approach to adopt in China, expatriate business leaders should endeavor to become acquainted with the three competing ideologies, the economic and political systems, and the characteristics of Chinese employees.

Summary

- Paternalistic leadership, which has traditionally been used in China, can still be found in contemporary Chinese organizations. It is a style that combines strong discipline and authority with fatherly benevolence and moral integrity. Chinese scholars regard it to be rooted in Confucian ideology and have identified its three constituent dimensions: authoritarianism, benevolence, and morality.

- Paternalistic leadership has long been accepted and practiced in China for two key reasons: one, it is in line with China's collectivistic and high power distance culture; and two, it is related to the Chinese cultural characteristic of valuing strong family bonds.

- Western scholars have leveled various negative criticisms at paternalistic leadership, mainly focused on issues related to its control over subordinates, the intent behind any benevolent behaviors, and the inequality of the power relationship between leaders and subordinates. Although many Western scholars have criticized paternalism on ideological and philosophical grounds, ironically, the management practices of Western organizations seem to have been absorbing the paternalistic ideology and increasingly taking paternalistic management approaches (e.g., the use of various work-life balance related HR policies and practices such as child care, health cash plans, fitness perks, and paid family leave) to help employees manage their personal responsibilities.

- Overall, research has shown that paternalistic leadership is positively related to numerous positive employee work outcomes (e.g., job satisfaction, commitment, and loyalty), particularly when employees hold high levels of respect for hierarchy and strongly rely on leaders for resources. The research findings suggest that it would be advantageous for expatriate business leaders to adopt a paternalistic leadership style when managing Chinese employees because of the collectivism and acceptance of hierarchy that are featured in the national culture, with Chinese employees tending to see the organizations for which they work as families and expecting their employers to look after their welfare.

- Paternalistic leadership can be an effective approach for modern businesses if the key criticisms leveled at it (i.e., control, the intent of benevolence, and the inequality of the power relationship) are correctly addressed. First, control should be used to promote employee welfare and to ensure that company policies are followed, rather than as a mechanism for employee compliance. Second, any benevolent acts should be motivated by genuine concern for employee welfare, rather than by instrumental objectives. Third, the power relationship between leaders and subordinates should be based on skill, knowledge, and experience levels, rather than on hierarchy and expectations of unconditional compliance.

- Four key leadership styles co-exist in contemporary China: (1) paternalistic, (2) communal, (3) market, and (4) hybrid. These are influenced by different ideologies and are prevalent in different organizational contexts in China. The first three are shaped respectively by Confucianism, socialism, and capitalism and are prevalent respectively in family-owned and private businesses, SOEs, and joint ventures and foreign-owned enterprises. The fourth type is the result of combinations of the other three and is developing in many Chinese organizations of different sizes.

- When considering the most suitable leadership style to adopt in China, expatriate business leaders should endeavor to become acquainted with the three competing ideologies, the economic and political systems, and the characteristics of Chinese employees, which are crucial to develop a better understanding of contemporary Chinese leadership.

References

Aycan, Z. (2006). Paternalism: Towards conceptual refinement and operationalization. In U. Kim, K. S. Yang, & K. K. Hwang (Eds.), *Indigenous and Cultural Psychology: Understanding People in Context* (pp. 445–466). New York: Springer.

Aycan, Z., Kanungo, R., Mendonca, M., Yu, K., Deller, J., Stahl, G., & Kurshid, A. (2000). Impact of culture on human resource management practices: A 10-country comparison. *Applied Psychology, 49*(1), 192–221.

Blokland, H. (1997). *Freedom and Culture in Western Society*. London: Routledge.

Cheng, B. S., Huang, M. P., & Chou, L. F. (2002a). Paternalistic leadership and its effectiveness: Evidence from Chinese organizational teams. *Journal of Psychology in Chinese Societies, 3*(1): 85–112.

Cheng, B. S., Shieh, P. Y., & Chou, L. F. (2002b). The principal's leadership, leader-member exchange quality, and the teacher's extra-role behavior: The effects of transformational and paternalistic leadership. *Indigenous Psychological Research in Chinese Societies, 17*, 105–161.

Cheng, B. S., Chou, L. F., Wu, T. Y., Huang, M. P., & Farh, J. L. (2004). Paternalistic leadership and subordinate responses: Establishing a leadership model in Chinese organizations. *Asian Journal of Social Psychology, 7*(1), 89–117.

Farh, J. L., & Cheng, B. S. (2000). A cultural analysis of paternalistic leadership in Chinese organizations. In *Management and Organizations in the Chinese Context* (pp. 84–127). London: Palgrave Macmillan.

Farh, J. L., Cheng, B. S., Chou, L. F., & Chu, X. P. (2006). Authority and benevolence: Employees' responses to paternalistic leadership in China. In A. S. Tsui, Y. Bian, & L. Cheng (Eds.), *China's Domestic Private Firms: Multidisciplinary Perspectives on Management and Performance* (pp. 230–260). New York: Sharpe.

Fleishman, E. A. (1953). The description of supervisory behavior. *Journal of Applied Psychology, 37*(1), 1–6.

Fu, P. P., & Tsui, A. S. (2003). Utilizing printed media to understand desired leadership attributes in the People's Republic of China. *Asia Pacific Journal of Management, 20*(4), 423–446.

Goodell, G. E., Aronoff, M. J., Austin, D. J., Cadeliña, R. V., Emmerson, D. K., Hansen, K. T., ... & Wiseman, J. A. (1985). Paternalism, patronage, and potlatch: the dynamics of giving and being given to [and comments and reply]. *Current Anthropology, 26*(2), 247–266.

House, R., Hanges, P. J., Javidan, M., Dorfman, P., & Gupta, V. (2004). *Culture, Leadership, and Organizations: The GLOBE Study of 62 Societies*. Thousand Oaks, CA: Sage Publications.

Jackman, M. R. (1994). *The Velvet Glove: Paternalism and Conflict in Gender, Class, and Race Relations.* Berkeley: University of California Press.

Li, Y., & Sun, J. M. (2015). Traditional Chinese leadership and employee voice behavior: A cross-level examination. *The Leadership Quarterly, 26*(2), 172–189.

Littrell, R. F. (2002). Desirable leadership behaviors of multi-cultural managers in China. *Journal of Management Development, 21*(1), 5–74.

McDonald, P. (2012). Confucian foundations to leadership: A study of Chinese business leaders across Greater China and South-East Asia. *Asia Pacific Business Review, 18*(4), 465–487.

Northouse, P. G. (1997). *Leadership: Theory and Practice.* Thousand Oaks, CA: Sage.

Padavic, I., & Earnest, W. R. (1994). Paternalism as a component of managerial strategy. *Social Science Journal, 31*(4): 389–405.

Pellegrini, E. K., & Scandura, T. A. (2008). Paternalistic leadership: A review and agenda for future research. *Journal of Management, 34*(3), 566–593.

Pellegrini, E. K., Scandura, T. A., & Jayaraman, V. (2010). Cross-cultural generalizability of paternalistic leadership: An expansion of leader-member exchange theory. *Group & Organization Management, 35*(4), 391–420.

Redding, G. (2002). The capitalist business system of China and its rationale. *Asia Pacific Journal of Management, 19*(2), 221–249.

Redding, S. G., Norman, A., & Schlander, A. (1994). The nature of individual attachment to the organization: A review of East Asian variations. *Handbook of Industrial and Organizational Psychology, 4*, 647–688.

Stogdill, R. M. (1974). *Handbook of Leadership: A Survey of Theory and Research.* New York: Free Press.

Tsui, A. S., Wang, H. U. I., Xin, K., Zhang, L., & Fu, P. P. (2004). "Let a thousand flowers bloom": Variation of leadership styles among Chinese CEOs. *Organizational Dynamics, 33*(1), 5–20.

Uhl-Bien, M., Tierney, P. S., Graen, G. B., & Wakabayashi, M. (1990). Company paternalism and the hidden-investment process: Identification of the "right type" for line managers in leading Japanese organizations. *Group & Organization Studies, 15*(4), 414–430.

Vroom, V. H., & Jago, A. G. (2007). The role of the situation in leadership. *American Psychologist, 62*(1), 17.

Wah, S. S. (2010). Confucianism and Chinese leadership. *Chinese Management Studies, 4*(3), 280–285.

Wu, T. Y., Hsu, W. L., & Cheng, B. S. (2002). Expressing or suppressing anger: Subordinate's anger responses to supervisors' authoritarian behaviors in a Taiwan enterprise. *Indigenous Psychological Research in Chinese Societies, 18*, 3–49.

Wu, M., Huang, X., Li, C., & Liu, W. (2012). Perceived interactional justice and trust-in-supervisor as mediators for paternalistic leadership. *Management and Organization Review, 8*(1), 97–121.

Yang, B. (2012). Confucianism, socialism, and capitalism: A comparison of cultural ideologies and implied managerial philosophies and practices in the PR China. *Human Resource Management Review, 22*(3), 165–178.

Yukl, G. (2013). *Leadership in Organizations* (8th ed.). Boston, MA: Pearson.

Zhang, Y., Huai, M. Y., & Xie, Y. H. (2015). Paternalistic leadership and employee voice in China: A dual process model. *The Leadership Quarterly, 26*(1), 25–36.

Bibliography

Hofstede, G. (2001). *Culture's Consequences: Comparing Values, Behaviors, Institutions and Organizations Across Nations*. Thousand Oaks, CA: Sage Publications.

Hunt, R. G., & Meindl, J. R. (1991). Chinese political economic reforms and the problem of legitimizing leader roles. *The Leadership Quarterly, 2*(3), 189–204.

Lin, C. (2008). Demystifying the chameleonic nature of Chinese leadership. *Journal of Leadership & Organizational Studies, 14*(4), 303–321.

Lytle, A. L., Brett, J. M., Barsness, Z. I., Tinsley, C. H., & Janssens, M. (1995). A paradigm for confirmatory cross-cultural research in organizational behavior. *Research in Organizational Behavior: An Annual Series of Analytical Essays and Critical Reviews, 17*, 167–214.

Ma, L., & Tsui, A. S. (2015). Traditional Chinese philosophies and contemporary leadership. *The Leadership Quarterly, 26*(1), 13–24.

McDonald, P. (2012). Confucian foundations to leadership: A study of Chinese business leaders across Greater China and South-East Asia. *Asia Pacific Business Review, 18*(4), 465–487.

Peng, M. W., Lu, Y., Shenkar, O., & Wang, D. Y. (2001). Treasures in the China house: A review of management and organizational research on Greater China. *Journal of Business Research, 52*(2), 95–110.

Triandis, H. C. (1989). The self and social behavior in differing cultural contexts. *Psychological Review, 96*(3), 506–520.

Wah, S. S. (2010), Confucianism and Chinese leadership. *Chinese Management Studies, 4*(3), 280–285.

Part III

Research Findings: Views and Experiences of the Expatriate Senior Managers and Chinese Employees

Chapter 6

The Views and Experiences of 391 Expatriate Senior Managers in Leading and Managing Chinese Employees

To explore the views and experiences of expatriate senior managers in leading Chinese employees, I analyzed the responses given by 391 such managers to the following three questions, as explained in Chapter 3:

- Is leading Chinese subordinates different from leading those in your home country?
- What are the similarities and differences?
- What are the challenges?

The result of the data analysis showed the following:

- 17 (4.1%) of the sample expatriate managers said that leading Chinese subordinates was **the same** as leading those in their home country.
- 235 (57.2%) of the expatriate managers said that leading Chinese subordinates was **very different** from leading those in their home country.
- 159 (38.7%) of the expatriate managers said that leading Chinese subordinates involved **both similarities with and differences from** leading those in their home country.

The similarities that were mentioned were mainly related to the common human traits and needs and to the general skills required for a leader. The differences covered several aspects which can be grouped into two broad categories relating to (1) Chinese culture and business practice and (2) the characteristics of Chinese employees.

Chinese culture and business practices wield a significant influence on the work attitudes and behaviors of Chinese employees; some of their work attitudes and behaviors were viewed as positive by the sample expatriate senior managers, and others as challenging. In this chapter, I present the views and experiences of the 391 expatriate senior managers in two parts:

- Part 1. Similarities in leading Chinese employees
- Part 2. Differences and challenges in leading and managing Chinese employees

In presenting the views and experiences of the sample expatriate managers, many direct quotes drawn from the expatriates' responses are used. The use of the expatriates' own words is intended to enable the readers to gauge the expatriates' perspectives and experiences in greater detail and to reach their own interpretations and judgments. I also hope that this approach will make my analysis more interesting to read. Where appropriate, the views expressed by the interviewed Chinese employees are added in order to help explain such employees' characteristics, such as the higher tendency to change jobs and the high degrees of loyalty afforded to people, rather than to organizations.

Part 1. Similarities in Leading Chinese Employees

As reported above, 17 (4.1%) of the sample expatriate managers said that leading Chinese employees was the same as leading those in their home country, while 159 (38.7%) said that there were both similarities and differences. The responses of those expatriates who reported varying degrees of similarities (including those who saw no differences at all) were mainly focused on two aspects, shared human traits and needs and the general skills required for a leader.

Shared human traits and needs

The expatriate managers said that leaders need to deal with the same employee traits and needs no matter where they are because they are leading "people" or "human beings" who share the same traits and needs.

They stated that leaders need to bear such shared traits and needs in mind and take them into consideration when performing their leadership roles. The mentioned traits and needs can be summarized as follows:

- the desire to do a good job;
- an appreciation of stability and a dislike for change;
- a willingness to learn;
- an appreciation for a clear direction and a sense of purpose;
- the desire to know one's role and responsibilities;
- the desire to be supported;
- the desire to be challenged and have a platform for growth;
- the desire for acknowledgment and to be rewarded for good work results;
- the desire to develop and progress their skills and career;
- the need for recognition;
- the desire to be financially rewarded;
- the desire to be treated with respect and fairness;
- the desire for a sense of belonging;
- the basic needs for survival (e.g., shelter, warmth, and safety/a safe environment);
- the desire for self-actualization and fulfillment;
- the desire to strike a satisfactory work–life balance;
- the desire for a leader that is trustworthy and capable of managing, inspiring, providing guidance, and communicating clearly.

The following are some quotes from the expatriates:

Wherever you are you are leading individuals. People are people. No difference between countries.

(German expatriate, 50–54 years old, Hospitality)

Similarities are that we are speaking about people and people have in general same needs for recognition, etc.

(Finnish expatriate, 45–49 years old, Industrial Automation)

My experience is that all staff, regardless of cultural background, take pride in their work and seek to do a good job.

(American expatriate, 40–44 years old, Architecture)

What is similar is they employees want to do a good job, they care about the quality of their work, their opportunity to advance, grow, and improve their resume as well as their quality of life.

(American expatriate, 60 years old or over, Financial Instruments)

Employees want to be inspired and have a "sense of purpose".

(German expatriate, 40–44 years old, Chemical)

Leadership is about inspiring people to want to perform to the max of their ability. One might argue that inspiring people varies from place to place, but having worked with people from all over the world my take on it is simply that people excel when given an opportunity to take owner- ship of a task, regardless of who they are or where they come from, i.e., avoiding micro-management.

(Norwegian expatriate, 40–44 years old, IT Consulting)

Similar is the expectation to get rewarded for good work and outstand- ing results.

(German expatriate, 35–39 years old, Marketing)

I think about this (simply) as human instincts. Those behaviors that we all share such as avoiding loss, forming coalitions, belonging socially, hierarchy status, emotions before reason, etc. People across all cultures will behave at work in certain ways and maybe it presents a little differ- ently in China. When I have been confused, I can usually seek out the motivation and explanation within the framework of instinct.

(Australian expatriate, 55–59 years old, Professional Services)

Similarities: All employees should be treated with respect and should be motivated positively to work to the best of their capacities.

(Dutch expatriate, 40–44 years old, Real Estate)

Similarities are usually obvious—ambitious employees want recogni- tion, promotion, success, and fulfillment; average employees want a work–life balance and a pay check at the end of the month without the need to stretch themselves. This is the same everywhere I think.

(British expatriate, 30–34 years old, Green Energy)

Similarities: the need for people development is the same: people want to grow and are willing to learn ... people need a sense of belonging to a team to work better...Regular feedback is very important to manage employees.

(Belgian expatriate, 30–34 years old, Machinery)

Similar is that we all want to work and earn money.

(No demographic information)

Similar—basic needs are the same (salary, recognition, progression, and support) as people are people.

(No nationality information, 45–49 years old, Education)

Similarities: People are motivated by money and recognition everywhere.

(American expatriate, 45–49 years old, Mobile Games Distribution)

Ultimately, we are all just people, seeking shelter, warmth, and sustenance. Any way to provide and protect these core requirements is going to yield good results.

(British expatriate, 30–34 years old, Tech/Fashion Accessories)

Similarities are people like to be in a safe environment, know clear roles and responsibilities, expect communication and equal support.

(Swiss expatriate, 50–54 years old, Packaging & Chemicals)

Employees need guidance, clear communication, and trust in leadership, so here no difference.

(German expatriate, 35–39 years old, IT)

Similarities are that both are appreciating a professional leader who knows what he is talking about.

(Israeli expatriate, 45–49 years old, Consulting)

All want to develop, look at their manager for support in this. When triggered and managed properly, will realize the same results (but through different ways)...

(Dutch expatriate, 40–44 years old, Real Estate)

The general skills required of a leader

The expatriate managers said that all leaders should have and use some general or universal leadership skills when managing or leading employees, regardless of nationality and culture. The leadership skills and approaches mentioned by the expatriates included the following:

- treating employees fairly and with the appropriate respect as individuals;
- building trusting working relationships with employees;
- dealing with interpersonal relations;
- providing employees with support, training, coaching, personal development, and regular feedback;
- demonstrating passion and integrity;
- effectively communicating any performance goals;
- providing clear goals, directions, and guidelines;
- being approachable and open;
- inspiring and motivating employees to perform to the best of their abilities;
- dealing with employee diversity (e.g., the motivated, the lazy, the bright, and the not-so-bright);
- providing employees with opportunities to take ownership of a task;
- leading by example.

The following are some quotes from the expatriates:

I believe leading employees in China is very similar to leading employees in my country and the other countries I have worked. If you show people respect, work to understand their life desires, and can lead them to work for a common good, the people will respond well and do the job.

(American expatriate, 55–59 years old, Manufacturing)

Leading Chinese employees is similar to leading Western employees from the point of view of the key factors at play of engaging each other. I mean respect and trust are universal for any sound manager and employee relationship.

(Belgian expatriate, 55–59 years old, Steel Wire)

There are many aspects of leadership that are generic, regardless of the nationality or culture of the employees. So, for example, giving clear direction, being careful to understand staff problems from all sides before making a judgment, being approachable and open, being a good judge of people and character apply in any context.

(British expatriate, 40–44 years old, Public Sector)

Similarities: to succeed with managing employees, one needs a great deal of passion, integrity, good attitude, no matter if you are in China or somewhere else.

(Italian expatriate, 50–54 years old, Medical Equipment)

The issues faced are all the same. Trying to communicate what you want done, getting them to actually do it, getting them to do it the way you want them to do it.

(American expatriate, 45–49 years old, Furniture Trading/ Manufacturing)

Similarities: All staff require the right motivation. Different techniques for different personalities. Some staff are keen to develop into leaders, others happy to remain a team member. Same in China and the UK.

(British expatriate, 35–39 years old, Construction)

Leadership requires a clear goal, good communication, and role definition no matter where you are.

(Australian expatriate, 35–39 years old, Entertainment)

Similarities: basic skills, disposition towards leadership.

(Italian expatriate, 35–39 years old, Machinery)

From the above, we can see that the leadership skills required of a leader are in line with the mentioned employee traits and needs. For example, employees want to be treated with respect and leaders thus need to possess the skills required to do so; they want leaders who can inspire them and leaders thus require the skills to motivate and inspire their employees to work to the best of their abilities; and they want to progress in their careers and leaders need to possess the ability to provide training, coaching, and career development opportunities. This clearly illustrates the importance, in the exercise of leadership, of addressing the traits and needs of employees.

Part 2. Differences and Challenges in Leading and Managing Chinese Employees

As reported at the beginning of this chapter, 235 (57.2%) of the expatriate managers said that leading Chinese employees differed greatly from leading those in their home country, while 159 (38.7%) said that there are both similarities and differences. The differences mentioned were mainly related to the Chinese employees' values, attitudes, behaviors, and approaches toward their jobs.

In this section, I will first report the different but positive characteristics of Chinese employees, as perceived by the sample expatriate managers. I will then report those different characteristics that were considered as challenging. Those expatriate managers who are or will be working in China should consider how to make the most of the positive employee characteristics in relation to organizational efficiency and how to compensate for or overcome the challenging aspects.

The positive characteristics of Chinese employees, as perceived by the expatriate managers

The expatriate managers mentioned two main different but positive characteristics of their Chinese employees: their tendency to work hard and their eagerness to learn.

Working hard

A good number of the expatriate managers praised their Chinese employees for being hard workers and for making fewer direct complaints than those from their home countries or others in which they had worked. The following are examples of what they said:

> *Chinese people are very hard working.*

> (German expatriate, 30–34 years old, Lodging)

Chinese staff normally work much harder vs western staff...

> (Dutch expatriate, 45–49 years old, Marketing Services/Consulting)

Chinese employees work harder.

> (American expatriate, 60 years old or over, Nuclear Energy)

People in China work harder and less direct complaints.

> (British expatriate, 45–49 years old, Advertising)

...most of my employees were very hard working and wanted to reach their goals, which is a major advantage.

> (German expatriate, 55–59 years old, Tourism)

Some of the expatriate managers said that their Chinese employees were willing to work well beyond normal working hours. The practice of working long hours, which is common in many Asian countries, was not something the expatriates had often encountered in their home or other Western countries. Some expatriates were impressed by their Chinese employees' willingness to devote their free time to work, be it during the weekend or late at night. Some expatriate managers said the following:

Compared to my home country, Chinese employees are willing to go to greater length to succeed and are much more flexible with regard to work hours to accomplish tasks.

> (Danish expatriate, 50–54 years old, Medical Devices)

Can call them late at night or weekend.

> (American expatriate, 60 years old or over, Solar Energy)

My Chinese colleagues...are hardworking, loyal, and willing to work extremely long hours without complaint.

> (Dutch expatriate, 45–49 years old, Hotel/Hospitality)

The Chinese employees' proclivity to work hard may be seen as a great advantage that expatriate managers can exploit when leading

Chinese employees. However, it cannot be taken for granted because Chinese employees will only work hard when their managers take the "right" managerial approaches suited to motivate them to do so. A Swiss expatriate said the following:

> *I have lead teams in a few different countries and it's different every time...If managed right, Chinese employees are however much more efficient and hardworking than Europeans.*

(Swiss expatriate, 35–39 years old, Automotive Services)

Eagerness to learn

Several expatriates observed that their Chinese employees were eager to learn new things. Some expatriate managers said the following:

> *It is pleasant working with Chinese employees as they are always eager to learn.*

(Belgian expatriate, 55–59 years old, Pharmaceuticals)

> *Chinese employees have a thirst to learn.*

(British expatriate, 45–49 years old, Financial/Accounting)

> *Chinese employees are much more eager to learn new things.*

(German expatriate, 50–54 years old, Consulting)

> *The younger generation in China is more open to learn new things, news styles, etc.*

(Dutch expatriate, 45–49 years old, Investment & E-commerce)

Some expatriates said that their Chinese employees' willingness and eagerness to learn was driven by their desire to gain more experience and to develop their skills and careers:

> *Chinese people are more willing to learn and to improve themselves.*

(No demographic information)

Chinese employees will invest (their time) to learn new things and get more experience...

(French expatriate, 35–39 years old, Food Industry)

...the large majority are keen to learn and want to develop their skills and career.

(British expatriate, 50–54 years old, Power Generation)

The Chinese employees' eagerness to learn and to develop as workers and individuals presents leaders with both positive and challenging aspects. On the positive side, it is always a pleasure for a leader to lead or work with employees who are motivated to learn and develop. On the challenging one, leaders will need to ensure that their employees are being given tasks or opportunities suited to help them to improve their skills and careers; failing to do so may cause employees to seek development opportunities elsewhere. As reported in the section below entitled "A greater focus on money, job titles, and personal benefits", the Chinese employees' desire to develop is one of the key reasons behind high employee turnover.

The challenging characteristics of Chinese employees, as perceived by the expatriate managers

The expatriate managers perceived a number of characteristics of their Chinese employees as very different from those of employees in their home countries. Such differences were viewed as being very challenging. In the following, I first list the top 10 such characteristics and then provide greater detail on them and explain why they were viewed as challenging. The suggestions made by the sample expatriates to the end of overcoming these challenges are reported in Chapter 9.

The top 10 challenging characteristics

(1) a high degree of respect for hierarchy and authority;
(2) a low tendency to engage in initiatives and proactiveness;
(3) the language spoken and an indirect communication style;

(4) the need to be given detailed instructions, monitored, and micro-managed;
(5) reservedness and inexpressiveness in communication;
(6) the high value placed on "face";
(7) lower levels of work competency and knowledge;
(8) a greater focus on money, job titles, and personal benefits;
(9) lower accountability;
(10) loyalty directed to people rather than to the organization.

A high degree of respect for hierarchy and authority

The challenging characteristic of Chinese employees most mentioned by the expatriate managers was their high respect for hierarchy and authority. A great number of them said that their Chinese employees were very respectful toward people higher up in the organizational hierarchy and they were used to following orders/instructions from superiors and to unquestioningly obeying any requests coming from the top. The following quotes illustrate the expatriates' views on the employee–manager relations in China when compared with those found in other countries:

In France you respect the boss but when you have something to tell him you can tell him without fear, in China the boss is like a god, and nobody can be against a decision taken by the boss.

(French expatriate, 50–54 years old, Railway)

In America, leaders and employees seek to like and be liked; in China, hierarchy and deference play a bigger role in employee–employer relations.

(American expatriate, 50–54 years old, Consulting)

Chinese are more Confucian in that they are more comfortable with a pyramid organizational structure with strong top-down guidance. Not so comfortable with matrix management structures common in Canada and US. Home country employees are relatively more comfortable with multi-reporting, flatter organizational structures.

(American expatriate, 60 years old or over, Financial Services)

Yes, there is a difference in leading, as Chinese employees are used to take orders and execute them. In Germany, you place a target and ask for solutions.

(German expatriate, 60 years old or over, Automotive)

Hierarchy and "the boss is always right" mentality are very much a part of most organizations that I have seen here. People rarely disagree with anyone in authority and are not used to answering questions like "what would you do?". Quite often, people go to their boss asking for the solution to a problem as opposed to coming with 2–3 options and then working through it together.

(No demographic information)

There is a higher power distance between employees and managers in China. Generally, employees will wait for managers to give direction prior to taking action. Some staff have no qualms with being inactive should no direction be given.

(American expatriate, 40–44 years old, Architecture)

I would say that differences exist in perception of hierarchy and collaborative work. In western culture, hierarchy seems to flatten more and more with development of horizontal organization while in China it remains highly vertical. Consequently, it requires one to clearly define what are the objective and missions and to follow up personally.

(No demographic information)

As mentioned in Chapter 4, Confucius's *wu lun* (five cardinal relationships) exert a profound influence on the past and current hierarchical system/relationship in Chinese families, organizations, and society as a whole. From a young age, Chinese children are taught that parents are superior to children and that bosses are superior to subordinates. They are also taught to honor their parents and respect their elders and superiors. Under this hierarchical societal structure, Chinese people take rank, age, and seniority seriously and give respect to those holding higher social status and to their elders. Those holding lower rank are expected to show restraint and to comply with the requests of those who they perceive as being superior to avoid offending them.

In line with this hierarchical structure, Chinese senior managers often assume an authoritarian stance in the workplace, making decisions and issuing orders with little consultation of their subordinates. This management tradition, however, has made most Chinese employees accustomed to relying on instructions from the top and to rarely take initiatives.

The Chinese employees' respect for seniority presents both good and challenging aspects. A good one is that the decision-making processes are usually very quick, as leaders do not need to take the time to consult the viewpoints of their employees or to explain the reasons for their decisions to persuade their staff. Two expatriates said the following:

In my experience, most Chinese employees are more likely to follow management-led initiatives without a lot of buy-in and persuasion time.

(British expatriate, 35–39 years old, Education)

Chinese Employees do have more reverence for their boss,....so it is an easy shortcut to use authority.

(No demographic information)

The Chinese employees' respect for hierarchy had posed the following two main challenges for the sample expatriate managers:

Challenge a: High respect for seniority and authority has become a hindrance to open communication and the sharing of ideas. The Chinese employees' respect and obedience toward authority and higher-ranking individuals have led them to hardly ever express their views. This was seen by the expatriates as a factor inhibiting the sharing of ideas and the creation of an open communication working environment. The following statements illustrate this challenge:

Chinese employees are taught to comply and they do not come forward with creative ideas or improvement suggestions.

(American expatriate, 45–49 years old, Heavy Manufacturing)

In China, the meaning and respect for hierarchy is higher than in other countries. This means that employees are often keen to obey without sharing ideas, counter-proposals...

(Italian expatriate, 30–34 years old, Consumer Industry)

Chinese employees have obedience in their DNA. They unquestioningly follow the tasks within their remit. They respect their leaders because they are their leaders rather than because they are deserving of respect. Any discussion of company improvement with them involves allusion, nuances, indirect allusion rather than simply speaking your mind.

(British expatriate, 60 years old or over, Education)

Too often they fear expressing their opinion freely and possibly disagreeing with their superior. Northern European company culture is very low hierarchy and encourages very open dialogue. This is not typical in China.

(Finnish expatriate, 40–44 years old, Steel)

Challenge b: Chinese employees tend to follow orders and not to challenge instructions. Another challenge resulting from Chinese employees' high respect for hierarchy and authority is that they tend to scrupulously follow their superiors' instructions or directions but seldom question or challenge them. As such, both good and bad instructions or orders from supervisors are accepted and followed by Chinese employees even if they think their supervisors are wrong. The following quotes illustrate this challenge:

Chinese employees will be more likely to be unquestioningly "obedient" than UK ones. So even if they think a leader's decision is a bad one, they'll go ahead and implement it regardless.

(British expatriate, 40–44 years old, Public Sector)

Also, they tend not to challenge decisions from above even if they realize that the decision is not the best one.

(No demographic information)

Chinese employees are extremely respectful of their superior. In many occasions, this leads to situations where the employee does not challenge the boss and follows blindly the superior's instruction.

(Spanish expatriate, 50–54 years old, Energy)

Chinese employees tend to relate to me as a "superior" more than a colleague. They seem to be more afraid of me and less likely to challenge me or ask questions.

(Canadian expatriate, 45–49 years old, Food and Beverage)

Too much respect of the hierarchy. No initiative or decision without the agreement of the boss. No contradiction, when the boss says something, there is no objection even if someone knows that the boss is wrong.

(French expatriate, 50–54 years old, Railway Industry)

In China, there tends to be a culture of following directions, and sometimes that means there is a risk of people doing things they don't believe in, or know will not work, because they don't want to contradict the boss.

(No demographic information)

In most situations, the Chinese employees' deep-rooted belief in compliance and obedience and in not challenging their supervisors makes the interaction between managers and subordinates a top-down one, with managers giving instructions and subordinates following them. This leads Chinese employees to rarely take any initiative, as explained in the next section.

A low tendency to engage in initiatives and proactiveness

The second most mentioned challenging characteristic was the Chinese employees' low tendency to engage in initiative taking and proactiveness. Many expatriates said that most of their Chinese employees rarely took any initiatives or acted proactively to deal with tasks, issues, and problems; instead, they expected to be given instructions as to how to complete a task. The following quotes illustrate the expatriates' views on this:

Over the past nine years, I have seen many similar patterns. This does not apply to all employees, but in general. Westerners are self-motivated, ready to research, learn new skills, and know they advance from their achievements. Chinese are often waiting for you to hand them the path of what to do on a day-to-day basis.

(American expatriate, 50–54 years old, Hospitality)

Although Chinese employees are very motivated, they need to be told exactly what to do and when to do it. In general, they are not proactive. They will approach the manager with a problem they encounter, rather than a problem + several possible solutions they find suitable.

(Dutch expatriate, 35–39 years old, Machine Manufacturing)

In China, in general, employees are either hesitating to take initiative or they are not taking it in the right place. Again, in most cases, they do not act as if they are managing their own territory.

(Turkish expatriate, 50–54 years old, Real Estate)

Unfortunately, the Chinese people expect the boss to think of every solution to a problem rather than propose a solution themselves.

(No demographic information)

Chinese employees obey more, they think less. They lack initiative, they like to be told what to do.

(Israeli expatriate, 35–39 years old, Luxury)

...in meetings, they are far less likely to contribute, and really are looking for you as the manager to just inform them and tell them what they need to do.

(American expatriate, 35–39 years old, Professional Services)

Chinese tend to adhere to boxes, sticking within defined areas of responsibility and not necessarily stepping beyond those "defined responsibilities". Foreign staff tend to engage these limits more and push beyond defined responsibility, if given the opportunity.

(American expatriate, 35–39 years old, Contract Manufacturing)

Chinese employees are not used to taking any initiative...Do not consider anything that obviously they will do because they often don't if not well instructed. Europeans are used to knowing what is necessary to do even if the leader didn't tell them all the procedure.

(No demographic information)

In Holland, employees need a leader, a coach, they are proactive and work themself, develop themself. They will discover their own mistakes and repair them until the result is satisfying. In China, employees need a boss. Someone who tells them exactly what to do. Own initiative is rather seldom.

(Dutch expatriate, 50–54 years old, Machinery)

Employees in my home country are more strongly opinionated and speak out directly when they can predict a weakness in any process. Chinese employees will generally wait until these weaknesses manifest themselves. Sad to say, the people I worked with are not proactive problem solvers in the same degree.

(No demographic information)

Two main reasons can explain such Chinese employee characteristics. First, the hierarchical system deeply embedded in Chinese society (see Chapter 4 and the section above) has led Chinese employees to become accustomed to following instructions, rather than taking initiatives. The cultural expectation is for employees to be submissive to authority and to follow their managers' instructions with unquestioning obedience. Should they not meet this expectation, they would be viewed as breaching the protocol of the supervisor–employee hierarchical relationship, which could expose them to unwanted criticism. As a result, most Chinese employees will not take any initiatives and get involved in issues or tasks that they perceive to fall outside of the scope of their positions.

The other reason for the Chinese employees' lack of initiative and proactiveness is believed to be the result of the rote learning approach taken by many Chinese education institutions. Chinese students often learn or memorize things by repetition, without an understanding of the reasoning or relationships involved in the material they are learning.

From primary school, Chinese students are required to follow the instructions they are given by their teachers; they are rarely encouraged to put forward or come up with ideas to solve problems. Due to their educational experience, many Chinese employees are accustomed to following instructions and do not have the confidence to perform tasks on their own when no advice or instructions are given by their supervisors. The following quotes from some expatriates illustrate their observations in this regard:

Chinese staff are much less able to think for themselves, come up with new solutions, think outside the box—in my view, again a result of an educational system that does not encourage creativity/free thinking.

(Dutch expatriate, 45–49 years old, Marketing Services/Consulting)

In my opinion, this has to do with the way they were educated in university. The professor provides the theoretical knowledge, and one is supposed to take this over. There are no group discussions or project groups where one has to come up with solutions to problems or issues.

(Dutch expatriate, 35–39 years old, Machine Manufacturing)

Chinese colleagues are the product of a relatively closed society and a very narrow education system, where they are conditioned to follow norms and not question anything or anybody...Initiative is a rare commodity. Creativity is equally rare...

(British expatriate, 60 years old or over, Education)

The major challenges faced by the expatriate leaders were that (1) they struggled to encourage or teach their Chinese staff to take initiatives and to dare to go ahead with a task in the absence of instructions on how to carry it out, and that (2) they found it difficult to delegate responsibilities or empower individuals, as their employees were not innovative and proactive in solving problems. The following quotes illustrate the challenges:

The biggest challenge from my experience is to get the employees to take more initiatives and come with solutions rather than problems.

(Dutch expatriate, 50–54 years old, Production of Food Products)

Chinese employees are not very innovative so it is more challenging to ask them to work through projects that are not defined in detail.

(British expatriate, 50–54 years old, Power Generation)

...more hierarchical and less proactive employees, takes more time to teach people and to motivate them to take decisions themselves.

(Dutch expatriate, 55–59 years old, Computer and Machinery)

The expectation of many employees is the leader will provide answers to problems instead of empowering teams to work together to solve problems. The words "initiative", "proactive" are things that are a real challenge to "teach" while empowering individuals here.

(Australian expatriate, 35–39 years old, Training and Development)

Anticipation, consistency, common sense are very common in daily western life where in China unless the boss has instructed you to do something, nothing will get done. Encouraging team members to be proactive and think ahead is something that most expats struggle with because Chinese hoteliers are more inclined to take orders from their boss and not necessarily be expected to do this on their own.

(New Zealander expatriate, 40–44 years old, Hospitality)

... it takes very long time to bring our Chinese employees to take initiatives in problem-solving issues and resolution of issues without having direct/immediate approval...The challenge becomes to achieve proactive efficiency.

(Canadian expatriate, 45–49 years old, Consulting)

The language spoken and an indirect communication style

The third most mentioned challenge was the official language spoken in China (i.e., Mandarin Chinese—普通话 in Chinese, pronounced *pǔ tōng huà*) and the communication style of their Chinese employees.

a. The language
Many expatriates perceived the Mandarin Chinese language as one of the biggest barriers and challenges for them. The quotes below illustrate the expatriates' perception:

Language is a big barrier.

(Spanish expatriate, 35–39 years old, Automotive)

Everything is grey because of the language difference (conceptual—pictorial).

(Belgian expatriate, 45–49 years old, Consultancy)

Communication is a challenge due to language impediments.

(Australian expatriate, 60 years old or over, Hospitality)

Challenges: the language structure is so much different (and we know it influences mental structure), it requires more energy to work with Chinese-speaking people than western people.

(French expatriate, 40–44 years old, Video Games)

The biggest challenge is and will be the Chinese language, especially reading...

(German expatriate, 50–54 years old, Hospitality)

Challenges...Inability to connect due to language limitations, and thereby being seen always as an "outsider".

(Indian expatriate, 35–39 years old, Media and Advertising)

The biggest challenge is the language as I speak rudimentary Chinese and 95% of my team does not speak English. Communication, and getting the message across, is a major issue that I deal with daily.

(Dutch expatriate, 45–49 years old, Hospitality)

Most of the participating expatriates had a low to intermediate level of fluency in Mandarin Chinese. Thus, many of them had to rely on translators or could only communicate with those Chinese employees who had a good command of English. However, translators did not often precisely interpret the points intended to be communicated, thus leading to a lack of understanding or misunderstandings and extra work. The following quotes illustrate this:

Well, the most obvious is the language difference. I often needed to use a translator that was often cumbersome.

(No demographic information)

Due to the language gap, almost all conversations are done through intermediaries, which leaves a lot unsaid, wrongly interpreted, and fosters lack of understanding and sometimes unnecessary extra work.

(Dutch expatriate, 40–44 years old, Hospitality)

A word can be translated, but may still have a meaning with a different feeling or specific meaning.

(American expatriate, 45–49 years old, Energy/Manufacturing)

Then of course there are the language and inference differences. Interpretation is much more important than translation.

(No demographic information)

Sometimes, the smallest mistake in translation can cause a big misunderstanding.

(Israeli expatriate, 30–34 years old, Luxury)

The challenges caused by the language difference were not only faced by those expatriates who spoke little Mandarin and needed a translator but also by those who did speak the language well. This was because, as non-native speakers, they may have missed or misunderstood some cues, nuances, details, meanings, messages, and concepts.

The first problem is language. I speak Chinese quite well, but some of the details I am still missing.

(German expatriate, 50–54 years old, Tourism)

The number 1 challenge is communication even if you speak good Mandarin, it is easy to cause misunderstandings.

(British expatriate, 45–49 years old, Power Generation)

The main challenge in China is language as even those who have a bilingual ability (Chinese/English) do not always understand the message you are trying to convey.

(British expatriate, 35–39 years old, Hospitality)

Even when you are able to 100% communicate in the employee's language, in my case Chinese, the gap somehow remains.

(No demographic information)

Furthermore, a lack of understanding and/or a misunderstanding could easily take place because either party—the expatriate managers, their subordinates, or both—was not communicating in its first language, for example, expatriates from non-English-speaking countries (e.g., Germany or France) communicating with their Chinese employees in English.

In many cases, both have to speak not in their mother tongue and this might be an additional risk for misunderstandings.

(Austrian expatriate, 45–49 years old, Automotive)

The language barrier is the most difficult one; most expat managers as well as Chinese employees are operating in another language than their mother tongue. The whole working relation is based on "translation".

(Belgian expatriate, 50–54 years old, Steel Wire)

Obviously, language creates a difference and my Chinese employees speak English as a second language and I do not speak Chinese well.

(Canadian expatriate, 40–44 years old, Food and Beverage)

There is the question of language, even in a company with English as the workplace language, because there is not always the same level of comfort and capacity of self-expression in a second language.

(British expatriate, 40–44 years old, Education)

b. An indirect communication style

Compared to the direct and self-assertive styles of communication adopted in many Western countries, the Chinese communication style tends to be indirect and reserved. A section below, entitled "Reservedness and inexpressiveness in communication", discusses this issue in relation to Chinese employees. In this section, the focus is on their indirectness in communication. Some expatriate managers said that their Chinese employees were indirect when communicating.

Chinese are not as direct in expressing ideas as western people.

(Italian expatriate, 30–34 years old, Machinery)

Chinese employees are not used to direct communication.

(Italian expatriate, 25–29 years old, Consulting)

In China, I needed to understand that people don't talk using the straight way to arrive to the point but a curve.

(Danish expatriate, 35–39 years old, Tourism)

Chinese people are usually not used to go straight to the point but rather loop around it when they need to describe some problems or job challenge.

(Italian expatriate, 25–29 years old, Consumer Industry)

The Chinese employees' indirectness in communication and their inclination to adopt a non-assertive approach and to avoid making direct criticisms were born out of the high value Chinese people place on maintaining face and harmonious social relationships, avoiding confrontations with others, and displaying respect for people (see Chapter 4 for these characteristics).

Several expatriate managers said that they had found their Chinese employees' indirectness to be challenging as it had been difficult for them to understand what their employees had intended to say and their opinions.

Most likely the biggest challenge is the indirectness of northern Asian cultures. So much can be lost in translation when messages from both sides are not fully understood.

(Australian expatriate, 35–39 years old, Hospitality)

The most difficult challenge is understanding the unsaid language and the exchange of information and opinion between colleagues.

(Italian expatriate, 35–39 years old, Telecommunication)

Chinese employees are not straight to the point, they are more diplomatic, dilute the information, and make it difficult to get real feedback of what is happening.

(French expatriate, 35–39 years old, Manufacturing)

This indirectness in communication was particularly challenging for those expatriates who, being used to a very direct style, had come to China expecting the "norm" to be the same as that found in their own countries.

The need to be given detailed instructions, monitored, and micro-managed

Linked to the lower propensity to take initiatives and exhibit proactiveness discussed above, the fourth challenging characteristic most mentioned by the expatriate managers was that their Chinese employees needed to be given detailed instructions, monitored, and micro-managed in order to ensure the completion of any tasks.

Many expatriates said that they needed to be highly specific in regard to what they wanted their Chinese employees to do and how to do it, to explain all tasks in detail, to provide clear directions, and to closely monitor progress. They had reached this conclusion because they had observed that their Chinese employees preferred and expected very clear and defined tasks, rather than being given a goal and then being allowed/expected to work independently to achieve it, and that they would lose their way or fail to complete a task should no specific guidance and direction be offered. The following quotes illustrate this:

You have to draw a very detailed roadmap for each task, even for excellent employees of high education. The same is true for other employees, who need a lot of supervision/control because they otherwise tend to stray out of bounds (in many ways of varying seriousness). Overall, Chinese staff need tighter reigns and a stricter leadership style in my experience, in order to keep the machinery moving smoothly.

(No demographic information)

The specifics of managing and leading our China employees are that they are very oriented towards task execution and how to execute the task to meet their boss's requirements. To that extent, I have observed my China colleagues being more secure when I give very detailed task instruction and framework. This is very different with my interactions with other countries where I can have discussion and have the teams understand the goal and give them more freedom to reach the goal.

(French expatriate, 25–29 years old, Fashion)

More accurate and precise direction expected by the Chinese. Big picture not as important as in Europe. You will not hear if something is not going well so more follow-up needed.

(Danish expatriate, 40–44 years old, Engineering)

Chinese staff require—and expect—a much higher level of detailed communication. In Finland, one usually only gives a rough outline of the target and then delegates authority and gives a high level of trust to the employee. In China, this approach usually leads to no or poor results. A colleagues told me: management in China is easy, just need to remember 3 words: follow-up, follow-up, follow-up.

(Finnish expatriate, 35–39 years old, Paper Machinery)

Chinese employees work much less independent and need more clear instructions and regular review of the progress.

(German expatriate, 50–54 years old, Automotive)

They feel more comfortable to execute detailed instructions rather than to be given a goal and propose a plan to achieve that goal.

(Italian expatriate, 40–44 years old, Manufacturing)

This is a generalization, but I have found that Chinese employees often need much more guidance and are much less self-motivated.

(American expatriate, 30–34 years old, Online Education)

Chinese employees expect rules, templates, detailed instructions for everything.

(German expatriate, 40–44 years old, Consulting)

Chinese employees require specific guidance and direction down to the task level... Much more direction and review required, usually on a daily basis.

(No demographic information)

Chinese employees expect rules, templates, detailed instructions for everything. Don't come up with own ideas, are less creative, innovative.

(German expatriate, 50–54 years old, Consulting)

Chinese employees want to be told step by step how to do something and if given a task they want to be told exactly how to achieve it. Whereas US employees take more initiative utilizing their own creativity to achieve the goal.

(American expatriate, 55–59 years old, Management Consulting)

The Chinese employees I interviewed, however, said that this attitude varied by individual, job position, nature of the job, and industry. For example, they said that those employees who were motivated to be high performers, held senior management positions, and worked in a creative industry would neither need nor expect to be given detailed instructions. They also said that most employees in non-management positions tended to be less independent and needed and/or expected to be given detailed task instructions.

So, what would happen should the Chinese employees not receive any specific and detailed instructions? Several expatriates said that the results would be poor or no work would get done. Two of them said the following:

Instructions must be much more detailed, otherwise results are poor, as Chinese are not used to create or optimized own workflows.

(German expatriate, 45–49 years old, Consulting)

Of course. I have to spend a lot of time every day to tell them the obvious. Otherwise they will not do it.

(German expatriate, 35–39 years old, Retail)

Several expatriate managers said that they had needed to resort to micro-management in order to ensure satisfactory task completion.

There is a need for higher direction and a degree of micro-managing to ensure work is completed to standard. Particularly when recommendations are sought that need to be based on limited information.

(New Zealander expatriate, 40–44 years old, Manufacturing)

I believe Chinese employees really expect a manager to lead them every day by going more to micro-management and micro-control level than what is required in Western Europe. More intermediate check points are required and also wanted by Chinese employees.

(Belgian expatriate, 30–34 years old, Steel Business)

Chinese need close/micro-management, most of Chinese can't work independently, you need to set tasks, review several times and check, you cannot 100% rely on them...

(Austrian expatriate, 25–29 years old, Facility Management and Engineering)

Much more general guidance and work-related supervision are needed, almost down to a micro-management level.

(No demographic information)

Chinese are less independent and unable sometimes to make independent decisions...Need to micromanage, need to have a one-on-one meetings to let people express ideas.

(Italian expatriate, 35–39 years old, Machinery)

As discussed earlier in this chapter, the main reasons for the need to give Chinese employees detailed instructions, to monitor their progress, and to micro-manage them are related to the hierarchical system, employee expectations, and the rote learning approach used in many Chinese education institutions. Some expatriates said that it could also be due to language issues as they were not fluent in Chinese and their Chinese subordinates were not fluent in English. Issues related to language and communication are discussed in the previous section of this chapter.

Many of the Chinese employees I interviewed agreed that the hierarchical system and the rote learning approach used had led many Chinese employees to become submissive to authority and to become accustomed to following instructions, rather than acting independently. In addition, they expressed that the Chinese employees' penchant to follow detailed instructions could also be due to wanting to complete a task correctly and efficiently and wanting to avoid taking responsibility for any mistakes, as most Chinese employees believe that their managers/leaders should make all decisions and take full responsibility for them.

The obvious challenge for the expatriate leaders was that, instead of empowering and delegating responsibilities, they had needed to be very hands-on and micro-manage by drawing up clear roadmaps, breaking down tasks into small chunks for each employee, giving specific and detailed instructions, and closely monitoring progress.

Although the expatriates said that this state of affairs was challenging, they also said that, once they had given detailed instructions or processes, their Chinese employees were very efficient in executing them. They said the following:

Once a working process is laid out clearly and followed up with daily, I think Chinese employees are very good at executing and following procedure.

(No demographic information)

Chinese employees are generally good in executing repetitive tasks, which means that they are handling very well redundant tasks when they know how to proceed... In this regard, the employee needs to be trained to know how to handle the task and of course, you need to ensure that the Chinese employees understand the process, because most of the time they will not tell you when they do not understand well (communication issue apart, there is also the "face" issue).

(French expatriate, 25–29 years old, Appliances)

Main difference is that most Chinese tend to be process driven rather than target driven...The good side is: Once you've set up a clear process, then things tend to run smoothly. The shortcomings: If the process is unclear, then you'll get nowhere and people may not innovate in a way to achieve a goal that has not been clearly segmented into an intermediate task.

(No demographic information)

Compared to my home country, the main difference popping in my mind is the need for Chinese people to have a clear framework. As long as the framework is clear, Chinese people are extremely efficient.

(French expatriate, 30–34 years old, Automotive)

Reservedness and inexpressiveness in communication

The fifth most mentioned challenging characteristic of Chinese employees was their reservedness and inexpressiveness in communication. A great number of the sample expatriates said that, when compared with their home country employees, their Chinese subordinates tended to not express their ideas as openly, did not proactively voice any questions and concerns, rarely confronted people with problems, and were less willing to or afraid of expressing their views in public forums. The following are some related quotes:

They are very reserved in their attitude, difficult to see what they think.

(American expatriate, 55–59 years old, Engineering and Construction)

Chinese do not give feedback, so you never know if they did the job or not. You always have to ask.

(Italian expatriate, 45–49 years old, Telecommunications)

In Israel, everyone has an opinion about how things should be done. In China, people are reluctant to offer a view, even when asked to.

(No demographic information)

Most striking is that most Chinese employees keep to himself/herself and are reluctant to share.

(Mauritian expatriate, 45–49 years old, Trading)

Chinese staff are much less vocal, and afraid to have an opinion.

(Dutch expatriate, 40–44 years old, Consulting)

In China, to find information you often have to ask; information is not given voluntarily.

(No demographic information)

Chinese staff tends to have a bit more problems bringing issues up (e.g., problems, concerns, doubts, etc.).

(Spanish expatriate, 20–24 years old, HR)

You never know what they really think. Not even as a boss, because they would never come with questions or opposite opinions.

(German expatriate, 45–49 years old, Machinery)

Maybe the biggest difference is the way employees speak out their opinion...Dutch employees are always debating, discussing and have a strong own opinion...I have learned that this goes differently in China. It is very easy to think your way is the best way, but that didn't work out in China...because things work differently, and we will never understand the real emotions or feelings of Chinese people.

(No demographic information)

I suppose generally the difference is that Chinese staff may not be as open to sharing their opinions with managers. There may be more which is discussed informally and behind closed doors in China, so you should be well connected to people at different levels in the organization to know what people really think/feel/want.

(No demographic information)

Chinese employee inexpressiveness or lack of voice in the workplace was thought by the expatriates to be the result of a combination of four reasons: hierarchy, language barriers, fear of losing face, and a desire to maintain a harmonious relationship.

Reason 1: Hierarchy. As mentioned in Chapter 4 and a section above (entitled "a high degree of respect for hierarchy and authority"), the hierarchical order emphasized by Confucianism has made hierarchical management a common practice in the Chinese workplace. Such a practice or tradition has made Chinese employees deeply respectful of power and status and submissive to authority to the extent that they do not think it is their place to make any suggestions or question authority in the decision-making process. The following quotes illustrate the expatriates' observation of the influence of hierarchy on employees' communication and idea sharing:

In China, the meaning and respect for hierarchy is higher than in other countries. This means that employees are often keen to obey without sharing ideas, counter-proposals, or other ways to face issues.

(Italian expatriate, 25–29 years old, Consumer industry)

Chinese have extremely high respect for hierarchy (which is good); however, occasionally this may preclude them from speaking up their ideas.

(No demographic information)

Chinese employees tend to be less vocal. They won't contradict their leader as much.

(No demographic information)

However, in China, I have found that many people will not ask questions once the leader makes a statement, rather they just do, leading to more challenges as a result of not really knowing how, but being afraid to ask.

(American expatriate, 40–44 years old, Real Estate)

Too often, they fear expressing their opinion freely and possibly disagreeing with their superior. Northern European company culture is very low hierarchy and encourages very open dialogue. This is not typical in China.

(Finnish expatriate, 35–39 years old, Steel)

The main difference is that Chinese have been taught to listen to the "boss". It takes much effort to get them to open up to speaking and sharing ideas.

(American expatriate, 55–59 years old, Manufacturing)

Reason 2: The language barrier. In addition to the hierarchical tradition, a lack of fluency in English is another reason for the Chinese employees' inexpressiveness in front of expatriate managers. Some expatriate managers said the following:

However, there is certainly a slight concern/fear among Chinese staff when speaking with a foreigner and language challenges are one of the key factors that stimulate this.

(British expatriate, 20–24 years old, Education)

I am all the time trying to change the communication culture to be more direct and faster. Language issues in some cases hold the process back...

(Finnish expatriate, 40–44 years old, Manufacturing)

I have tried encouraging my Chinese team members to be more vocal in their opinions in public forums. I realized that they have some good ideas and thoughts, when I discuss with them in private, but are unable to bring it out in front of clients or senior bosses, due to two reasons. 1. Culturally, it's not good for employees to disagree/voice out their opinion without knowing what the boss says./2. Most of them are not very comfortable with fluent spoken English.

(Indian expatriate, 30–34 years old, Media and Advertising)

Reason 3: Fear of losing face. Chinese employees' fear of losing face is another key reason for their inexpressiveness, particularly in public settings. As discussed in Chapter 4, face is highly valued by the Chinese; as such, it is carefully protected and maintained, and most people will go to any length to avoid losing face. The Chinese people's fear of losing face, however, has led them to not speak up in public to avoid saying the wrong things and embarrass themselves or others. Such fear has also led them to not admit any lack of skills, understanding, and knowledge in relation to a task. Some expatriate managers said the following:

Communication is a challenge not just verbally but also in a cultural aspect of losing face. If problems come up, we see more hide the issue rather than address challenges and ask for support and solve the issue.

(Swiss expatriate, 45–49 years old, Packaging & Chemicals)

...a Chinese employee will not easily tell you if he has not understood as he will think he will make you lose face if he does not understand.

(No demographic information)

The other such issue arises when the Chinese employee does not understand the concept or have the specific knowledge required to complete a task. They do not come out and seek help. Instead, they will just be quiet and let the deadline pass. After this happens, they will then, usually only when queried, explain they lacked the skill, did not understand, etc.

(American expatriate, 55–59 years old, Finance and others)

More details pertaining to the issues related to face are presented in the next section, entitled "The high value placed on face".

Reason 4: To maintain harmonious social relationships. China's cultural emphasis on maintaining harmonious social relationships discourages people from expressing disagreement. For the Chinese people, expressing different opinions means disagreeing, which would harm relationship harmony and cause confrontation. To avoid this, most Chinese employees will choose to remain silent. Some expatriates stated the following:

They are more concerned with preserving harmony than challenging others.

(No demographic information)

Direct questioning to solve an issue was often perceived as confrontation...

(British expatriate, 40–44 years old, Financial Services)

The Chinese want harmony, stability, a sense of where they fit into the group and display the usual Confucian belief that they should not question or challenge older or more senior people.

(British expatriate, 55–54 years old, Education and E-commerce)

Their Chinese employees' inexpressiveness and unwillingness to speak their minds had presented three main challenges for the expatriate managers.

Challenge 1: The expatriates had been unable to get feedback or viewpoints from their staff. This has hindered any attempts to produce ideas among staff. A British expatriate stated the following:

Although this sounds slightly cliché, Chinese employees tend to follow the requirements of their job description to the point. For creative positions such as marketing, this can be a tough obstacle when trying to generate ideas among staff.

(British expatriate, 20–24 years old, Education)

In addition, it had affected various HR processes, such as team building and performance management. An Australian expatriate said the following:

This big one for me is the cultural norm that you do not admit fault or speak your true feelings while at work…This has a huge impact on many contemporary western leadership models. The connection or impact can be visualized if thinking through how effective western HR processes are in China for team building, trust and empowerment, performance management, reward and recognition, and continuous improvement.

(Australian expatriate, 50–54 years old, Professional Services)

Some expatriate managers said that their Chinese employees would not provide their inputs in discussions, particular in meetings, even when they were aware of problems or had ideas for making improvements. They said that meetings were ineffective because most employees, if not asked directly, would not voice their concerns or provide inputs, but just attend passively.

…many do not speak up in group meetings at all when you know they have an opinion.

(British expatriate, 50–54 years old, Advertising and Marketing)

It is not effective to have open (group) discussions, since people are reluctant to provide their (sincere) input during such discussions.

(Dutch expatriate, 35–39 years old, Real Estate)

...they do not ask many questions and are not very open during meetings and discussions.

(French expatriate, 45–49 years old, Electrical Insulation)

...within meetings unless directly asked to comment, Chinese staff will most likely sit through the meeting without saying anything at all and making notes. It is not that they are incapable, quite the contrary.

(British expatriate, 20–24 years old, Education)

Challenge 2: The impossibility to address problems in a timely fashion. This was due to employees not reporting and even hiding problems. The expatriate managers said that most of their Chinese employees would keep quiet if something went wrong, which could lead to bigger problems.

One challenge with Chinese employees is that they never tell you what is wrong with the task or express that they can't achieve something.

(American expatriate, 55–59 years old, Management Consulting)

If a problem arises, it could be difficult to realize it because people wouldn't let it reach the top.

(No demographic information)

Biggest challenge here was to have people advise if there was an issue, rather than to try and hide a much larger potential problem.

(Australian expatriate, 35–39 years old, Education)

And sometimes the communication with Chinese employees is not as open as I wish it would be. Everyone makes a mistake once in a while and I would appreciate if I am told about the mistake from one of my employees, but it happened more often in China than in Germany that the mistake was hidden.

(German expatriate, 50–54 years old, Tourism)

What is different and was the most difficult thing for me to get used to is the typical employee be they an office worker or a scientist with a PhD in China will not report problems unless asked specifically about a matter. It could be something as simple as a sample or shipment being held up due to customs. The product being received may be critical to completing a task on time. Yet the Chinese employee will more often than not withhold any such problem until the due date is past. It is almost as if they do not want you to see they need help to resolve something. Contrast this to people who have worked for me from Europe or the US and you almost have the opposite. They will typically want to seek a resolution to anything blocking their success.

(American expatriate, 55–59 years old, Finance and others)

Challenge 3: A lot of effort went into encouraging Chinese employees to speak up and share ideas. The Chinese employees were reticent to be open, exchange ideas, and speak up their ideas and opinions for fear of being wrong. The expatriates thus needed to put a lot of effort to encourage their Chinese employees to speak up and share ideas. Some expatriate managers said the following:

...one needs to put in a lot of effort to get Chinese staff to contribute to meetings and share their opinion.

(No demographic information)

Challenges—to make Chinese staff confident to speak up and bring forward solutions to problems and not just to follow the Policies.

(Australian expatriate, 30–34 years old, Human Resources)

The challenge is to let everyone express their views in a personal manner.

(French expatriate, 40–44 years old, Luxury)

Challenges: ...Courage to challenge and express own ideas. Develop confidence to exchange ideas or different opinions on a subject.

(Australian expatriate, 55–59 years old, Automotive)

The high value placed on "face"

The sixth most mentioned challenging characteristic was the great importance attached to "face" (*mianzi*) by Chinese employees in their working
lives. As explained in Chapter 4, "face" is highly valued by Chinese
people as it represents one's esteem, honor, reputation, and social prestige.
Many expatriate managers said that their Chinese employees saw "face"
as something extremely important to uphold. An Italian expatriate rightly
illustrated the importance of face to Chinese people:

> *Then I understood that if you want to destroy the spirit of a man in
> China, it's enough to let him lose the face. So I have been very careful
> in treating people.*

(Italian expatriate, 40–45 years old, Mechanical Engineering)

The Chinese people's preoccupation with avoiding loss of "face"
causes Chinese employees to behave differently from their Western counterparts. The resulting behaviors have been seen as uncommon and possibly unacceptable in Western workplaces. For example, to avoid risking
loss of "face", many Chinese employees will exhibit behaviors such as not
speaking in meetings in order to avoid saying something wrong, not taking initiatives to avoid making mistakes, not admitting to any lack of
skills or knowledge in relation to a task, not asking for help if they
encounter a problem, and coming up with excuses when things go wrong.
Some expatriate managers said the following:

> *Chinese are very sensitive about losing face and professional
> appearance...*

(American expatriate, 50–54 years old, Industrial Manufacturing)

> *Chinese employees don't feel comfortable if taking own decisions due to
> fear of losing face.*

(No demographic information)

> *Chinese do not want to lose the face, so even if something is not clear
> they will not tell you. You have to check.*

(Italian expatriate, 45–49 years old, Telecommunications)

There is always the issue of "face" as well, which comes up regularly in meetings. Generally in China, staff do not want to ask questions during the meeting.

(Australian expatriate, 30–34 years old, Training and Development)

Many expats feel insecure at not knowing whether a local team believes in your plan or strategy. As culturally locals believe it's best to tell the boss what he/she wants to hear than engage in direct feedback that may lead to losing face.

(British expatriate, 45–49 years old, Recruitment)

No one will ever admit that they don't know how to do, instead of asking for assistance and help. Some of the people stubbornly refuse to be helped, because they live in the clouds and will never accept failure, their level of pride is too high.

(German expatriate, 50–54 years old, Hospitality)

Chinese employees will often say "yes" in order to save face, even when they know the correct answer is no.

(New Zealander expatriate, 40–44 years old, Manufacturing)

The direct western approach can come across in China as being disrespectful or arrogant and in most cases a loss of face value... Chinese people thrive more in group participation where success is shared and celebrated as a team. Targeting individuals in my experience came across as the boss isolating the abilities and performance of one individual which leads to loss of face value.

(New Zealander expatriate, 35–39 years old, Hospitality)

The passive behaviors resulting from Chinese employees' preoccupation with "face saving" and "avoiding loss of face" were regarded by many sample expatriates as one of the major challenges linked to leading/managing their Chinese employees. The following quotes illustrate the expatriates' experience on how issues related to "face" had led to operational errors and affected organizational efficiency.

In the USA we are direct, aren't overly concerned with the concept of losing face, and want to solve the problem in as short a time as possible. In China people are much less direct and avoid losing face, which often leads to unnecessary delays to avoid fault/blame/responsibility.

(No demographic information)

This has to do with the Face-Loss Syndrome here in China. They are more concerned not to lose face or their value and are rather taking a higher risk of making endless sums of mistakes and producing a huge quantity on operational errors on all levels.

(German expatriate, 50–54 years old, Hospitality)

Another major challenge was the issue with "face". As a young Caucasian having worked in several Western countries, this was something difficult for me to understand and I often had to ask for help from supervisors on how I can approach this particular employee.

(Finnish expatriate, 25–29 years old, Hospitality)

Challenges: wanting to save face, they will say anything, not always the truth...

(French expatriate, 45–49 years old, International Trade)

Lower levels of work competency and knowledge

The seventh challenge most mentioned by the expatriate managers was that they felt that the work competency and knowledge of their Chinese employees were lower than those found in their home or other countries in which they had worked. They said that the average Chinese employee lacked (a) professional knowledge and experience; (b) problem-solving skills; (c) critical thinking; and (d) international experience and perspectives. The following quotes illustrate the expatriates' views on each of these four aspects, with some stating that such inadequacies varied by employee age, educational level, and geographical location:

a. Professional knowledge and experience

Chinese graduates typically have lower core knowledge than Western graduates, less prepared for the work environment.

(American expatriate, 35–39 years old, Architecture & Interior Design)

Professional maturity of the teams can be a challenge at times.

(American expatriate, 40–44 years old, Technology)

...most without long years of professional experiences need more guidance and coaching. Also, new graduates are not well prepared for the industry needs and therefore we have to educate them from basics, e.g., working behavior, communication, etc.

(Swiss expatriate, 45–49 years old, Packaging and Chemicals)

b. Problem-solving skills

Chinese engineers are excellent at following step-by-step instructions but not good at creative problem-solving by themselves.

(American expatriate, 55–59 years old, Automotive and Energy)

Differences: Greater structure required, less autonomy expected, less creative thinking and problem-solving on the part of the employee.

(British expatriate, 30–34 years old, Media)

...the ability to address the bottleneck is much lower as this is something people would rather dodge than address. Everything beyond the well-defined square meter and role is a risk and is, based on education, not something to be explored. And, there are generations of difference between people only 5 years apart or 50 km apart (city, outskirts, countryside, etc.).

(Belgian expatriate, 40–44 years old, Consultancy)

At the same time I tell people the problem, I have to tell them the solution...majority is and was not trained to solve problems, they can do what they have learnt or experienced.

(Austrian expatriate, 40–44 years old, Hospitality)

It is challenging to ask Chinese employees to brain storm on a solution or come up with ideas to different scenarios that can solve a certain problem.

(Danish expatriate, 35–39 years old, Food)

c. Critical thinking

There is no critical thinking introduced into the Chinese education system. People just absorb data, memorize it, thinking that this will be sufficient for survival.

(German expatriate, 55–59 years old, Hospitality)

Analytics capabilities barely exist in China, same as creativity. This has to be taught.

(German expatriate, 40–44 years old, Manufacturing)

I work in the creative industry and would say that the "average" Chinese is not as creative as its western counterpart and many are unable to "think outside the box".

(British expatriate, 55–59 years old, Advertising and Marketing)

Chinese colleagues are the product of a relatively closed society and a very narrow education system, where they are conditioned to follow...The greatest challenge is summed up by the phrase "tell me what you want me to do and I'll do it". Little role for initiative or critical thinking.

(British expatriate, 60 years old or over, Education)

d. International experience and perspectives

The typical education level and international business acumen is VERY low among ordinary Chinese. To what extent this is the case depends on location, department, etc. China is not the same in Shanghai, Wuhan, or Jiaxing.

(Norwegian expatriate, 35–39 years old, Manufacturing)

Chinese employees often lack experience & an international perspective, thus you have to guide them through the process & regularly "check in" with them.

(Australian expatriate, 30–34 years old, Recruitment)

There is a clear difference as the level of education as well as amount of exposure of working for international companies is limited.

(Dutch expatriate, 30–34 years old, Hospitality)

The inadequacies mentioned above are likely to be the result of a combination of two key factors. First, the education system in China does not adequately equip students with problem-solving skills, analytical and team working ones, and those needed to apply theories to practices. Some expatriates commented the following:

Education—according to my work experience as well as socializing amongst Chinese and foreigners in China, there is a lack of how to apply theoretical and memorized data/information/knowledge and transfer this in such a manner as to make it workable, practical, and applicable for use. For some reason, the education system in China is set up and operated in such a way that they have forgotten to link the theoretical with the practical. This is visible across all industries and on all levels of education and levels of hierarchy.

(German expatriate, 55–59 years old, Hospitality)

Education of Chinese employees does often not fit requirements for international working environment, e.g., language, communication skills...

(Luxembourgian expatriate, 45–49 years old, Iron and Steel)

The way of thinking is usually quite narrow in China and people have quite good theoretical knowledge, but sometime common sense and skills in actual practice are missing.

(Finnish expatriate, 30–34 years old, Machinery)

The locals...struggle with moving from conceptual thinking to practical application. Especially middle management operates at low efficiency.

(Danish expatriate, 40–45 years old, Retail)

The Chinese schooling system is not built up on individual thought and learning patterns or connections; the Chinese schooling system (majority) is still build up on "learn what I tell you to learn and remember".

(Austrian expatriate, 40–44 years old, Hospitality)

Second, the Chinese employees' lower levels of work competency and knowledge may be due to their business skills, knowledge, and acumen not having been honed in step with China's fast-developing socioeconomic environment. Despite the abundance of organizations and job opportunities, many employees still have limited experience and professional knowledge of the industry in which they operate.

Mainly due to the job market situation, employees in Europe tend to be over-qualified compared with their Chinese peers. This means that, basically, leading employees in Europe requires less technical attention.

(No demographic information)

In China, as in many developing countries, many employees have limited experience in using the product/service they are involved in developing/delivering. This means that many assumptions taken for granted elsewhere need to be defined in detail.

(No demographic information)

The challenge resulting from Chinese employees' lower levels of work competency and knowledge is the need for expatriate managers to provide more guidance, coaching, and training on the aforementioned work skills. The following quotes illustrate the views expressed by some expatriates:

The way we adjust is that we deliver more training to Chinese employees than for any other employees in our Group.

(French expatriate, 25–29 years old, Fashion)

In China...employees tend to be rather under-qualified for their position requirements. This means that managers/leaders must do much more training and coaching in China than they would elsewhere.

(No demographic information)

The challenge is to develop independent thinking by the Chinese employee in such a way that he or she is able to solve new problems and tasks in daily work.

(No demographic information)

I implemented reporting, meeting rules, standard management processes, e.g., minutes and action plans...We need more time for relevant trainings, social and soft skills besides the traditional technical or professional developments. Communication and sharing is a challenge since this was never a focus in Chinese education, e.g., an engineer (PhD) needs to be able to present his research results and application engineers should be able to write a comprehensive report to customers in order to "sell" his topic and value. This needs to be developed from scratch.

(Swiss expatriate, 45–49 years old, Packaging and Chemicals)

...by providing more training and by making the employee understand that China is now a global power and that they have embraced the "market economy system" and that requires for them to adapt to international standard of approaches, performances, processes, and procedures, and of course quality. In fact, we told the key people to forget their past experiences at Chinese universities, and state-owned companies, and to look to the future...

(American expatriate, 55–59 years old, Advertising)

Given that the development of professional skills takes time, some expatriates said that they had had to adjust their expectation and themselves.

I had to adjust my...overall expectations of what seems to be high-level education is not quite the same here in comparison to the western world...Most of all, I had to greatly cut down my expectations of what most people say they know and what they actually can do. As mentioned above, they most likely have the theoretical knowledge but have no idea of how to transfer this knowledge into a practical approach.

(German expatriate, 55–59 years old, Hospitality)

I didn't try to change Chinese employees apart from intensive technical training. I found it was less frustrating and more effective to change my own methods and expectations to match my teams.

(American expatriate, 55–59 years old, Automotive and Energy)

A greater focus on money, job titles, and personal benefits

The eighth challenging characteristic most mentioned by the expatriates was that their Chinese employees placed greater emphasis on extrinsic rewards such as money, job titles, and benefits, and less on intrinsic rewards such as recognition and job satisfaction. Some expatriates commented the following:

> *The employees need motivation. But the motivation in China is more related to salary and environment. Less related to job recognition.*

(Belgian expatriate, 30–34 years old, Finance)

> *Chinese employees respond more to economic incentives, while European employees respond more to "soft" values (i.e., more time off work).*

(Danish expatriate, 35–39 years old, Tourism)

> *...all has to be adapted in KPI towards bonuses or money, verbal praise is not so accepted if doesn't come with more income or money.*

(Chilean expatriate, 35–39 years old, Automation)

> *Another one is that Chinese (not all) managers pay more attention to their title than to their responsibility towards direct reports.*

(French expatriate, 50–54 years old, Automotive)

> *Also, the same employee would be highly entrepreneurial and self-motivated if he/she can share in the company's profits or at least the fruits of his own direct efforts, while he will totally switch off his brain and wait for commands when he is on a basic salary.*

(Italian expatriate, 35–39 years old, FMCG)

Some of the expatriates said that their Chinese employees held a sense of entitlement to advancement and unrealistic expectations for promotions and salary increases even in the absence of any skill or performance improvement.

The Chinese work for two months and think they deserve a raise, promotion, and more responsibility.

(American expatriate, 45–49 years old, Hospitality)

There are also high expectations in salaries and salary increases, in spite of a lack of improvement in performance.

(No demographic information)

...employees seem to believe they are entitled to advancement—concept of earning it is absent...

(American expatriate, 40–45 years old, Information Technology)

You need to carefully manage expectations as often Chinese employees expect promotions & salary increases quickly.

(Australian expatriate, 30–34 years old, Recruitment)

I also find many to be...very demanding from a salary expectations perspective even when they may not be deserving of promotions or more money. And then there is the problem with titles (bigger titles) which seem to mean as much to the majority as money does.

(British expatriate, 50–54 years old, Advertising and Marketing)

What do Chinese employees do if their expectations for promotions and salary increases are not met? They leave the organization! Several expatriate managers said that some of their employees had left their company for a small increase in salary elsewhere. Some said that the desire of some employees to maximize their income could even see them engaging in illegal practices, such as taking bribes and gifts. The following quotes illustrate the experiences of some expatriates:

They care more about title and about salary. They will leave a place they like for the smallest upgrade.

(Israeli expatriate, 30–34 years old, Luxury)

Most of young talent move from one company to other just for few more RMB, retention is a critical factor.

(No demographic information)

Developing local staff is a challenge as also often they will seek alternative employment on the basis of a small pay increase.

(Australian expatriate, 30–34 years old, Financial Services)

...turn over in China as a whole leads people to jump around for better titles and small monetary increases...

(American expatriate, 30–34 years old, Research/Consulting)

Challenges are motivation and learning...Some motivation comes with money/promotion opportunities. Others need attention. Yet others do not believe in waiting one year for either promotion or raise and resign (5 employees have done this) within eight months saying they "cannot get ahead in our company" by this system.

(American expatriate, 45–49 years old, Hospitality)

There is also a higher propensity of employees to switch to other companies for a small increase in salary.

(Italian expatriate, 35–39 years old, FMCG food)

In terms of differences, the main factor is the culture—the fact that "It's OK" to leave a job for a 10–15% pay increase, regardless of the effect it has on your long-term career or on the company you leave behind. "It's OK" to leave a job at New Year as that's when the job market is at its most aggressive. "It's OK" to give and accept bribes of cash, gifts, and favors, as long as you don't get caught. These all have a powerful effect on how things operate.

(British expatriate, 25–29 years old, Tech/Fashion Accessories)

I tried to be motivative, I tried to teach them a lot, I tried to have them involved, but the average employee is only looking for personal gain and how he can minimize the input to maximize the money, this also including illegal practices.

(German expatriate, 30–34 years old, Retail)

As can be seen from the above quotes, the expatriates perceived that their Chinese employees' focus on money, job titles, and personal benefits had led to high turnover rates. They viewed this as one of the biggest challenges from the perspectives of employee development and retention. However, do Chinese employees leave their jobs mainly for money and job titles, as stated by the expatriates? Or are there any other reasons for the high employee turnover rates?

The 11 Chinese employees I interviewed indicated that the reasons for employee turnover vary from individual to individual, but they did agree that money was an important motivator. They said that living expenses and property prices in China, particularly those found in urban areas, had increased dramatically following the fast economic development, which had pressurized people to focus on seeking opportunities to make more money and that the abundant job opportunities found in the large coastal Chinese cities had made it possible to move to jobs involving higher pay.

Another key reason mentioned by the interviewees was that many foreign MNCs, particularly product-based ones, are losing their competitive advantage in terms of the ability to attract and retain employees. They said that some Chinese companies and state-owned enterprises (SOEs) have become, or are developing into, global business entities, and are providing employees with attractive career advancement opportunities and very competitive compensation packages, which, in some cases, include stock options. Although most foreign knowledge-based MNCs (e.g., finance and consultancy) still maintain their competitiveness in terms of employee compensation, this development has enticed many Chinese employees who used to work for foreign MNCs to move to Chinese MNCs or SOEs. Two interviewees said that they themselves had made such a move for better compensation, career prospects, and person–organization cultural fit. They said that the organizational culture found in Chinese organizations fit them better than that of foreign MNCs.

The other reasons for employee turnover mentioned by the interviewees were the pursuit of better staff development opportunities, work-related stress, the desire to find a job that fit one's interests, and poor working relationships between managers and employees.

The Chinese interviewees suggested that, in order to reduce turnover rates, foreign MNCs would need to provide employees with competitive monetary rewards, good benefits, and opportunities for staff development and career advancement, rather than reserving senior positions for expatriates.

Lower accountability

The ninth challenging characteristic mentioned by the sample expatriate managers was their Chinese employees' lower accountability compared with that found in their own home countries. Some of the expatriates said that most Chinese employees were unwilling to or afraid of taking any responsibility and that they did not seem to understand that any tasks delegated to them were their responsibility. They thus were not prepared to accept any responsibility. The following quotes illustrate the expatriates' observation:

> *I have encountered that employees have little or no experience in identifying problems and finding solutions and they don't accept the responsibility for a task.*

(No demographic information)

> *I am trying to get people to take more responsibility for their work and the mistakes. Sometimes, there was an attitude of I'll do the work and it is someone else's job to see if there are any mistakes.*

(American expatriate, 40–44 years old, Furniture Trading/
Manufacturing)

> *No one truly wants to embrace responsibility and if they do, they focus on the small details rather than the big picture.*

(British expatriate, 35–39 years old, Advertising)

> *In China, people do not like to take decisions nor want to own responsibility for actions/decisions.*

(German expatriate, 25–29 years old, Consumer Electronics)

> *Another key difference is that most Chinese employees are afraid of responsibility, or don't really understand what it is. They often look to their managers/supervisors to make decisions and execute—they are afraid to take decisions by themselves.*

(British expatriate, 25–29 years old, Green Energy)

Also, generally there isn't a very strong culture of accountability in China—people are still used to a culture where they get paid for showing up every day regardless of outcomes, so people who are supposed to deliver sales or KPIs sometimes don't get the point and don't see that they're not doing their job. I've had to terminate people who don't understand this.

(No demographic information)

There is an absence of accountability, and in over more than a decade it has not become clear to me why a straightforward order and/or point of training will be instantaneously and blatantly disobeyed or reversed mere seconds after having confirmed that the information has been heard and understood.

(No demographic information)

Very different: Israeli employees like to have the freedom to makes decisions by themselves, take responsibility, be mission oriented, and decide on the tasks by themselves. They are not afraid to fail. Chinese seem to prefer being told what to do and not take responsibility for making their own decisions—they are task orientated.

(Israeli expatriate, 35–39 years old, Technology Investment Banking)

In general, my Italian colleagues would act and take decision more or less independently in a situation of emergency under their management, while Chinese colleagues would rather avoid taking unnecessary responsibilities.

(Italian expatriate, 35–39 years old, Energy)

Have tried to increase individual instead of collective accountability. Needed to do this to increase rate of progress. Chinese staff are reluctant to accept personal accountability but also reluctant to impose individual accountability on others. Basically did not work.

(Australian expatriate, 45–49 years old, Insurance)

Why do Chinese employees fall short in accountability? A key reason is the **hierarchical structure** found in Chinese society. Most Chinese employees are accustomed to following the instructions given by their supervisors and thus most perceive that any work outcomes are the responsibility of their leaders. Some expatriate managers said the following:

> *People expect decisions to be made for them in China. There is a lack of desire to take responsibility for decision-making.*

(Australian expatriate, 30–34 years old, Wholesale/Retail FMCG)

> *Allowing Chinese colleagues to take ownership of their area of responsibility is harder, decision-making tends to be referred upwards rather than taking ownership.*

(British expatriate, 40–44 years old, Metals)

> *Chinese company culture has tendency to try to upwards delegate all decisions if possible—the boss decides.*

(Finnish expatriate, 35–39 years old, Steel)

> *My Chinese colleagues have a tendency of waiting to be led with too few showing self-starting capabilities, they prefer to defer decision-making or shouldering responsibilities...*

(Dutch expatriate, 40–44 years old, Hospitality)

> *Chinese employees will be more likely to be unquestioningly "obedient" than UK ones. So even if they think a leader's decision is a bad one, they'll go ahead and implement it regardless—the responsibility is not theirs, but the leader's.*

(British expatriate, 35–39 years old, Public Sector)

Another key reason for the Chinese employees' low accountability is their **risk avoidance and fear of being punished** for making mistakes. Some expatriate managers stated the following:

> *The employees in China are more careful with risk taking which also leads to less accountability.*

(Finnish expatriate, 40–44 years old, Industrial Automation)

Avoidance of risk taking in China is another difference that goes along with an aversion towards ownership and accountability.

(American expatriate, 45–49 years old, Automotive)

Chinese do not take any additional responsibility as they are afraid of being punished.

(Polish expatriate, 50–54 years old, Automotive)

One of the challenges associated with low accountability is a **lack of initiative** on the part of the employees (see the section on "a low tendency to engage in initiatives and proactiveness" above). Some expatriate managers thus had to take care not only of the strategic decisions but also of the routine ones.

Everyone "administers" (= do what I'm told to do), few take responsibility, and accountability is an unknown trait...Little role for initiative or critical thinking.

(British expatriate, 60 years old or over, Education)

Primary difference is less ability for Chinese staff to take initiative and responsibility for projects and to plan. Chinese workers are more single task oriented and used to the boss making even routine decisions.

(American expatriate, 45–49 years old, Consulting)

Another challenge faced by the expatriates was the **difficulty encountered in training their staff to become accountable** because making changes that affect culture and values is arduous.

I am changing the work practice within my organization...The efficiency and accountability in the organization was not at the level I expected... The challenges are that to change a culture takes a long time and that people are changing too often in the organization.

(Finnish expatriate, 40–44 years old, Industrial Automation)

One thing that is very important to note is all these situations are not because of people's lack of ability, it is the result of thousands of years of cultural coding and to break it in a way where people don't fear judgment takes time and support.

(British expatriate, 35–39 years old, Advertising)

...many Chinese employers like to publicly shame people as examples to other employees. This culture makes it very hard for Chinese employees to take responsibility.

(British expatriate, 25–29 years old, Green energy)

The greatest challenges I faced in this were in terms of values; those are difficult to change in people because they are much more deeply rooted than say, behaviors. The best example leading to the need for change was getting Chinese employees to "embrace" the value of "Accountability". The message from the rest of society and that which seems to be rewarded is the ability to avoid accountability. Having people be responsible for themselves, their mistakes or shortcomings in particular, is challenging in any society, but doubly so in Chinese society where it is not rewarded or valued.

(American expatriate, 55–59 years old, IT)

Yes, because their background and approach to their jobs are different. It is harder to teach them to ask questions, to be proactive in their responsibilities, and to accept ultimate responsibility for their projects.

(American expatriate, 55–59 years old, Healthcare)

Loyalty directed to people rather than to the organization

The tenth challenging characteristic mentioned by the expatriate managers was that their Chinese employees exhibited high loyalty to people (e.g., their bosses and direct line managers) but not to the company as a whole. The following quotes illustrate the expatriates' views on the loyalty orientations of their Chinese employees:

Chinese employees are usually more loyal to their managers than to the wider company.

(British expatriate, 25–29 years old, Green Energy)

High loyalty to people in China, in U.S. higher loyalty to company.

(No demographic information)

Germany: people are loyal to the company. China: people are loyal to the direct boss or those who hired them.

(German expatriate, 40–44 years old, Home Appliance Manufacturer)

Chinese staff tends to be more loyal on the personal level while German staff is more loyal to the company.

(German expatriate, 25–29 years old, Consulting)

Many Chinese colleagues have little loyalty towards the company and change jobs frequently.

(Luxembourgish expatriate, 45–49 years old, Iron and Steel)

Chinese employees are interested in short-term returns and have problems to invest in long-term relationships with the company. Relationships are with people, not with the company.

(French expatriate, 45–49 years old, Electrical Insulation)

The Chinese employees' loyalty to people rather than to organizations can be due to three reasons.

Reason 1: Relationships being built on personal connections between "people". As mentioned in Chapter 4, China is a relationship-based society and the related social relationships are always built up from and on a personal level. Thus, people are the subjects with which relationships are built, whereas organizations are seen as mere legal entities. All of the Chinese employees I interviewed agreed that Chinese employees tend to be loyal to people rather than to the company, although two of them also said that some younger employees are loyal neither to people nor to the company, as they work purely to advance their own career aspirations. They said that they learned from, interacted with, and got support from their direct managers on a day-to-day basis, and thus naturally felt loyal toward them, while the company was seen as too remote from their daily working lives and thus not deserving of loyalty. By showing loyalty to their managers/supervisors, Chinese employees build *guanxi* (relation-ships) with them; this helps them to establish not only good working relationships but also personal ones. Some of the Chinese employees said that maintaining a good *guanxi* with their managers/supervisors could help their career advancement in the current organization or in a different one by following them there.

Reason 2: The reciprocity of *renqing*. *Renqing* (commonly interpreted as a "favor" that one can give or receive) is an important medium of social exchange in China (see Chapter 4). It is a social capital found in one's *guanxi* web that can be used and benefited from; it is also a debt or obli-gation one "owes" to a previous donor of *renqing*. Most Chinese employ-ees will show loyalty toward and work harder for supervisors who have helped them develop skills and knowledge and/or provided them with personal assistance, as they feel obliged to repay the *renqing*. The reci-procity of *renqing* is essential for building and maintaining *guanxi*. Relationships are maintained or strengthened through reciprocity pro-cesses, while failure to reciprocate can weaken or damage them.

Reason 3: Confucius's teachings in respect to *wu lun, ren,* and *li*. As discussed in Chapter 4, Confucianism is the dominant and most influential ideology in China. Confucius's *wu lun* (i.e., the five cardinal human rela-tionships) have shaped the hierarchical relationships found in past and present Chinese families, organizations, and society as a whole. The role-based expectation for the emperor–minister relationship—which can be translated into the modern employer–employee one—is that the emperor, who assumes a superior role, holds power and authority over ministers and owes them protection; correspondingly, the ministers, who occupy an inferior role, are expected to be obedient and loyal to their superiors. In Confucius's view, an ideal leader is one who demonstrates *ren* (i.e., benevolence and humaneness), while the followers, in return, are expected to be loyal and deferential. Confucius saw *li* (i.e., right and appropriate behaviors) as fundamental to proper governmental leadership, with the leader treating the subordinates with propriety and respect and the subor-dinates loyally serving the leader. In brief, "loyalty" was seen by Confucius as a virtue expected of followers in the leader–follower rela-tionship; this expectation still influences the thinking and behaviors of Chinese employees.

Challenges

The main challenge associated with the Chinese employees' tendency to be loyal to people, rather than to the company, is **high staff turnover**. When their "bosses" or "leaders" leave the company, some Chinese employees will also resign, which is not good for the growth and operation of organizations. Some expatriate managers said the following:

> *Leading Chinese employees is somewhat different than leading employees in Australia. To put it in oversimplified terms, Chinese employees work for their leader, whereas in Australia employees tend to work for their organization. This causes many challenges—for example, you cannot replace a leader and easily expect their reports to keep working for your organization. You will have to earn their loyalty all over again. If a leader leaves the organization, then lots of work has to be done for employee retention. Expect many people to leave.*

(Australian expatriate, 45–49 years old, Telecommunications)

> *Differences: Chinese employees usually follow the leader (I'd better say "their boss") rather than processes, so sometimes it is not easy to let the organization improve.*

(Italian expatriate, 45–49 years old, Medical Equipment)

> *But one of the challenges with younger Chinese is the lower commitment to the company, they can change jobs very easy...Chinese employees are less loyal to their employer, ready to move when opportunities come...*

(Dutch expatriate, 40–44 years old, Investment & E-commerce)

Nevertheless, the loyalty felt by Chinese employees to people can still be beneficial to the business. Some expatriate managers said that their Chinese employees were very loyal and worked hard when they trusted and/or believed in a leader.

> *The positive thing is that Chinese employees can also be very loyal as long as they perceive you as a boss who can bring the business (and thereby themselves) forward. In this case, they invest themselves personally in the business and work hard and unquestioningly until the task at hand is done.*

(No demographic information)

Chinese employees work extremely hard and if provided the right environment, recognition, and incentives are very loyal.

(Australian expatriate, 45–49 years old, Consulting)

Chinese are very loyal and committed if they trust you. More time needs to be spent on gaining their trust, i.e., prove you are there to support them and protect the team. Communication and interaction needs to take into account high context and low context, so care needs to be made to ensure that what I want to say is fully understood.

(No nationality information, 40–44 years old, Education)

Please see Chapter 9 for the suggestions made by the expatriates in relation to gaining the trust of Chinese employees.

Summary

This chapter presented the views and experiences of 391 expatriate senior managers in leading/managing their Chinese employees.

- Over half (57.2%) of the expatriate managers said that leading Chinese subordinates differed greatly from leading employees in their home countries; about two fifth (38.7%) said that leading Chinese subordinates presented both similarities and difference compared to leading those in their home countries; only 4.1% said that leading Chinese subordinates was the same as leading those in their home country.

- The similarities mentioned were mainly related to the employees' common traits and needs and the general skills required for a leader. The expatriate managers said that they were leading "people" or "human beings" who shared the same traits and needs. Thus, leaders, regardless of where they are, need to deal with the same employee traits (e.g., the desire to do a good job, the desire to be supported) and needs (e.g., for recognition and financial rewards). In terms of the leadership skills required, the expatriate managers said that all leaders should possess and use general or universal leadership skills (e.g., treat employees fairly and provide clear directions) when managing or leading employees, regardless of nations and cultures.

- The differences mentioned by the expatriate managers covered both the positive and challenging characteristics of their Chinese employees. The positive characteristics included a tendency to work hard and an eagerness to learn. A good number of the expatriate managers praised their Chinese employees for being hard working, expressing fewer direct complaints, and being more willing to work long hours than those in their home countries or other countries in which they had worked. Several expatriates said that their Chinese employees were eager to learn new things and to learn from experienced managers in order to gain more experience and develop their skills and careers.

- The expatriates mentioned a number of challenging characteristics of their Chinese employees. The top 10 such characteristics and their associated challenges are summarized as follows:

(1)   **High levels of respect for hierarchy and authority:** Many of the expatriates observed that their Chinese employees were very respectful toward people higher up in the organizational hierarchy and that they were unquestioningly obedient to any orders/ instructions coming from the top. Influenced by Confucius's *wu lun* (five cardinal relationships), hierarchical relationships are still commonplace in Chinese families, organizations, and society as a whole. Chinese employees' high respect for hierarchy and authority, however, had resulted in two main challenges for the expatriates. First, it had constrained open communication and the sharing of ideas, as their Chinese employees hardly ever expressed their views or challenged the viewpoints of their superiors even when they were aware that the latter were wrong. Second, it had led Chinese employees to rely upon and to scrupulously follow any instructions coming from the top, while rarely taking initiative.

(2)   **A lower propensity to engage in initiatives and proactiveness:** Many of the expatriate managers stated that most of their Chinese employees rarely took any initiatives or acted proactively to deal with tasks and problems; instead, they expected to be given detailed instructions as to how to complete a task. The Chinese employees' lower levels of initiative and their tendency to wait for instructions from their mangers/supervisors were thought to be due to the hierarchical system deeply embedded in Chinese society, whereby those in lower positions are expected to submit to authority and to unquestioningly obey the instructions of those in higher positions. The expatriates commented that it was also due to the rote learning approach used in many Chinese education institutions, which rarely encouraged students to come up with ideas to solve problems. The Chinese employees' lack of initiative and proactiveness was seen as a challenge by the expatriate leaders because they found it difficult to delegate responsibilities or empower individuals and struggled to encourage or teach their Chinese staff to take initiatives.

(3)   **The language spoken and an indirect communication style:** Many expatriates perceived the Mandarin Chinese language as one of the biggest barriers and challenges for them, one faced not only by those expatriates who spoke little Mandarin and needed a

translator but also by those who did speak the language adequately because, being non-native speakers, they may miss or misunderstand some cues, nuances, details, meanings, messages, and concepts. Chinese employees' indirectness in communication, in contrast to the direct and self-assertive style commonly seen in many Western countries, was also seen as a challenge by many of the expatriate managers, who found it difficult to understand the views of their Chinese employees and what they intended to say. This characteristic of Chinese employees is born out of the high value placed by the Chinese on maintaining face and harmonious social relationships, avoiding confrontations with others, and displaying respect for people.

(4) **The need to be given detailed instructions, monitored, and micro-managed:** The main reasons for this characteristic were said to be associated with the hierarchical system, employee expectations of being given detailed instructions, the language barrier, and employee intentions to complete a task correctly and efficiently and to avoid taking responsibility for any mistakes. The challenge for the expatriate leaders was that, instead of empowering and delegating responsibilities, they needed to be very hands-on and micro-manage by drawing up clear roadmaps, breaking down tasks into small chunks for each employee, giving specific and detailed instructions, and closely monitoring progress. Nevertheless, some expatriates said that, once they had received detailed instructions or processes, their Chinese employees were very efficient in executing them.

(5) **Reservedness and inexpressiveness in communication:** A great number of the expatriates said that their Chinese subordinates rarely expressed any ideas or viewpoints, did not proactively voice any questions and concerns, rarely confronted people with problems, and were rather unwilling to or afraid of expressing their views in public settings. Chinese employees' inexpressiveness or lack of voice in the workplace was thought to be the result of a combination of hierarchy, language barriers, fear of losing face, and a desire to maintain relationship harmony. Chinese employees' inexpressiveness and unwillingness to speak their minds had presented the expatriates with three main challenges.

First, they were unable to get their subordinates' feedback or viewpoints, which was an obstacle when trying to produce ideas among staff. Second, any issues or problems could not be addressed in a timely fashion, which could lead to bigger problems, as their employees would not report and even hide problems. Third, a lot of effort was needed in order to encourage their employees to speak up and share their ideas.

(6) **The high value placed on "face":** Many of the expatriate managers said that their Chinese employees placed a very high value on "face" (*mianzi*) and saw it as something that was extremely important to uphold. Face is highly valued by Chinese employees as it represents one's esteem, honor, reputation, and social prestige. Chinese employees' careful maintenance of and preoccupation with avoiding loss of face causes them to behave in ways that would be unacceptable in Western workplaces. For example, to avoid losing face, they will rarely speak in meetings to avoid saying something wrong; they rarely take initiatives to avoid making mistakes; they will not admit to any lack of skills or knowledge in relation to a task; and they will not ask for help if they encounter a problem. The passive behaviors resulting from Chinese employees' efforts to "avoid losing face" were regarded by many sample expatriate managers as a major challenge, as they had the potential to cause operational errors and to affect the efficiency of the organization.

(7) **Lower levels of work competency and knowledge:** Many of the expatriate managers felt that the work competency and knowledge of their Chinese employees, although varying by age, educational level, and geographical location, were generally lower than those found in their home countries. Four aspects were mentioned: (a) professional knowledge and experience; (b) problem-solving skills; (c) critical thinking; and (d) international experience and perspectives. The Chinese employees' lower levels of work competency and knowledge may be due to a combination of two key factors: one, the education system in China, which does not equip students with abilities such as problem-solving and analytical and team working skills; two, Chinese employees' business skills, knowledge, and acumen have not kept pace with China's

fast-developing socioeconomic environment. The challenge resulting from the Chinese employees' lower levels of work competency and knowledge was the need for expatriate managers to provide more guidance, coaching, and training.

(8) **A greater focus on money, job titles, and personal benefits:** Many of the expatriate managers said that their Chinese employees placed greater value on extrinsic rewards—such as money, benefits, and job titles—and less on intrinsic rewards such as recognition and job satisfaction. Some said that their Chinese employees held unrealistic expectations in regard to promotions and salary increases, even in the absence of any skills or performance improvements, and that some of them had left the company in pursuit of a small salary increase. The expatriates commented that their Chinese employees' focus on money, job titles, and personal benefits had resulted in high employee turnover rates, which were viewed as one of the biggest challenges from the perspectives of employee development and retention. The interviewed Chinese employees agreed that money was a key reason for employees leaving for other companies, but they also pointed out that many foreign MNCs were losing their competitive advantage in terms of the ability to attract and retain employees, as some Chinese MNCs and SOEs were providing them with attractive career advancement opportunities and very competitive compensation packages and Chinese employees tended to find a better person–organization cultural fit in the latter.

(9) **Lower accountability:** Many sample expatriate managers said that, compared with their home country counterparts, most of their Chinese employees exhibited lower accountability—i.e., they were unwilling or afraid to be accountable and seemed unaware that any tasks delegated to them were their responsibility. One of the reasons for the Chinese employees' lower levels of accountability is considered to be China's hierarchical social structure, whereby Chinese employees are accustomed to following the instructions given by their leaders and perceive that any work outcomes are the latter's responsibility. Another key reason is considered to be Chinese employees' risk avoidance tendencies and their fear of being punished for making mistakes. The

challenges associated with such low accountability were a lack of initiative from the Chinese employees and the efforts needed to train them to become accountable because of the difficulties involved in culture- and value-related changes.

(10) **Loyalty directed to people rather than to the organization:** A number of the expatriate managers said that their Chinese employees exhibited high levels of loyalty toward people (e.g., their bosses and direct supervisors), but not toward the company. Three reasons can explain this state of affairs. The first is related to the subjects with which Chinese people build relationships. China is a relationship-based society and Chinese social relationships are always built on personal connections between people, so people are the subjects of relationship building, whereas organizations are seen as mere legal entities. The second reason is associated with the reciprocity of *renqing* (favors) which is an important medium of social exchange and is essential for building and maintaining *guanxi* in China. Most Chinese employees will show loyalty toward supervisors who have helped them in their professional and/or personal domains as they will feel an obligation to repay the *renqing*. The third reason is related to Confucius's teachings in respect to *wu lun, ren*, and *li*. "Loyalty" was seen by Confucius as a virtue expected of followers in the leader–follower relationship. The main challenge associated with Chinese employees' loyalty to people—rather than to organizations—is high staff turnover rates. Some employees will resign when their "bosses" or "leaders" leave the organization. Nevertheless, the very positive aspect that stems from their loyalty to people is that Chinese employees are very loyal and work hard when they trust and/or believe in their leader.

Chapter 7

Degrees and Patterns of Cross-Cultural Leadership Behavior Adjustment

When leading and managing Chinese employees in China, expatriate managers need to deal not only with cultural differences but also with the many unique characteristics of Chinese employees, such as a high respect for hierarchy and reservedness in communication (see Chapter 6 for such characteristics). Do expatriate managers adjust their own leadership approaches and/or change (or try to change) their Chinese staff? If so, to what extent do they adjust? What are the patterns of their adjustment? How and why do they adjust? This chapter presents my research findings related to these questions, organized into five sections. The first section reports the degree to which expatriate managers adjust their leadership behaviors; the second presents the patterns of their adjustment; the third explains the reasons for each pattern; and the final two sections present the top 10 aspects in relation to which the expatriate managers had adjusted their own leadership approaches and had changed (or had tried to change) their Chinese subordinates, respectively.

Research Findings in Relation to the Degree of Leadership Behavior Adjustment

In my study, I defined the concept of cross-cultural leadership behavior adjustment as the process by which expatriate business leaders change their own leadership behaviors and/or the behaviors of their host country subordinates, as discussed in Chapter 2. Paired-sample t tests were

Table 1. Results of paired-sample *t* tests, leaders' self-assessment.

		Paired differences			
		Mean	SD	df	*t*
Pair 1	Task-oriented (current) −Task-oriented (past)	0.73	1.27	383	11.34***
Pair 2	Relations-oriented (current) −Relations-oriented (past)	0.62	1.28	386	9.50***

Note: Task-oriented: *N* = 384; Relations-oriented: *N* = 387.
***P < .001 (two-tailed).

Table 2. Results of paired-sample *t* tests, subordinates' assessment.

		Paired differences			
		Mean	SD	df	*t*
Pair 1	Task-oriented (current) −Task-oriented (first 3-month)	0.29	1.02	303	5.01***
Pair 2	Relations-oriented (current) −Relations-oriented (first 3-month)	0.26	0.74	300	6.06***

Note: Task-oriented: *N* = 304; Relations-oriented: *N* = 301.
*** P < .001 (two-tailed).

performed to analyze the degree to which the expatriate business leaders had adjusted their leadership behaviors by comparing their past and current ones. The quantitative responses provided by both the expatriate senior managers and their directly reporting Chinese subordinates were analyzed. Please see Chapter 3 for the methods used for data analysis.

Tables 1 and 2 present the results of the paired *t* tests. In regard to the leaders' self-assessment, the mean scores for *current* and *past* behaviors presented significant differences in regard to task-oriented ($t = 11.34$, $p < 0.001$) and relations-oriented behaviors ($t = 9.50$, $p < 0.001$). The results indicate that the expatriate leaders had adjusted their behaviors in both categories. With regard to the results of the subordinates' assessment, significant differences in the mean scores for the *current* and *first 3-month* behaviors were also found in both categories (task-oriented: $t = 5.01$, $p < 0.001$; relations-oriented: $t = 6.06$, $p < 0.001$). Thus, the subordinates' assessment also shows that the leaders had adjusted both categories of their leadership behaviors.

In brief, the results of the statistical analyses show that the expatriate managers had significantly adjusted their leadership behaviors in leading and managing their Chinese employees. The results of the analysis of the qualitative data—aimed at exploring the patterns of leadership adjustment—presented in the next section also show that most of the expatriate leaders had significantly changed their leadership behaviors. Although Situational Leadership Theories (see Chapter 2) advocate that leadership behaviors need to be adjusted according to situations, there is a lack of research on whether leaders—particularly those working in different cultural settings—actually do so. My research addressed this gap and provided empirical evidence showing that expatriate senior managers do adjust their leadership behaviors when working in unfamiliar cultural settings.

Research Findings in Relation to the Pattern of Leadership Behavior Adjustment

This section presents the findings pertaining to the expatriate senior managers' patterns of cross-cultural leadership adjustment. As explained in Chapter 3, the expatriate managers' adjustment patterns were analyzed by organizing the ratings of the expatriate managers' degree of leadership behavior adjustment and the degree to which they had changed (or had attempted to change) their subordinates in the 2 × 2 matrix shown in Figure 1.

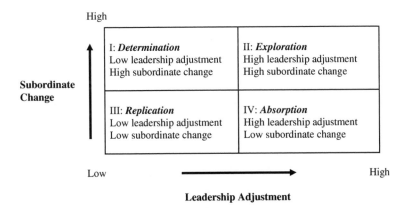

Figure 1. Patterns of cross-cultural leadership behavior adjustment, derived from Nicholson (1984).

The four quadrants indicate different patterns of adjustment:

- *Determination* (quadrant I; low leadership adjustment, high subordinate change)—This pattern emerges when expatriate leaders actively change their subordinates but make little adjustment to their own leadership approaches.
- *Exploration* (quadrant II; high leadership adjustment, high subordinate change)—This occurs when expatriate leaders significantly change both their leadership approaches and their subordinates.
- *Replication* (quadrant III; low leadership adjustment, low subordinate change)—This pattern transpires when expatriate leaders make few leadership adjustments and make little change to their subordinates.
- *Absorption* (quadrant IV; high leadership adjustment, low subordinate change)—This comes to light when expatriate leaders modify their leadership approaches but make few changes to their subordinates.

The statistical results of the analysis of the 391 expatriate managers' responses are presented below. Figure 2 shows the proportions by which the expatriates demonstrated each of the four patterns of adjustment:

(1) 309 (79.1%) expatriate managers—indeed the overriding majority—displayed the *exploration* pattern of adjustment (i.e., they had made adjustment to both their leadership approaches and their subordinates);
(2) 45 (11.5%) displayed the *absorption* pattern (i.e., they had largely adjusted their leadership approaches but not their subordinates);
(3) 21 (5.3%) displayed the *determination* pattern (i.e., they had made little adjustment to their leadership approaches but had actively tried to change Chinese employees); and
(4) 16 (4.1%) displayed the *replication* pattern (i.e., they had made little adjustment to both their leadership approaches and Chinese employees).

The results show *exploration* as the dominant pattern displayed by the leaders (79.1%); *absorption* as the second pattern, albeit far less common than the dominant one, with only 11.5% of the managers exhibiting it; and only small numbers demonstrating the *determination* and *replication* patterns (5.3% and 4.1%, respectively). In other words, the results show that most of the expatriate senior managers had simultaneously adjusted their

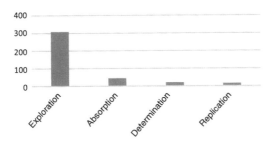

Figure 2. The proportions of each pattern of cross-cultural leadership adjustment displayed by the expatriate managers.

own leadership approaches and had changed (or had tried to change) their Chinese employees, slightly over 10% of them had adjusted their leadership approaches but had made few changes to the behaviors of their subordinates, while a small proportion of them had either actively tried to change their subordinates or had implemented very little self-adjustment and subordinate changes.

The expatriate senior managers' decisions on whether to adjust, and to what degree, themselves and/or their subordinates, and hence their patterns of adjustment, had been influenced by various internal and external factors. In the next section, the reasons behind each pattern of adjustment are reported.

The Reasons Behind Each Pattern of Leadership Adjustment

In this section, the reasons underpinning the adoption of each of the four patterns of adjustment are explained. Table 3 provides a summary of such reasons. As in Chapter 6, many direct quotes from the expatriates are used. The use of the expatriates' own words is intended to make the analysis interesting to read and to enable readers to formulate their own interpretations and judgments.

The exploration pattern of adjustment (high leadership adjustment, high subordinate change)

The research findings showed that 309 expatriate senior managers (79.1%) had simultaneously adjusted their own leadership approaches and changed

Table 3. Summary of the reasons underpinning each pattern of leadership adjustment.

Pattern of leadership adjustment	Reasons for adjusting leadership behavior	Reasons for changing (or trying to change) employees
Exploration 309 expatriates (79.1%)	(Degree of adjustment: High) They had adjusted their leadership because: • they had felt it was important to respect and adapt to the local culture and practices and to meet the expectations of Chinese employees for a leader; • they had wanted to get good results.	(Degree of change: High) They had changed (or had tried to change) their employees in order to: • improve employee performance; • meet customer expectations.
Absorption 45 expatriates (11.5%)	(Degree of adjustment: High) They had adjusted their leadership because they had felt it was important to align their leadership approaches with the local culture and practices, rather than to try and change them.	(Degree of change: Low) They had not changed (or tried to change) their employees because they had sensed it would have been difficult to do so.
Determination 21 expatriates (5.3%)	(Degree of adjustment: Low) They had made low degrees of leadership adjustment because: • they had perceived that many aspects of their leadership were generic and could thus be applied to all contexts, regardless of the nationality or culture of the employees;	(Degree of change: High) They had changed (or had tried to change) their employees because they believed that some characteristics of their Chinese employees needed to be changed in order to work more effectively.

- they had perceived that what was required was a change in "how" leadership was "delivered" according to the characteristics of employees and organization, rather than to their own leadership approaches;
- they had trusted their subordinates to perform.

Replication
16 expatriates
(4.1%)

(Degree of adjustment: Low)
They made low degrees of leadership adjustment for different individual reasons; for example, because they had perceived that their leadership approach fit with the Chinese work culture, and thus no adjustment was needed; they had perceived that their leadership approach would work for anyone, regardless of nationality or gender; they had wanted to remain true to themselves.

(Degree of change: Low)
They had not changed (or tried to change) their employees because they had thought that:
- it would be impossible to change their Chinese employees' work approach due to the embeddedness of Chinese traditions;
- it would not be worth changing their Chinese employees due to the high employee turnover rates.

(or tried to change) their Chinese employees. They had done so because they had felt that both these strategies were needed. On the one hand, they had adjusted their leadership because (1) they had felt that it was important to respect and adapt to the local culture and practices and to meet the expectations of their Chinese employees for a leader, and (2) they had wanted to get good results. The following quotes reflect these reasons:

The reason behind this leadership adjustment is due to cultural differ-ence that must be respected here in mainland China. The direct western approach can come across in China as being disrespectful or arrogant and in most cases a loss of face value.

(New Zealander expatriate, 40–44 years old, Hospitality)

To work in China, you need to get familiar with the business culture and learn the language, respect the local customs, and be ready to learn, as you would do in any other country outside your native country.

(Italian expatriate, 40–44 years old, International
Government Cooperation)

Need for adjustment is based on cultural expectations. How criticism and praise are given is different between China and my home country. Also, people in China are a bit more sensitive to criticism, and more difficult to build back up, after receiving criticism. Personal feelings can get in the way easily.

(American expatriate, 30–34 years old, Education)

I think the biggest thing, which impacts a need for adjustment, is expec-tations as a leader of the organization, and early life learning/teaching, which is very different from our leadership expectations. Adjust through experience and hard learning myself.

(No demographic information)

Yes, when I had to be a leader in a Chinese team, I approached it differ-ent than when I approach other cultures teams. Different cultures require always different strategies!

(Venezuelan expatriate, 30–34 years old, Urban Planning &
Architecture)

...you must adapt your leadership style in China. You have to be much more specific, much more clear and cannot expect too much initiative from the employee as many seem not to know by themselves what is expected and how to go about it. The need to adjustment is led by the mere fact that many Chinese employees do not perform as expected and projects especially time and qualities are not being met.

(Israeli expatriate, 45–49 years old, Consulting)

I had to become more flexible and dedicate more time to manage the team, and to get deeper in some business what I was not doing in France. I also have to change my way to take decision, I need to explain more and see some key people before the meeting took place, it is a loss of time but needed to have successful results.

(French expatriate, 50–54 years old, Railway)

On the other hand, they had changed (or had had change) their subordinates because they had wanted to improve employee performance and to meet customer expectations. The following quotes illustrate this:

Yes, we changed employees as well as practices. We have changed procedures and gave much more training. The need for change was that performance was poor. We replaced employees that did not show willingness to make an effort and for the rest we provided extra benefits and training.

(Israeli expatriate, 45–49 years old, Consulting)

I did not want to change Chinese employees for the sake of changing them or for making them closer to what I would like them to be. I just tried to do it to improve their performance and therefore the performance of my department and of the company I worked for.

(Italian expatriate, 35–39 years old, Pharma)

... have tried to change the approach to ideas discussion, and the self-confidence of the employees by giving more structure to the team, by letting the employees express anonymously their ideas ... the change was needed to improve the efficiency of the employees.

(Italian expatriate, 35–39 years old, Machinery)

The need for change was obviously the lack of results. No company can be efficient with such an attitude. Sometimes you cannot change people behavior/attitude, so you must replace them.

(French expatriate, 55–59 years old, Automotive)

What led the need for change: Our clients like confident people who have an opinion.

(Australian expatriate, 55–59 years old, E-commerce)

Instigate change by showing a different (better) way and the need for change. Typically the need for change is led by our clients' requirements.

(British expatriate, 35–39 years old, Construction)

In hotels changes are also required as more and more foreign corporate clientele increases year on year as economic opportunities continue to grow in China.

(New Zealander expatriate, 40–44 years old, Hospitality)

To summarize, the expatriates had displayed the *exploration* pattern of adjustment (i.e., they had simultaneously adjusted their leadership approaches and tried to change their Chinese employees) because, on the one hand, they had felt that it was important to respect and adapt to the local culture and practices and to meet the expectations of their Chinese employees for a leader, and, on the other hand, they had wanted to improve employee performance and to meet customer expectations.

The absorption pattern of adjustment (high leadership adjustment, low subordinate change)

It was found that 45 expatriates (11.5%) had not tried to change their subordinates but had adjusted their own leadership approaches. They had done so due to two main reasons: first, they had felt that it was important to align their leadership approaches with the local culture and practices, rather than to try and change them, and second, they had sensed that it would be difficult to change their Chinese subordinates. Over half of them expressed the belief that the local culture and practices were not for them to change, but to adapt to, and that understanding the Chinese mindset and adjusting one's own leadership was the only way to effectively lead people in China. The following quotes illustrate such views:

I have lived in Greater China for nearly 15 years. The culture and the way things are done here are not for me to change. It is something which I have learned to adapt to and have enjoyed the steep learning curve which I believe I still am on. In my experience, my team have appreciated every effort that I have made to try and understand where they are coming from and I believe it to be one of the major contributing factors to many successful relationships.

(South African expatriate, 35–39 years old, Water Filtration)

You cannot change a culture and I have witnessed other expatriate managers try and fail in their attempts to change this. The best expatriate managers in China are those who have taken the time to get to know their staff and learnt more about Chinese language and culture. Knowledge of this will make it easier for Chinese employees to feel you are interested in them and their country which will lead to a more motivated and happy workforce.

(British expatriate, 20–29 years old, Education)

I think you have to understand as much as you can about how business and hierarchy work in the Chinese mindset. I find myself being far more strategically minded here, I have to remember the rules of business, etiquette, and corporate culture differ from back in the UK. I have to adjust, no other way, adjust or fail.

(British expatriate, 30–34 years old, Recruitment)

The other main reason that had led the expatriates to adapt their leadership, but not to try to change their Chinese subordinates, was that they had perceived it as difficult, if not impossible, to change their Chinese employees due to the latter's deeply embedded cultural values.

I didn't try to change Chinese employees apart from intensive technical training. I found it was less frustrating and more effective to change my own methods and expectations to match my teams.

(American expatriate, 55–59 years old, Automotive and energy)

No, I haven't. It's very much limited to change people. It's more a compromise....

(German expatriate, 50–54 years old, Machinery)

Hard to change people's fundamental values. Cannot change people.

(No demographic information)

To be honest, I think that trying to change Chinese employees' working practice is of an enormous difficulty hence I went to try to reach an understandable point of a good compromise. We enhanced our communications and understanding in an amazing way thanks to the stimulation I gave to them to be more open in share ideas and comments.

(Italian expatriate, 55–59 years old, Mechanic)

To summarize, those expatriates who had displayed the *absorption* pattern of adjustment (i.e., who had largely adjusted their leadership but had made little change to their Chinese subordinates) had done so mainly because they had perceived that it was important to align their leadership approaches with the local culture and practices and because they had felt that it would be difficult to change the deeply embedded local culture and work practices.

The determination pattern of adjustment (low leadership adjustment, high subordinate change)

A combination of four reasons was found to have led 21 expatriates (5.3%) to maintain their leadership approaches while actively trying to change their subordinates. First, six of them had maintained their leadership approaches because they had perceived that many aspects of their leadership were generic and could thus be applied to in any contexts. These expatriates' universalistic view is illustrated in these two quotes:

There are many aspects of leadership that are generic, regardless of the nationality or culture of the employees. So for example, giving clear direction, being careful to understand staff problems from all sides before making a judgment, being approachable and open, being a good judge of people and character apply in any context.

(British expatriate, 40–44 years old, Public Sector)

I did not change much because I think good management techniques are the same everywhere and work everywhere.

(French expatriate, 50–54 years old, Electrical Insulation)

Although they hadn't thought it necessary to adjust their leadership, they did affirm the importance of being aware of cultural differences and of different employee characteristics.

Second, three expatriates expressed that adjustments in leadership were not necessary and that what was required was a change in the way it was delivered according to the characteristics of the employees and organization. An expatriate said the following:

...the leadership style is defined by the personality of the leader. What is different is the delivery of that style according to the maturity of the staff and organization. Some leaders tell, some ask, some threaten, some cajole, some punish, some reward, etc. When entering a new organization I have to gently transition the existing staff to my own way of working; too fast and people can't focus on their work, too slow and the company doesn't grow. Much like with parenting, the nuances are more important than the theory.

(British expatriate, 45–49 years old, Automotive)

Third, four expatriates had not felt the need to change their leadership because they trusted their subordinates to perform:

I have not adjusted my leadership approach. Trust leads to trust. Respect breeds respect.

(Danish expatriate, 50–54 years old, Medical Devices)

My management style is open and built on trust. No need to adjust this for Chinese employees.

(Dutch expatriate, 50–54 years old, Chemical)

Fourth, most of the expatriates expressed the belief that some characteristics of their Chinese employees needed to be changed in order to work more effectively. For example, they had felt that their Chinese subordinates needed to be more proactive and confident and to take responsibilities, instead of waiting for instructions from their supervisors. They had tried to bring their Chinese employees to adopt what they believed to be good ways of working. To do so, they had encouraged their subordinates to challenge opinions, take responsibilities, and work independently, and they had provided mentoring and coaching. Two expatriate managers said the following:

> *I've tried to encourage them to challenge more, and I've tried to encourage them to feel more ownership and sense of personal responsibility for the overall team and its objectives, rather than just their individual objectives. There are many ways to do this, including personal mentoring, group events, providing encouragement and criticism of individuals and the whole team in equal measure.*

(British expatriate, 40–44 years old, Public Sector)

> *I require people to work independently. I don't want to be a "boss". I don't believe in a top-down approach. I believe in sharing knowledge and experience to develop faster... To a certain extent I try to coach them, this takes more time and effort in China than in my home country.*

(Dutch expatriate, 40–44 years old, Architecture/Construction Sector)

Taken together, these expatriates displayed the *determination* pattern of adjustment (i.e., they had maintained their leadership approaches and had actively tried to change their subordinates) because (1) they had perceived that their leadership approach could be applied anywhere, regardless of the nationality or culture of the employees; (2) they had felt that it was only necessary to change the way leadership was delivered; (3) they trusted their subordinates to perform; and (4) they believed that some characteristics of their Chinese employees needed to be changed in order to make their work more effective.

The replication pattern of adjustment (low leadership adjustment, low subordinate change)

A small number of the expatriates (16, 4.1%) said they had neither changed their own leadership behaviors nor the behaviors of their subordinates. There were different individual reasons behind their conviction that it was unnecessary to adjust their leadership: one said that his leadership approach fit the Chinese work culture; another that a *leader's leadership will work for anyone, regardless of nationality or gender*; a third said that he had tried to find a common language when working with Chinese subordinates; and a fourth said that he had hired more expatriates who were better able to accommodate his leadership approach. An expatriate had kept his leadership approach as he had thought that it was important to be true to himself; he stated the following:

> *Most important is to be yourself. If you try to be someone you are not, you will be quickly outed as inauthentic. People can spot a bullshitter a mile away—in any culture. You will be more effective as an ugly American than as someone pretending to be Chinese.*

(American expatriate, 55–59 years old, Accounting)

A young expatriate expressed a similar view, saying it was important for him to behave according to his own values and that he was looking for an organization that would fit them. He stated the following:

> *I am trying to find other overseas companies rather than changing my values.*

(Nepalian expatriate, 20–29 years old, Events & Conferences)

Turning to the reasons why 16 expatriates hadn't changed (or tried to change) their subordinates, some hadn't done so because they had thought that it would be impossible to change their Chinese employees' work approach due to the deeply embedded Chinese traditions. An expatriate said the following:

> *I believe that it is not possible to change everything about Chinese workers' approach to the job, as much of it is rooted in millennia-old traditions.*

(Danish expatriate, 40–44 years old, Tourism Sector)

An expatriate had thought that changing his Chinese employees was not worth the effort due to the high employee turnover rate.

Not worth spending time...the annual employee turnover in China is approx. 4–5 times higher than the one in West.

(40–44 years old, no other demographic information)

The reasons why these expatriates had not changed their Chinese subordinates may sound passive to many, but the expatriates had perceived that their "inaction" was a practical measure they had taken as a result of their evaluation of the local reality.

In brief, the reasons why these expatriates had displayed the *replication* pattern of adjustment (i.e., they had made little adjustment or changes to both their leadership approaches and their Chinese employees) had included the following: their perception that their leadership approach fit the Chinese work culture, thus making any adjustment unnecessary; their desire to be true to themselves; their conviction that it would be impossible to change their Chinese employees' work approach due to the deeply embedded Chinese traditions; and their assessment that it was not worth trying to change their Chinese employees due to the high employee turnover rate.

Section summary

The reasons underpinning each of the four patterns of adjustment reported above highlight how a combination of various internal and external factors had influenced the expatriate senior managers' decisions on whether to adjust their behaviors and/or their subordinates, thus informing the pattern of adjustment. For example, internally, the managers' own perceptions of the need to adapt to local culture and to meet the expectations of their Chinese employees, and of the best way to manage them, had influenced their decisions on whether to adjust their own approaches and/or the behaviors of their subordinates. Externally, for instance, the characteristics of their Chinese employees—such as reservedness in communication, high dependence, and low proactiveness—and the need to improve employee performance had also influenced the leaders' decisions on whether to change their own leadership approaches and/or their subordinates.

The next two sections present the top 10 aspects in regard to which the expatriate managers had adjusted themselves and had changed (or had tried to change) their Chinese employees, respectively.

The Top 10 Aspects in Regard to Which the Expatriate Managers Had Adjusted Themselves

There were various aspects in regard to which the expatriates said they had made adjustments. The top 10 most mentioned are listed in the following, after which details on the top five are provided:

(1) Style of communication
(2) Higher levels of patience
(3) A higher frequency of monitoring and following up
(4) Specific and detailed task instructions
(5) Greater directiveness and control
(6) Greater indirectness, politeness, friendliness, and gentleness
(7) Less delegation, a more hands-on approach
(8) The adoption of a more fatherly or brotherly role
(9) More time spent in being available to the team
(10) Greater use of micro-management

Style of communication

Communication was the aspect of adjustment in which the expatriates most mentioned they had engaged. The need to adjust their style of communication had arisen as a result of not only language differences but also of cultural ones. First, in relation to language differences, the Chinese language fluency of most of the expatriate managers had ranged from "no proficiency" to "professional working proficiency", while most of their Chinese employees possessed low to medium levels of English fluency and were particularly weak in regard to listening comprehension. Thus, language differences had created situations in which a total or partial lack of understanding had occurred regularly on both sides.

Many expatriates said that, to improve understanding, they would repeat themselves several times and check regularly whether they had been understood. The following quotes illustrate how language differences had led the expatriates to adjust their approaches:

Because of language issues, I try to repeat questions and main topics several times and make sure everybody understands.

(French expatriate, 50–54 years old, electrical insulation)

The language barrier is the most difficult one, most expat managers as well as Chinese employees are operating in another than their mother tongue. The whole working relation is based on "translation"...What I have seen done is adjust my communication in different ways. Checking understanding of my audience in a non-patronizing way. Working with focus groups where they can use their own Chinese language (free flow of ideas) and only needed to report back in English.

(Belgian expatriate, 55–59 years old, Steel)

Be culturally aware and contextualize yourself and your ideas. Simplify your language and repeat yourself 10x more than you think you should. This is not a failing of the employees, but rather my lack of ability to adequately communicate in Chinese.

(American expatriate, 45–49 years old, Technology)

In addition to repeating themselves and checking understanding, some expatriates had given more detailed information, spent more time communicating with their Chinese employees, and held both formal and informal meetings. The following quotes illustrate the efforts they had made in communicating with their Chinese employees:

I did some adjustment on communication, by over communicating, using as much as possible chalk & boards, avoiding or reducing to the minimum, conf calls on important issues.

(Brazilian expatriate, 55–59 years old, No industry information)

To adjust I spend longer explaining my requirement, back it up with additional communication (email, etc.) and check, check, check as often as daily to make sure everything is on track.

(Australian expatriate, 55–59 years old, Professional Services)

I tend to be more descriptive in explaining what I expect from them and pamper them, so they understand what is expected from them and feel more valued.

(French expatriate, 35–39 years old, Management consulting)

I clearly explain the task, i.e., what is the task, what is the expected result, and what is a good result, the deadline as well as what is the intention of the task (why it is needed) so that the employee can make her/his expected contribution to the overall goal.

(No demographic information)

More detailed communication, more follow-up, clarity on responsibility. Use meetings as formal forums to give info, use informal meetings/ one-on-one sessions to get input.

(Danish expatriate, 50–54 years old, Consulting)

Some expatriates had adjusted by listening more attentively and speaking more slowly.

I adjust by listening more and taking every idea very seriously and talking about what we should do. It takes a little extra time in the beginning but by gaining the people's trust it works well in getting much done.

(American expatriate, 55–59 years old, Manufacturing)

Yes, one general change is related to communication. As a foreigner with limited Chinese, communicating to staff working in a second language requires more patience & better listening.

(American expatriate, 30–34 years old, IT)

I have to adjust the speed I am talking in English and try not to use too many long or complicated words so that my staff can fully get my meaning.

(British expatriate, 60 years old or over Export and manufacture)

Second, differences in cultural factors had also led the expatriates to adjust their style of communication. As mentioned in Chapter 6, most Chinese employees have a high respect for authority and are very protective of their "face". These two employee characteristics lead Chinese employees to always respond affirmatively and uncritically to their supervisors' instructions or to not ask any questions even when they do not understand something when communicating with their expatriate managers. Such behaviors are intended to show respect to their supervisors and/ or to save their own face by avoiding showing they have not understood, but they do make it difficult to achieve mutual understanding and effective communication. A French expatriate said the following:

> *Lot of adjustments are needed. The first one might be related to the communication, ensuring that the information is clearly understood, without a long practice a lot of foreigners might think that when a Chinese says yes to them, it means that they understood everything and say yes. The reality is different and foreigners have to find if yes means yes or yes but if you could make it more clear it will be better. Then using English or Chinese also leads to some misunderstanding and it is important to explain the same thing in different ways to ensure a common understanding.*

> (French expatriate, 30–34 years old, Distribution)

Higher levels of patience

The second most mentioned adjustment by the expatriate managers involved their becoming more patient. There were four main reasons for said adjustment: (1) communication problems caused by language differences; (2) the need to give detailed and precise instructions; (3) the longer waits for results and the need to invest in employee training; and (4) the need to understand and accept local practices.

First, language differences had led many of the expatriates not only to adjust their commutation style, as mentioned in the last section, but also to adjust their levels of patience. The expatriates had felt that more patience was needed when communicating with their Chinese employees because either they themselves or their Chinese employees (or both) were communicating in a language that was not their native one. They thus needed to be patient in order to ensure that they had clearly communicated what they wanted to convey to their Chinese subordinates. Two expatriates said the following:

> *More patience when speaking with employees. I need to always remind myself that I am the one who does not speak the language of the country (Chinese) and problems with communication are partly caused by my*

ignorance. This can be challenging when under time pressure or working on critical tasks.

(Canadian expatriate, 45–49 years old, Food and Beverage)

The biggest change is to be patient, working alongside Chinese employees can be frustrating both because of subtle differences in the language and translation. Clear concise communication is a must in China, whereas in your own language you may be able to just tell someone to do something, in China you need to be very clear.

(British expatriate, 45–49 years old, Metals)

The second reason that had led the expatriate managers to increase their level of patience was the need to give precise task instructions to their Chinese subordinates. As described in Chapter 6, most Chinese employees are accustomed to following their supervisors' instructions, rather than taking initiatives. Many of the expatriates had found that, in order to ensure that the work would be done, they had to give detailed task instructions and, in some cases, to repeat such instructions several times, which had compelled them to become more patient. Some expatriates stated the following:

My Chinese staff would like to be told exactly what to do, they don't want to discover and learn. So I do not assume they know what I know, I have to be very precise in my directions. Be more patient, and nurturing, try to use SOP to educate employees.

(American expatriate, 45–49 years old, Mobile Games Distribution)

I'm more patient with Chinese employees than I am with foreign employees. But perhaps the most important difference is that thinking outside the box is not what Chinese employees excel at. Therefore, sometimes you need to lead by showing them specific examples of what you are looking for or where you want the organization to be headed to.

(No demographic information)

I had to be more patient, to repeat many times my instructions, be sure they have understood, check and recheck things done.

(Italian expatriate, 55–59 years old, Automotive)

I had to adjust it a lot. In Western business communication, a manager can ask his employees for their opinion or their plan of approach in their job. In the beginning, I got a lot of silence when asking my employees for this. They simply said: "You are the boss, you just tell me what to do."

(Dutch expatriate, 35–39 years old, Machine Manufacturing)

In order to ensure that their employees would understand what was expected of them, some expatriates had developed tools (e.g., checklists) and structured their requirements, and had then presented them to their employees in small, manageable increments.

I try to be more patient and develop further our process into smaller sub-process. I create lots of checklists and formatted document to ensure method and process are respected. Adjustment are made everyday depending on how the tasks are successfully completed or not.

(French expatriate, 30–34 years old, Consulting)

You have to adjust, be more patient. Structure your demands and present them in "chewable portions", follow up regularly...

(Austrian expatriate, 40–44 years old, Automotive)

The third reason that had led the expatriates to adjust their levels of patience was the longer waits for work results and the need to invest in employee training. Four expatriates expressed that they had needed to adjust their expectations and wait more patiently for results:

I also learned to be more patient and I expect that the work will not be completed on time or to my expectation. Therefore, I lowered my expectation and give it more patience with being persistent.

(Swiss expatriate, 40–44 years old, Education)

I need to be more patient understanding that in China the results may come, but will take longer to happen.

(Spanish expatriate, 30–34 years old, FMCG Non-food)

Third is patience. I accepted already that we cannot expect the same efficiency as in my home country.

(Turkish expatriate, 45–49 years old, Real Estate)

To adjust you need to be ready for the simplest task to take longer. Patience and humility are needed, arrogance and a brash approach will get you nowhere. Taking time and checking you are understood and that you also understand is necessary.

(No demographic information)

Several expatriates said that they had had to be more patient in training their Chinese employees. The following quotes illustrate this:

I find more time is spent in China educating on the opportunities and challenges but through this, the China colleagues are more aware of the SWOT and risks. Patience is very much needed to work in this manner but the results can be equally rewarding.

(American expatriate, 55–59 years old, Industrial Manufacturing)

I did adjust. Be willing to teach and bring people up to owning a problem or situation. You have to adjust otherwise it creates a losing proposition for both sides. My biggest adjustment was patience.

(American expatriate, 45–49 years old, Chemical)

Still adjusting yes: must be far more patient, far more repeats required. And maybe some adjustment in tolerating more employees sometimes moving to wrong directions requiring me to take a more active role in guidance than just coaching.

(Finnish expatriate, 50–54 years old, Engineering Business)

The fourth reason that had caused the expatriates to increase their levels of patience was that they had found that their Chinese employees had different ways of doing things, and that they thus needed to understand and accept such differences. Some expatriates said the following:

I do think leading Chinese employees is different from leading employees in my home country. Maybe the biggest different is the way employees speak out their opinion, want to be heard, do this their own way, even when the leader has decided to do it this way...I have to be more patient and I have learned that this go differently in China. It is very easy to think your way is the best way, but that didn't work out in China. You have to rely on and trust Chinese people because things work differently...

(No demographic information)

You need to become more patient and you need to understand and accept the cultural differences.

(No demographic information)

Have to be more patient while also keeping an open mind to better understand where my Chinese colleagues are coming from and how a different approach would be better received.

(No demographic information)

More patience and trying to understand the context better in seemingly strange situations.

(Lebanese expatriate, 30–34 years old, Online Games)

A higher frequency of monitoring and following up

The third most mentioned adjustment by the expatriates involved more frequently monitoring and following up. They had made this adjustment because of three main reasons: (1) to ensure that their employees had understood the task instructions and objectives; (2) to provide their Chinese employees with more much needed guidance; and (3) to ensure that the work would be done and to the expected quality.

Ensuring that the employees had understood the task instructions and objectives

Some expatriates said they had had to follow-up more in order to ensure that their employees had understood the task instructions and objectives.

They had needed to do so because Chinese employees often respond affirmatively and uncritically to instructions, rarely asking questions, voicing concerns, and raising issues.

> *They are less comfortable in raising problems and issues unprompted...I have to ensure we all understand each other and what has been agreed. Sometimes you get a yes but on further probing there is not full understanding beneath it.*

> (British expatriate, 50–54 years old, Engineering)

> *Instructions and communication need to be closely monitored to ensure a clear understanding on both sides of the message being relayed.*

> (Australian expatriate, 60 years old or over, Hospitality)

> *The main adjustment from a project management standpoint is that you have to learn not to make assumptions about requests and demands being fully understood. The key terms I believe are active listening and follow-up. Each act of communication needs to end with a confirmation of the understanding. Each process needs to have daily follow-up built into it. By internalizing these practices, many problems can be prevented.*

> (No demographic information)

Providing Chinese employees with more guidance

Another reason that had prompted the expatriates to engage in more frequent monitoring and following up was that they had felt that their Chinese employees needed more specific instructions and more guidance. Three of the expatriates—a Finn, an Israeli, and a German—compared their home country employees with their Chinese subordinates to illustrate this point:

> *Chinese staff require—and expect—a much higher level of detailed communication. In Finland, one usually only gives a rough outline of the target and then delegates authority and gives a high level of trust to the employee. In China, this approach usually leads to no or poor results. A colleagues* (sic) *told me: management in China is easy, just need to*

remember 3 words: follow-up, follow-up, follow-up...Personally, I find it very frustrating to keep following up on all projects and being involved in detailed issues.

(Finnish expatriate, 40–44 years old, Paper Machinery)

In Israel, everyone has an opinion about how things should be done. In China, people are reluctant to offer a view, even when asked to. In Israel, the manager's role is to reign in the employee's initiatives and channel them into the right direction. In China, what you don't define and ask for specifically, does not get done...This means that many assumptions taken for granted elsewhere need to be defined in detail. Define every task in detail; follow up in detail (not just "how did it go"). Never assume people understood what you mean. Always confirm, in detail.

(No demographic information)

Chinese employees need more guidance whereas German employees like to take over more responsibility and work more independently... Yes, needs to be adjusted. Explaining the work process more detailedly and controlling the work more frequently.

(German expatriate, 30–34 years old, Executive Search/HR Consulting)

Several other expatriates also expressed the view that Chinese employees needed more guidance and therefore more follow-up. The following quotes illustrate their views:

The difference is that the Chinese employee needs to have a strong guidance to do his work, with clear in-between steps with defined in-between results. The challenge is to develop independent thinking by the Chinese employee in such a way that he or she is able to solve new problems and tasks in the daily work...adjustment necessary. In the daily work there is a strong control mechanism necessary.

(Dutch expatriate, 45–49 years old, Engineering)

The stage of independence is different here in China and people, most without long years of professional experiences, need more guidance and coaching. Also, new graduates are not well prepared for the industry needs and therefore we have to educate them from basics, e.g., working behavior, communication, etc. ...More coaching and follow-up are needed instead of delegation and forgetting. If we are expecting results to be delivered on time, it needs to be followed up and supported.

(Swiss expatriate, 50–54 years old, Chemicals)

A lot more guidance and communication of clear expectations is needed. While in Europe I can say to some/many employees: This is what I expect as an end-result, come to me if you need help/have questions, this approach does not work in China. A lot closer management is needed to achieve results. Part of this is cultural, part is also a language issue in my experience...A lot closer follow-up...

(Austrian expatriate, 35–39 years old, Manufacturing)

Ensuring that the work would be done and to the expected quality

Some expatriates said that they needed to follow up progress in order to ensure that the work would be completed and to a specific level of quality. The following quotes illustrate this:

I learned to be 100 percent clear, and need to follow up in order to make sure the task has been completed. Often an OK in China does not mean that the task has been completed.

(Swiss expatriate, 40–44 years old, Education)

I had to follow up closely on all work I delegated, ensure it is done correctly and timely, I have to go into details. Back home general directions were sufficient, here it will spell trouble.

(Mauritian expatriate, 50–54 years old, Trading)

I have to be more disciplined about checking to see if the work is achieving the "end result" I hope to achieve. More follow-up.

(Canadian expatriate, 45–49 years old, Food and Beverage)

Leading Chinese people that had no exposure to Europe for some years is like being a teacher in kindergarten, or school, depending of the level of maturity of the company organization. ... follow up daily on every-thing, no trust that things are done as agreed and in the agreed timeline. You become a control person if you want things done in time and in a specific quality.

(German expatriate, 45–49 years old, Home Appliance Manufacturer)

I tend to have a lose leadership style in which I prefer to give lot of autonomy to my employees, I see myself a leader mainly as a coach and facilitator to make sure my people can work efficiently. I had to move to a more controlling manager, closer follow-up on what people do to make sure that the quality of the delivered work meets my requirements.

(Belgians expatriate, 35–39 years old, Steel Business)

Specific and detailed task instructions

The fourth most mentioned adjustment that the expatriates said they had made involved a shift from giving employees autonomy and delegating responsibilities to giving them specific and detailed instructions. They had made this adjustment because they had observed that their Chinese subor-dinates were less independent, rarely took initiatives, and expected to be given specific instructions. The discussion of these characteristics of Chinese employees can be found in Chapter 6. The following quotes illus-trate how some expatriates had had to give specific and detailed instruc-tions or directions in order to compensate for the characteristics of their Chinese employees:

In China, I found I had to be very detailed and prepared, with a clear plan to move forward. My Chinese employees wanted more structure, and guidance, with clear direction on what I expected. They were also reluctant to challenge this.

(British expatriate, 45–49 years old, Financial/Accounting)

You must adapt your leadership style in China. You have to be much more specific, much more clear and cannot expect too much initiative from the employee as many seem not to know by themselves what is expected and how to go about it.

(Israeli expatriate, 45–49 years old, Consulting)

I have to put a much higher importance on the grade of detail of my questions, directives, and instructions. A regular follow-up is absolutely necessary. My management system is much more detailed and rigid than it was before.

(German expatriate, 35–39 years old, Maritime)

I have to adjust my intent. I cannot assume anyone will understand the intent of my orders. The Chinese were raised and educated not to question or care about intent. So we need to be specific in a laborious way. We cannot presume they will understand why we want what we want.

(No demographic information)

Adjust: my communication needs to be complete, more detailed. Nothing is implicit here. Need for adjustment: if not, nothing happens.

(French expatriate, 50–54 years old, International Trade)

Leading the team is not different, all the same skills apply but many are just not used to working and having that total independence ...I find you need to be more specific, don't assume your message was understood, break it down to most basic instructions.

(Irish expatriate, 40–44 years old, Hospitality)

But perhaps the most important difference is that thinking outside the box is not what Chinese employees excel at. Therefore, sometimes you need to lead by showing them specific examples of what you are looking for or where you want the organization to be headed to.

(No demographic information)

...sure it is, particularly the aspect setting a direction and cutting tasks into small pieces and providing individuals detailed instructions...I have adjusted my approach from a collaborative problem solving in a

giving-time-frame approach towards giving detailed instructions to individuals monitoring the details.

(Dutch expatriate, 40–44 years old, International Trade)

Several expatriates said that, in China, the leadership approach needs to be more akin to that of a teacher who gives detailed instructions and full explanations.

...the leader must behave to some extent like a teacher, explaining what is expected, to which level of detail...This is less leading with a vision, but rather giving directions every 5 minutes to make sure the team goes in the right direction at the right pace.

(No demographic information)

Need to be more of a teacher in China, have loads of patience and be much more specific when briefing them on a task.

(Australian expatriate, 55–59 years old, Ecommerce)

Chinese employees need to be told in detail how the task has to be performed...The leadership approach is more that of a teacher than of a manager. It is difficult to avoid micro-managing in China and I am not sure if leading by example really works in China.

(Italian expatriate, 35–39 years old, Pharmaceutical)

In China I need to teach my staff more basic things and it takes more time to get things done.

(German expatriate, 40–44 years old, Automotive)

Greater directiveness and control

The fifth most mentioned adjustment that the expatriates said they had made involved becoming more directive and controlling. This adjustment had mainly been due to the hierarchical practices found in China. As explained in Chapter 4, Confucius's *wu lun* (five cardinal relationships) have shaped the past and current hierarchical system/relationship found in Chinese families, organizations, and society as a whole. In the Chinese business context, senior managers often assume an authoritarian stance, making decisions and issuing orders with little consultation of their subordinates. On the other hand, subordinates are expected to show loyalty and obedience to their leaders, and to comply with their requests. The following quotes show how the hierarchical tradition has led Chinese employees to expect detailed instructions from their managers, hence leading to the need for expatriates to become more directive and controlling.

Leading Chinese employees is different from leading employees in my home country. A key difference is the hierarchical and paternalistic culture found in many Chinese businesses. Staff expect to be given clear direction and tend to want to push decision-making upwards...I have to be more directive in general—people are more comfortable being told what to do and how to do it.

(British expatriate, 45–49 years old, Financial Services)

The difference is in expectation of management, which is more hierarchical approach in China...Challenges are to delegate responsibility. I had to adjust my leadership approach. I have a more detailed and direct leadership approach in China.

(Finnish expatriate, 45–49 years old, Industrial Automation)

In China the employees wait for me to make decisions, in the West the employees act according to their sphere of competence. Had to adjust a lot. After target setting, control and supervision are very important.

(Swiss expatriate, 55–59 years old, Construction)

Chinese do not take any additional responsibility as they are afraid of being punished...I had to adjust my management style into very detailed controlled, direct supervision dictatorial punishment management style.

(Polish expatriate, 55–59 years old, Automotive)

Another consequence of China's hierarchal tradition is that most Chinese employees have become accustomed to *not* taking initiatives, which had also led the expatriates to become more directive and controlling in order to ensure that the work would be done. Some expatriates said the following:

> *Chinese employees are afraid to take independent decisions. Afraid to make mistakes and therefore also do not learn from their mistakes... Have to tell more what to do. Have to be tougher, less nice, when reprimanding to ensure messages get across. With senior management, have to spend more effort in creating comfort level of making own decisions. With junior management and below need to do more procedures, very specific processes, to ensure things get done right.*

(Dutch expatriate, 40–44 years old, Hospitality)

> *Primary difference is less ability for Chinese staff to take initiative and responsibility for projects and to plan. Chinese workers are more single task oriented and used to the boss making even routine decisions. It takes time to train staff to think and act independently, think holistically about underlying business problems, and decompose abstract projects into a sequence of activities and milestones that they are responsible for managing...find I sometimes need to act like a "boss" in the Chinese definition to get an appropriate response.*

(American expatriate, 50–54 years old, Consulting)

> *There is less independent initiative. You have to draw a very detailed roadmap for each task, even for excellent employees of high education. The same is true for other employees, who need a lot of supervision/ control because they otherwise tend to stray out of bounds (in many ways of varying seriousness). Overall, Chinese staff need tighter reigns and a stricter leadership style in my experience, in order to keep the machinery moving smoothly.*

(No demographic information)

> *In China the meaning and respect for hierarchy is higher than in other countries. This means that employees are often keen to obey without sharing ideas, counter-proposals or other ways to face issues...I need to take decisions that could be usually be taken by my cooperators. Also, the sense of priority is quite different and often needs to be passed with a Top-Down approach.*

(Italian expatriate, 30–34 years old, Consumer Industry)

The Top 10 Aspects in Regard to Which the Expatriate Managers Had Changed (or Had Tried to Change) Their Chinese Employees

The expatriates said that they had changed or had tried to change various aspects related to the characteristics of their Chinese employees. The top 10 most mentioned aspects are listed below, with greater details then provided for the top five:

The expatriates had changed or had tried to change their Chinese subordinates to make them:

(1) More direct and vocal in communication
(2) More independent
(3) Responsible and accountable
(4) More critical thinkers
(5) More proactive in taking initiatives
(6) Brave in accepting failure, taking risks, and making changes
(7) More structured workers and thinkers
(8) More confident
(9) Less hierarchical and bureaucratic thinkers and actors
(10) Collaborative workers

Making Chinese employees more direct and vocal in communication

The most mentioned aspect in respect to which the expatriates said they had changed or tried to change their Chinese subordinates involved making them more direct and vocal in sharing their viewpoints or raising problems. As mentioned in Chapter 6, many of the expatriates said that their Chinese subordinates did not proactively voice concerns and ask questions, and were unwilling to and/or afraid of expressing their views, particularly in public forums.

To encourage their subordinates' expressiveness and directness, most expatriates had tried asking them for their opinions, encouraging them to voice their views, and reinforcing the importance of sharing ideas. However, their endeavors did not seem to have been successful in effectively changing their Chinese employees due to the Chinese social norm or practice of being reserved in communication. The following quotes illustrate this:

> *Chinese staff are much less vocal, and afraid to have an opinion. They defer to senior people much quicker vs western employees...we very much encourage the team to become more independent, think for themselves and speak up. This is a long-term process that is not quick or easy—and it requires a 'safe environment' where they feel they can share their opinions.*

(Dutch expatriate, 45–49 years old, Marketing services/Consulting)

> *I have tried encouraging my Chinese team members to be more vocal in their opinions in public forums. I realized that they have some good ideas and thoughts, when I discuss with them in private, but are unable to bring it out in front of clients or senior bosses...*

(Indian expatriate, 35–39 years old, Media and Advertising)

> *Try to get Chinese employees to speak up, to offer opinions, very difficult.*

(American expatriate, 60 years old or over, Accounting)

> *Chinese employees require more support to build confidence in their own opinions and to be able to express these with confidence. Breaking from the group mentality is a challenge.*

(Australian expatriate, 50–54 years old, Consulting)

> *I have explicitly told local team members that I will not always have the foresight to come to each of them or recognize if there is an issue with them, a client, or a project so I need them to be more vocal (this does not work). Changing social norms is a long haul and needs to be engrained in the overall company and values.*

(American expatriate, 35–39 years old, Research/Consulting)

> *I have reinforced the importance of providing complete information or saying they do not know—if they do not know. I have modeled what the*

consequence of making decisions on incomplete or wrong information would be.

(New Zealander expatriate, 45–49 years old, Manufacturing)

Only one expatriate said that he had succeeded in making his Chinese subordinates "open up". His approach involved providing his employees with "daily" opportunities to "practice" and "learn" "how to" share ideas and voice concerns, thus going a step further than merely "encouraging" them to do so or "reinforcing" the importance of doing so. Simply "encouraging" Chinese employees to share their views seems likely to be less effective than giving them opportunities to "practice and learn" how to do so as they are not accustomed to being direct and vocal in sharing their viewpoints and thus will not feel comfortable doing so. The successful expatriate explained his approach in the following quote:

I try hard to get my Chinese people to open up and feel comfortable. To do so I cannot be harsh or short with answers. I am usually very quick with a response but now I wait longer to gauge reactions and see how the people feel...I had daily meeting with my staff to get them to talk to each other and me with problems. It took time but after a month or two the people started to discuss problems and it was successful as they started to find ways to help themselves and other team members.

(American expatriate, 55–59 years old, Manufacturing)

Making Chinese employees more independent

The second most mentioned aspect in regard to which the expatriates said they had changed or tried to change their Chinese subordinates involved making them more independent. As mentioned in Chapter 6 and in a section above (entitled "specific and detailed task instructions"), many expatriates felt that their Chinese subordinates were accustomed to waiting for instructions from their managers. To change this, they had tried to make their Chinese employees more independent, think for themselves, and make decisions. The expatriates said that they wanted their Chinese employees to work independently as they believed that everyone in an organization should have the knowledge and the ability needed to work independently and make decisions, rather than wait for supervisors' decisions or directions.

> *I require people to work independently. I don't want to be a "boss". I don't believe in a top-down approach. I believe in sharing knowledge and experience to develop faster.*

(Dutch expatriate, 40–44 years old, Architecture/Construction)

> *I must make much time to ensure people feel trust in talking and working independently. The people have much to offer but the traditional Chinese boss does not listen or respect...The need for adjustment comes from my desire to get the employees to get engaged with their work and not wait for direction.*

(American expatriate, 50–54 years old, Manufacturing)

> *I have made them more independent and self-guided. This was due to my reluctance to "decide" everything.*

(Finnish expatriate, 45–49 years old, Construction)

> *Try to promote more independence. Independent decision making. Cannot run the whole business by myself. Team has to be able to be adaptable to a varied set of circumstances and be able to respond to it in an appropriate manner.*

(Dutch expatriate, 40–44 years old, Hospitality)

> *Yes, the biggest change has to be to allow them to work on their own volition. Teaching to work more independently without the need to refer back for decisions...Employees were taught to think about the cost of a decision, and the boundaries in which a decision can be made before referring back up the management chain.*

(British expatriate, 40–44 years old, Metal)

The expatriates had used several approaches to try to make their Chinese employees more independent. For example, they had tried delegating, asking questions, giving freedom, and providing training and coaching. The following quotes illustrate such approaches:

I always delegate as much as it is safe to do so. I let them work the problem and don't Micro-manage them. I want the Result to be in a certain range—the rest is up to them. Some people are not comfortable with this kind of "freedom"—but only by letting them make mistakes employees will have a greater understanding of the impact of their actions (or no actions for that matter). Some People like this creative atmosphere and grow—not quickly—but sustainable—then you can have people working for you 10–15 years (and of course you have to pay fair).

(Austrian expatriate, 45–49 years old, Trade)

Main change was giving employees enough space and confidence to make their own opinions, devise their own solutions, and have a comfortable and non-critical environment in which to err safely.

(No demographic information)

Instead of giving a direct action and solution, I guide my team to find the solution on their own. I do so by asking questions.

(Brazilian expatriate, 30–34 years old, Chemicals)

Tried to give more responsibility and decision-making by themselves and implement open feedback.

(German expatriate, 30–33 years old, Executive Search/HR Consulting)

I gave my employees responsibility and trained them to take pride in their own projects. I would sometimes not help them in times where I felt it was better for them to learn by making mistakes.

(American expatriate, 30–34 years old, Hospitality)

I give staff freedom, but they have to be able to deal with this freedom. To a certain extent I try to coach them, this takes more time and effort in China than in my home country.

(Dutch expatriate, 40–44 years old, Architecture/Construction)

Although some expatriates said that it took time and effort to make their Chinese employees more independent, other had been successful in doing so. The expatriates said the following:

Try to change so employees can try to think more for themselves by empowering them. It helped although there have been errors along the way but we've been patient and this has paid off in time. One way has been to give stock options to key employees within the organization as well as give them free flexibility in the working hours with the hope to get better productivity.

(Venezuelan expatriate, 40–44 years old, Marketing)

I put more and more responsibilities on them. Otherwise I would have to do all decisions by myself. Now they decide on daily business by themselves and only report the results to me. In the beginning they were not used to take responsibilities at all but now it works very well.

(German expatriate, 55–59 years old, Automotive)

I was able after a certain amount of time to let them become more independent, make decisions on their own, make planning, use project management skills. And again, I need to be very patient with them. I can't expect them to do things the second time right after pointing out the issue.

(Dutch expatriate, 30–34 years old, Machine Manufacturing)

However, some expatriates had found that it was not always possible to get Chinese employees to work independently as they preferred their supervisors to make decisions and give instructions. Some expatriates said the following:

I have tried to make my Chinese staff more autonomous and give them the power and flexibility to achieve goals using their own methods. I have also encouraged staff to look further than the immediate goal and try to "think like a boss" and figure out what the next step would be. This is often met with mixed results and generally the Chinese staff prefer a step-by-step guide to how to do their job.

(Australian expatriate, 35–39 years old, Entertainment)

I tried to get people working more independently and creatively by demonstrating through my own actions and praising those who do make improvements. The challenges were that many staff do not like the risk that this autonomy entails. They prefer for me to make the decisions instead.

(No demographic information)

I tried to change the continuous need for the boss to make decision... Sometimes I succeed in letting my Team decide...sometimes, unfortunately not.

(Italian expatriate, 30–34 years old, Consumer industry)

Making Chinese employees responsible and accountable

The third most mentioned aspect in which the expatriates said they had changed or tried to change their Chinese subordinates was making them responsible and accountable. Many expatriates said their Chinese subordinates had little or no sense of accountability and thus needed to be changed. The expatriates' perspective on the accountability of their Chinese employees can be found in the section on "lower accountability" in Chapter 6.

The expatriates had taken various approaches (e.g., employee accountability statements, checklists, project management templates, and career development road maps) to ensure that their subordinates would feel responsible and accountable for the outcomes of their tasks. The following quotes show what they had done or tried:

We shifted from having "Job Descriptions" to "Employee Accountability Statements". The idea is to have each employee understand what are the desired "end result" opposed to assigning specific tasks.

(Canadian expatriate, 45–49 years old, Food and Beverage)

I am trying to get people to take more responsibility for their work and the mistakes. Sometimes there was an attitude of I'll do the work and it is someone else's job to see if there are any mistakes. If you design the work so that the mistakes are clearly obvious and the person realizes that mistakes will be caught and that they will be held responsible then things get better. It takes a lot of time to design a good process so that mistakes are easily recognizable. Also I believe putting in checklists for people to follow and sign off builds responsibility. If you say you went through the checklist, but the error still got through, it is fairly obvious you lied about following the checklist and should be held accountable.

(American expatriate, 50–54 years old, Furniture Trading/
Manufacturing)

I've tried to encourage them to feel more ownership and sense of personal responsibility for the overall team and its objectives, rather than just their individual objectives. There are many ways to do this, including personal mentoring, group events, providing encouragement and criticism of individuals and the whole team in equal measure. And being very careful to model behaviors myself that I want team members to display.

(British expatriate, 40–44 years old, Government)

The most important thing for me to change was to get the managers below me to take responsibility for their work and to readily lead projects...At first I tried to understand better why they didn't want to take responsibility. Once this was done, I had to work on two aspects to get them to develop: Practical and Mental. The practical side meant giving them a career development road map to show that I was interested in helping them develop and not just giving them more work to do; so if they met targets they could expect a promotion and pay rise. It also meant working closely with them to go through their workload, and then give them clear responsibilities, while moving some tasks to other people. Mental was creating the right atmosphere for them to take responsibility and be willing to lead. This meant that they had to feel safe in making decisions in the knowledge that I would support them if they failed and not throw them down a hole; also that they should get achievement for their efforts.

(British expatriate, 30–34 years old, Green Energy)

Yes—try to get them to plan and take more responsibility...Provide project management templates, starting with small projects for them to complete. Find they need a lot more hand holding to get the hang of it.

Of course, give them a bit of a break since they have to do this in foreign language. Also give them room to make mistakes and learn from them.

(American expatriate, 50–54 years old, Consulting/Technology Transfer)

One thing that I have very much worked on to change is "responsibility" as a team and owning problems in the office, and to ensure we provide solutions for every problem. Too often I have heard "meiyoubanfa" (Chinese for 'No way possible'). Building a cohesive team who mutually trust, from my experience, has been a real challenge. How I went about changing things—spent more time individually with members to understand how they feel about responsibility, while also explaining that us, as a company, a small one, we need to take ownership and make decisions by ourselves / on our own sometimes. Getting the team to understand that they can make a decision (within boundaries) was a big step in them owning their position in our company.

(Australian expatriate, 35–39 years old, Training and Development)

The expatriates' attempts to make their Chinese employees more accountable had taken time and effort. Had they been successful in this? Some had. The following quotes illustrate their experiences:

I have changed their approach and explained to them that they are fully accountable for what they are doing, and they must stop looking for my agreement for each decision. It took time, but finally it happened and those who could not integrate this new way of working have left the company.

(French expatriate, 50–54 years old, Railway)

Yes, we have changed our employees a lot in the last 10 years (or better they changed slowly themselves). Employees learned to work in a team in which there is not a "I am the boss and you have to do what I say" attitude, but which builds on self-responsibility and personal involvement, means coming up independently, without special request, with needed action plans and solutions or showing up innovations or better ways to solve problems. And they learned and understood that mistakes are part of a learning process and allowed and never have to be covered.

(Swiss expatriate, 50–54 years old, Apparel and Fashion)

We have consciously tried to change the organization to utilize the inherent strengths and skills of our Chinese team. We have been explicit about the manner and specifically what the US organization needs to do differently, or not at all, to allow the Chinese team to take the leadership and responsibility. This has been successful and staff feel they have the support of the whole organization, both in China and in the USA.

(Australian expatriate, 40–44 years old, Building Products)

There are adjustments necessary. I was used to work as the leader of a team, rather than the all-knowing boss. But since I have made this adjustment in other countries before, it came quite easily. My experience is that after a while the employees actually enjoy working with more responsibilities and initiatives as it helps them develop quicker by themselves. It requires extensive coaching in the beginning, but with substantial payback in the end as the group will become more productive.

(Dutch expatriate, 45–49 years old, Production of Food Products)

I have identified multiple employees I believed to carry much potential. For them I increased my demands, and tried to change their sense of personal responsibility and leadership. I believe I convinced them to stop seeing their job as a 9-to-5, and see it as an opportunity to inspire others and derive a sense of meaning from.

(No demographic information)

However, other expatriates' efforts had not paid off.

I come from a culture where it doesn't matter where or when you work, as long as you get stuff done. I tried doing this in China—it doesn't work. People here need order. They need to come to the office, on time, do their work, and go home.

(Israeli expatriate, 35–39 years old, Luxury)

Have tried to increase individual instead of collective accountability. Needed to do this to increase rate of progress. Chinese staff are reluctant to accept personal accountability but also reluctant to impose individual accountability on others. Basically did not work.

(Australian expatriate, 50–54 years old, Insurance)

Tried to provide more responsibility to the employees on their outcomes as they expected a more prescriptive approach on their tasks...Hired employees who would embrace this approach better; worked directly with those who could embrace it and tried to make them role models to the others...There was no real challenge with the employees embracing it; the real challenge was in the inability and failure of some of the executives (foreigners incl.) to lead this change.

(Lebanese expatriate, 30–34 years old, Online Games)

Making Chinese employees more critical thinkers

The fourth most mentioned aspect in which the expatriates said they had changed or tried to change their Chinese subordinates involved making them more critical thinkers. They had done so as they had felt that their Chinese employees lacked in critical thinking and tended to take the easy route of waiting for their managers to come up with solutions, instead of discussing and finding solutions to problems themselves. The following quotes illustrate the views of some of the expatriates:

Challenges center on getting employees to use critical thinking, taking some risk and making decisions. They always want the boss to decide.

(American expatriate, 50–54 years old, Pharmaceutical)

Chinese employees have obedience in their DNA. They unquestioningly follow the tasks within their remit. They respect their leaders because they are their leaders rather than because they are deserving of respect... The greatest challenge is summed up by the phrase "tell me what you want me to do and I'll do it". Little role for initiative or critical thinking.

(British expatriate, 60 years old and over, Education)

Challenges to me are the lack of autonomy, pro-activity and critical thinking. I tend to see that my Chinese employees tend to not go in depth in their reflection and always keep a superficial approach.

(French expatriate, 30–34 years old, Consulting)

The expatriates had taken various approaches to make their Chinese employees think more critically. For example, they had encouraged them to think and ask "why" questions, challenged them to think and find solutions, and asked them to be more critical about their own work. Some expatriates said the following:

I'm trying to actively engage them into the work. I'm trying to make them think more critically. I ask them "why are you doing it this way". "Why is this rule in place", "What are the benefits of this procedure", etc.

(Swiss expatriate, 40–44 years old, Education)

Tried to have people understand "WHY" and not just "WHAT" and also encouraged them to be open in asking questions to understand "WHY" and explain the same to their team as well.

(Indo-Canadian expatriate, 45–49 years old, FMCG)

I challenge them to think, to find solutions, go back to the basics. Follow a concept and reflect everything to that concept.

(Dutch expatriate, 50–54 years old, Machinery)

Also for them to challenge their own work effort to include more necessary details and thought about options and strength and weakness of options.

(American expatriate, 50–54 years old, Energy/Manufacturing)

The expatriate's efforts to make their employees think more critically had been met with various measures of success. It had been dependent on the individual employees' skills and had been hampered by their deep-rooted habit of *not* thinking critically. The following two quotes illustrate the expatriate managers' experiences:

Key changes I have tried are to get the employees to think more critically and take initiative. In some cases this works, in others it has not—this depends significantly on the employee and their skill.

(American expatriate, 35–39 years old, Professional Services)

I have put rather some efforts to develop a "critical thinking" (why are we....., what is the consequence of...)...This was a hard nut to crack as—rather naturally—without management it easily results in "loose sand", everyone doing his own thing based on own small piece of his idea/ interest...I could not really in all cases "change" it but manage it within controllable limits... "Improvements" were small (some more than others); I do not believe in miracles and a manager shouldn't overestimate his/her influence on his people, especially as a foreigner; Chinese habits are deeply rooted and the family/social circle of people are far more influential.

(Dutch expatriate, 35–39 years old, Metal Finishing)

Making Chinese employees become more proactive in taking initiatives

The fifth most mentioned aspect in relation to which the expatriates said they had changed or tried to change their Chinese subordinates involved making them more proactive in taking initiatives. The need for this change had stemmed from their observation that most of their Chinese employees rarely acted proactively and were used to passively waiting for their supervisors' instructions/commands and to let their supervisors or managers make all the decisions (see the section on "a low tendency to engage in initiatives and proactiveness" in Chapter 6 for more details). They had wanted their employees to work proactively for their own benefit and for that of the organization. The following quotes illustrate their views and efforts in relation to this change:

What I often miss with my Chinese colleagues is the willingness to work pro-actively and with tasks that are not specifically described in his/her job description...Constantly working on proactivity...

(Swedish expatriate, 45–49 years old, Retail)

More accurate and precise direction expected by the Chinese ... You will not hear if something is not going well so more follow-up needed. ... Tried to change the culture to be more proactive and more open to learning from mistakes.

(Danish expatriate, 45–49 years old, Engineering)

In China I have had to make certain expectations that we assume are normal in western office environments clear. Below I've described two main areas I try and work with my Chinese directs on. These challenges are by no means unique to Chinese employees, but they do tend to be a bit more prevalent. 1. Be proactive. It's a complex lesson, but there are two parts. One, There's no need to grin and bear a fundamentally flawed work situation. If there is something wrong, they should let someone know as soon as possible. Two, employees are expected to assess whether they actually need someone's help to fix a work problem. If there is a problem (or opportunity) that they can make forward progress on, then they have a responsibility to try and tackle that challenge.

(American expatriate, 25–29 years old, Business Intelligence)

I believe the best working environment is one where all employees root for each other's success and take a proactive role in advancing both the company's interest as well as each other's careers within the company. The initial state of the team was one where people came in to do their jobs, I tried to change that into an environment where people were changing their professional careers, by becoming more delivery-driven, cooperate, and think beyond the business of the day.

(No demographic information)

The expatriate managers had taken approaches such as building their employees' self-confidence to take on responsibilities, rewarding them for any independent and proactive work, empowering them, and providing training. The following quotes illustrate such approaches:

Chinese company culture has tendency to try to upwards delegate all decisions if possible—the boss decides... It takes effort to counter this by building trust in employees to take responsibility and reward them for independent and proactive work. Making mistakes needs to be made acceptable and even encouraged.

(Finnish expatriate, 40–44 years old, Steel)

I encourage Chinese employees to find ways to improve the workflow. As they know the daily routines better than me, they see how they can save time, avoid mistakes, get better results.

(German expatriate, 45–49 years old, Consulting)

Empower them to speak up openly and bring in ideas to solutions. Become more proactive and find their own way to deal with issues.

(No demographic information)

...tried to get employee to act more as a team and less individually or by department and to think more proactively...Through training and team training...leadership and example...

(Italian expatriate, 45–49 years old, Financial Services)

Summary

- This chapter reported the findings of the degrees and patterns by which the 391 expatriate senior managers had adjusted or changed their leadership in response to the differences between their own perceptions and standards and the Chinese cultural specificities and the characteristics of their Chinese employees.

- Two dimensions of the expatriate senior managers' adjustment were analyzed: the first was the extent to which they had changed their own leadership approaches (leadership adjustment); the second was that to which they had change (or had attempted to change) their Chinese subordinates (subordinate change). The expatriates' patterns of adjustment were analyzed using a 2 × 2 matrix based on these two dimensions.

- **Degrees of leadership behavior adjustment:** based on quantitative assessments drawn from 391 expatriate business leaders and 356 Chinese subordinates, the statistical results show that the vast majority of the former had *significantly* adjusted their leadership behaviors when leading and managing Chinese employees.

- **Patterns of leadership behavior adjustment:** the results of the analysis of the 391 expatriate managers' responses show the following:

  o the overriding majority of the expatriate senior managers (79.1%) had simultaneously adjusted their own leadership approach and changed (or tried to change) their Chinese employees, thus displaying the *exploration* pattern of adjustment;

  o over a tenth of them (11.5%) had largely adjusted their leadership approaches but had not tried to change their subordinates, thus displaying the *absorption* pattern;

  o a small proportion of them (5.3%) had made little adjustment to their leadership approaches but had actively tried to change their Chinese employees, thus displaying the *determination* pattern; and

  o another small proportion of them (4.1%) had made little adjustment to both their leadership approaches and their Chinese employees, thus displaying the *replication* pattern of adjustment.

- **The reasons underpinning the different patterns of leadership adjustment**
  - o Expatriates who had displayed the *exploration* pattern of adjustment, on the one hand, had adjusted their own approaches because they had felt it was important to respect and adapt to the local culture and to meet their Chinese employees' expectations of a leader; and, on the other hand, they had tried to change their Chinese employees in order to improve employee performance and to meet customer expectations.
  - o Expatriates who had displayed the *absorption* pattern of adjustment had done so because they had felt that it was important to align their leadership approaches with the local culture and practices, and because they had judged that it would have been difficult to change their Chinese subordinates.
  - o Expatriates who had displayed the *determination* pattern of adjustment had done so because they had perceived that many aspects of their leadership were generic and could thus be applied to all contexts, regardless of the nationality or culture of the employees, and that some characteristics of their Chinese employees needed to be changed in order to work more effectively.
  - o Expatriates who had displayed the *replication* pattern of adjustment had done so for various reasons; for example, they had wanted to remain true to themselves, they had deemed it impossible to change their Chinese employees' work approach due to the latter's deeply embedded traditions, and they had considered that it was not worth changing their Chinese employees due to a high employee turnover rate.
  - o A combination of various internal and external factors had exerted a strong influence on the expatriate managers' patterns of adjustment. Internally, for example, the managers' own perceptions of the need to adapt to the local culture and to meet their Chinese employees' expectations, and of the best way to manage, were found to have influenced their decisions in relation to whether to adjust their own behaviors and/or their subordinates. Externally, for instance, the characteristics of their Chinese employees—such as reservedness in communication, high dependence, and low proactiveness—and the

need to improve employee performance had constituted external factors that had influenced the leaders' decisions in regard to whether to change their own leadership approaches and/or their subordinates.

o In responding to those internal and external factors, most of the expatriate managers had chosen to simultaneously adjust their own leadership approach and to change (or try to change) their Chinese employees. They had adjusted themselves in aspects such as their style of communication and levels of patience, and in relation to providing detailed instructions, and they had changed (or had tried to change) their Chinese employees in aspects such as encouraging them to be more vocal, independent, accountable, and proactive.

- **The top 10 aspects in relation to which the expatriate managers had adjusted their leadership approaches were as follows:**
  (1) Style of communication
  (2) Higher levels of patience
  (3) A higher frequency of monitoring and following up
  (4) Specific and detailed task instructions
  (5) Greater directiveness and control
  (6) Greater indirectness, politeness, friendliness, and gentleness
  (7) Less delegation, a more hands-on approach
  (8) The adoption of a more fatherly or brotherly role
  (9) More time spent in being available to the team
  (10) Greater use of micro-management

- **The top 10 aspects in regard to which the expatriate managers had changed (or had tried to change) their Chinese subordinates were intended to (try to) make them:**
  (1) More direct and vocal in communication
  (2) More independent
  (3) Responsible and accountable
  (4) More critical thinkers
  (5) More proactive in taking initiatives
  (6) Brave in accepting failure, taking risks, and making changes
  (7) More structured workers and thinkers
  (8) More confident
  (9) Less hierarchical and bureaucratic thinkers and actors
  (10) Collaborative workers

Chapter 8

What Chinese Workers Value in a Job and Expect of Their Leaders, and What Satisfies Them

The work values and expectations held by employees influence their attitudes and behaviors in the workplace. Motivating Chinese employees to achieve their work goals requires knowledge of what they value in a job and what they expect of their supervisors. It is also necessary to know the extent to which the fit between expected and observed leadership behaviors is associated with employee satisfaction. This chapter reports my research findings on these aspects.

This chapter is organized into four sections. The first presents the findings of prior research conducted on the key job aspects valued by Chinese workers, while the second is focused on the leadership attributes and behaviors expected by Chinese workers. The third section reports my findings on the expectations held by a sample of 237 Chinese employees in relation to the leadership behaviors of their expatriate supervisors. The fourth presents the result of my analysis in relation to the fit between the Chinese employees' expected and observed leadership behaviors and how such a fit is associated with their work satisfaction. This chapter concludes with a discussion of the importance of meeting employee expectations of leadership behaviors in order to enhance the positive emotional state felt by Chinese employees toward their expatriate supervisors.

What Chinese Workers Value in a Job

Recent studies have found that some aspects of the work values held by contemporary Chinese employees differ substantially from traditional ones. Traditional Chinese work values, which are embedded in Confucian teaching, include hard work, thrift, endurance (patience and persistence), collectivism (prioritizing group goals over personal interests), and social harmony (Lu *et al.*, 2011). In the traditional collectivist and relation-oriented Chinese society, employees were expected to work for the good of the organization, to devote themselves to their jobs, to work diligently, and to maintain harmonious work relations (Lu *et al.*, 2011).

In the 1980s, to measure and evaluate cultural values within the setting of the Chinese social value system, Michael Bond and his colleagues conducted a pioneering and influential study, The Chinese Value Survey, in 22 countries (see, Bond & Hwang, 1986; Hofstede & Bond, 1988; Chinese Culture Connection, 1987). The researchers found that a set of values they labeled as "Confucian work dynamism" was highly correlated with the striking economic growth observed in the so-called Four Asian Dragons (Hong Kong, Singapore, South Korea, and Taiwan) between 1965 and 1985. Confucian work dynamism, which was constructed by the researchers to reflect indigenous Chinese culture, is composed of eight heavily Confucian items, such as ordering relationships, thrift, persistence, having a sense of shame, reciprocation, personal steadiness, protecting one's "face", and respect for tradition. They commented that, although comprehensible, these eight items may be cumbersome and peculiar to the Western mentality. They further concluded that these Confucian-based work values shaped Chinese workers' work ethic and helped to cultivate motivated, dedicated, and responsible individuals who contributed to their organizations' successes and to China's economic growth.

Although the traditional work values mentioned above are still prevalent in contemporary Chinese society, monetary rewards have also become a highly valued work aspect. Zhang *et al.* (2019), who drew upon data sourced from the 2015 International Social Survey Program (ISSP) and analyzed a sample of 17,938 individuals from 36 countries and regions, found that the top three work attributes valued by Chinese employees are high income, job security, and promotion opportunities. They also found that Chinese workers value monetary rewards much more than intrinsic ones such as job satisfaction, which their sample Chinese employees ranked significantly lower than their counterparts from other countries. The researchers stated that Chinese workers see pay as a very important element of a job and tend to judge their current salaries as inadequate. The strong interest shown by Chinese workers in monetary work aspects is consistent with the phenomenon whereby many young people in China today choose their college majors mainly on the basis of their related potential income levels and job security, and not so much in relation to non-monetary aspects (Cao, 2009).

Nie and Sousa-Poza (2017) analyzed data drawn from the 2012 China Labor-Force Dynamic Survey (CLDS) and examined what Chinese workers expect from their jobs. In the survey, the perceived importance of six different work motives was assessed, such as (1) making a living; (2) achieving inner peace; (3) meeting more people; (4) earning respect; (5) satisfying (one's own) interests; and (6) realizing (one's own) potential. They found that the financial aspect—making a living—was ranked highest, the third motive—meeting more people—was ranked lowest, and that the other four motives were ranked with about the same importance in between. This emphasis on the financial aspect represents a shift away from and a contradiction of the intrinsic motivators valued in traditional Confucian society.

Overall, the findings of recent research indicate that contemporary Chinese workers, unlike their ancestors and their counterparts in other countries, value monetary work aspects much more than non-monetary ones.

A high proportion of the expatriate managers who took part in my research also pointed out that their Chinese subordinates cared for and focused more on monetary rewards than those in their own home countries and that they would promptly switch jobs for small salary increases or slightly better promotion opportunities. The details of these findings can be found in the section on "a greater focus on money, job titles, and personal benefits" in Chapter 6.

Nevertheless, some expatriate managers in my research said that, in addition to monetary rewards and similar to their counterparts in other countries, their Chinese employees also valued recognition for their achievements and opportunities for career progression, personal growth, and self-actualization. These findings can be found in the section on "Similarities in leading Chinese employees" in Chapter 6.

The Leadership Attributes and Behaviors Expected by Chinese Workers

Managers and supervisors are a vital part of the daily working lives of employees and, as such, play a crucial role in shaping the latter's work attitudes and behaviors (Yukl and Gardner, 2019). This is because the various tasks included in managers' duties (e.g., allocating resources, setting work targets, conducting performance appraisals, and authorizing pay raises and benefits) can directly affect their employees' daily work experience (Yukl and Gardner, 2019; Marstand *et al.*, 2017; Lord & Brown, 2001; Henderson *et al.*, 2008). The ways in which expatriate managers behave in discharging their duties can thus significantly influence the work attitudes and behaviors of their Chinese employees. In this section, the findings of prior research on the leadership attributes and behaviors deemed desirable by Chinese workers are presented.

Several studies have found that authoritarian and paternalistic leadership styles are the most pervasive in Chinese business organizations and that most Chinese employees expect their leaders to demonstrate them (Bond, 1996; Hui & Tan, 1996; Scott *et al.*, 2003; Walder, 1988; Farh & Cheng, 2000; Li & Sun, 2015). In other words, Chinese employees expect their leaders to exhibit strong authority and fatherly benevolence, i.e., they want leaders who are not only able to take decisive action, provide instructions for improvement, and reprimand poor performers (Farh & Cheng, 2000; Tsui *et al.*, 2004) but also to provide their subordinates with care, support, and protection in both the work and non-work domains (e.g., Farh *et al.*, 2008; Gelfand *et al.*, 2007; Redding *et al.*, 1994). In the work domain, leaders are expected to provide job security, coach their subordinates, promote career development, fix any errors, and avoid embarrassing their subordinates in public (Farh & Cheng, 2000; Zhang, *et al.*, 2015). In the non-work domain, they are expected to treat their subordinates as family members, assist them in times of personal crises, and show holistic concerns that go beyond formal hierarchical relationships (Farh & Cheng, 2000; Farh *et al.*, 2008; Wang & Cheng, 2010). Such expectations reflect the Chinese cultural characteristics of strong familial ties, paternalistic control, high power distance, and submission to authority (Farh & Cheng, 2000; Li & Sun, 2015).

Although research has shown that many Chinese employees accept the authoritarian behaviors of their Chinese supervisors/managers, several studies have also found that authoritarian leadership is associated with various negative employee work attitudes and behaviors. For example, Tsui *et al.* (2004) found that, although the authoritarian behaviors of Chinese CEOs are often viewed as perfectly legitimate, they usually result in mere employee obedience and compliance, rather than commitment. Authoritarian leadership behaviors were also found to be "negatively" associated with team member commitment to and satisfaction with team leaders (Cheng *et al.*, 2002a), loyalty toward leaders, trust in leaders, and organizational citizenship behaviors (Cheng *et al.*, 2002b). It should be noted that, with the development of Chinese society, the younger generation is much less willing to accept authoritarian leadership behaviors and the obedience toward their supervisors traditionally expected of them.

In contrast to authoritarianism, the other leadership trait commonly demonstrated by Chinese leaders—fatherly benevolence—tends to elicit positive responses from Chinese employees and balances out any negative effects of the former. Chinese workers often show gratitude to leaders who exhibit benevolence and strive to reciprocate it by working diligently and meeting expectations (Farh & Cheng, 2000). Leader benevolence has been found to be positively associated with Chinese subordinates' identification and compliance with and gratitude toward their leaders (Cheng *et al.*, 2004).

In addition to being authoritarian and paternalistic, Chinese employees expect their leaders to be moral and upstanding. They expect their leaders to hold high moral standards, to be self-disciplined and unselfish, and to lead by example; they hope for leaders who treat subordinates fairly, keep their promises, put collective interests ahead of personal ones, do not abuse their power for personal gain, do not mix personal and business interests, and act exemplarily in both their professional and personal lives (Farh & Cheng, 2000; Wu *et al.*, 2012; Niu *et al.*, 2009; Lin, 2008). Confucian teachings, which emphasize that a leader should show moral integrity and be self-restrained, trustworthy, impartial, and honest toward both fellow colleagues and subordinates, are a key factor that has contributed to Chinese workers' expectations of the morality and integrity of leaders (Littrell, 2002). Chinese employees expect their managers to exemplify said Confucian ideology of sound moral conduct (Littrell, 2002). See Chapter 5 for Confucian teachings and traditional Chinese leadership.

From the expected or desired leadership attributes and behaviors discussed above, we can see that Chinese employees accept and expect their *Chinese* leaders to exhibit strong authority, fatherly benevolence, and moral principles. But do Chinese employees expect their *expatriate* managers or supervisor to do the same? The next section reports my research findings on the expectations of Chinese employees toward the leadership behaviors of their expatriate supervisors.

The Findings of My Research on the Expectations of Chinese Employees Toward the Leadership Behaviors of Their Expatriate Supervisors

Research has shown that the expectations and attitudes held by Chinese employees toward expatriate managers differ from those they hold toward local ones. These have been found to be influenced by factors such as any ethnocentric attitudes of employees and the extent to which expatriate managers respect local customs and are fluent in the local language (Templer, 2010; Varma *et al.*, 2011). What leadership behaviors do Chinese employees then expect of their expatriate supervisors? Is the fit between expected and observed leadership behaviors associated with Chinese employee satisfaction? This section reports the results of my analysis of Chinese employee expectations of the leadership behaviors of their expatriate supervisors. The next section reports my findings on how the fit between Chinese employee expected and observed leadership behaviors is associated with their degree of satisfaction with their jobs and supervisors.

The results reported here and in the following section are based on the responses given by 237 Chinese employees who reported directly to 40 expatriate senior managers, with a mean of 5.9 subordinates per leader (range: 3–17). Table 1 presents the profiles of the Chinese employees. It shows that 54.4% were female, nearly four-fifths (79.3%) were aged between 20 and 39, around 86% held at least a university degree, and over half (56.1%) had worked in their respective organizations for more than 2 years.

I asked my sample Chinese employees to assess two categories of leadership behaviors: task-oriented (four question items) and relations-oriented (five question items) (see Appendix B for the nine questions). I assessed these two dimensions of leadership behaviors because they are the most commonly examined in leadership research and because they have been found to reflect the authoritarian and paternalistic leadership behaviors—i.e., those most commonly found in the Chinese context (Tsui

Table 1.   Sample Chinese employee demographics.

		No. of respondents (Total = 237)	Percentage (%)
Gender			
	Male	103	43.5
	Female	129	54.4
	No info.	5	2.1
Age			
	20–24	19	8.0
	25–29	53	22.4
	30–34	66	27.8
	35–39	50	21.1
	40–44	26	11.0
	45–49	12	5.1
	50–54	3	1.3
	55–59	1	0.4
	≥60	1	0.4
	No info.	6	2.2
Educational level			
	High School	1	0.4
	College	18	7.6
	University	135	57.0
	Masters	61	25.7
	PhD	10	4.2
	Others	5	2.1
	No info.	7	3.0
Tenure (years)			
	<1	52	21.9
	1–2	47	19.8
	2–5	74	31.2
	5–10	44	18.6
	≥10	15	6.3
	No info.	5	2.1

et al., 2004). As mentioned in Chapter 2, task-oriented leadership behaviors—which are mainly aimed at the efficient improvement or accomplishment of tasks—include organizing and planning work activities, assigning tasks, setting priorities, and monitoring operations and performance to improve efficiency. On the other hand, relations-oriented behaviors—which are mainly concerned with the establishment of mutual trust, cooperation, commitment, and job satisfaction—include providing support and encouragement, showing trust and respect, consulting with subordinates, empowering people, and providing coaching and mentoring.

As explained in Chapter 3, I asked my sample Chinese employees to provide *three distinct answers* to the nine question items—i.e., the extent to which they felt their leaders (a) were *currently* adopting each behavior (*current*); (b) had adopted each behavior *during their first 3 months* working in the subsidiaries (*first 3-months*); and (c) *should have adopted* each behavior (*expected*)—on a 7-point Likert scale (1 = to an extremely small extent; 7 = to an extremely large extent). I used their responses to the *expected* questions to perform an analysis of the leadership behaviors they expected of their expatriate leaders, the result of which is reported below in this section. I used their responses to the *expected* and *current* questions to analyze how the fit between expected and observed leadership behaviors is associated with employee satisfaction; the result of this analysis is presented in the next section.

I first summed up the sample Chinese employees' responses to the *expected* questions and then calculated their means, which I found to be 5.50 and 5.53 for task- and relations-oriented leadership behaviors, respectively. This indicates that Chinese employees expect their expatriate supervisors to demonstrate rather **strong** task- and relations-oriented leadership behaviors. This finding is in line with those of previous research, which found that most Chinese employees expect their leaders to demonstrate strong authority and fatherly benevolence (see, e.g., Bond, 1996; Hui & Tan, 1996; Farh & Cheng, 2000; Li & Sun, 2015). In other words, the Chinese employees' ideal leaders are those who, on the one hand, show strong authority and demand that their subordinates effectively complete their tasks (task-oriented), and, on the other hand, provide their subordinates with care, support, and protection (relations-oriented).

Will Chinese employee satisfaction be higher when their expatriate supervisors meet such expectations? The next section presents my findings on this.

The Results of My Analysis of the Association Between Employee Satisfaction and the Fit Between Chinese Employee Expected and Observed Leadership Behaviors

In this section, I first briefly explain the importance of the fit between expected and observed leadership behaviors and the contribution of my study as one of the first to examine such aspects in a cross-cultural setting. Following this, I report my findings on how the job and supervisor satisfaction of my sample 237 Chinese employees was associated with the fit between their expected and observed leadership behaviors.

As reviewed in Chapter 2, Lord's Implicit Leadership Theory and House's Culturally Endorsed Implicit Theories of Leadership both suggest that a good fit between the leadership behaviors demonstrated by leaders and those expected by followers can yield higher degrees of employee satisfaction and performance. A small number of empirical studies have examined the effects of such a fit on employee work outcomes (Lambert *et al.*, 2012) and found that the greater the fit, the higher the employee performance, commitment, and job satisfaction (see, e.g., Epitropaki & Martin, 2005; Subramaniam *et al.*, 2010; Lambert *et al.*, 2012). However, those studies were mainly conducted in *mono-cultural* settings, and only limited research has been hitherto conducted in *cross-cultural* ones. Overall, very little is known about whether host country employee satisfaction is associated with the fit between the leadership behaviors they expect and those demonstrated by their expatriate supervisors.

As part of my research on the leadership behaviors of expatriate managers in China, I examined how Chinese employee satisfaction is associated with the fit between expected and observed expatriate supervisor leadership behaviors. This aspect needs to be examined because research has found that the expectations and attitudes held by employees toward expatriate managers differ from those they hold toward local ones, as mentioned at the beginning of the previous section.

As mentioned in the last section, 237 Chinese employees were asked to provide assessment on the leadership behaviors they expected their expatriate supervisors to demonstrate and on those they had actually observed. In addition, they were asked to indicate their degree of *job satisfaction* (three question items) and of *satisfaction with their expatriate supervisor (supervisor satisfaction)* (three question items), as explained in Chapter 3. The question items can be found in Appendix B.

Job satisfaction is defined as *a pleasurable or positive emotional state resulting from the appraisal of one's job or job experiences* (Locke, 1976: 1300); supervisor satisfaction refers to the positive emotional state felt by employees as a result of the fulfillment of their expectations by their supervisors. I examined these two aspects of employee satisfaction because both can be directly influenced by leadership behaviors through their direct effect on employee daily work experience.

I analyzed the data by means of polynomial regression analyses and response surface modeling. Any readers interested in the analysis process and in the detailed results of the statistical analysis should contact the author.

The results of the data analyses showed that Chinese employee satisfaction with expatriate supervisors is high in the presence of high degrees of fit between expected and observed leadership behaviors. This confirms the argument, made by Implicit Leadership Theory, that leaders demonstrating leadership behaviors that match their followers' expectations can elicit favorable employee outcomes (House, 1971; Lord *et al.*, 1986; Masterson & Lensges, 2015; Yukl and Gardner, 2019). This argument is based on the reasoning that individuals are likely to feel satisfied when working with supervisors who represent the traits and skills they would expect from people in leadership positions (House *et al.*, 2004; Yukl and Gardner, 2019; Marstand *et al.*, 2017; Lord & Brown, 2001; Henderson *et al.*, 2008; Meglino *et al.*, 1992).

However, the results of my analysis *failed* to show an association between Chinese employee "job satisfaction" and the fit between expected and observed leadership behaviors. This may be due to the fact that many contemporary Chinese employees do not see job satisfaction as a valuable or meaningful aspect of their working lives. As presented in the first section of this chapter, recent studies have found that many Chinese workers, unlike their counterparts in other countries, value monetary work aspects (e.g., high income and promotion opportunities) much more than job satisfaction. If job satisfaction is not cared about or valued by employees, then factors such as leadership behaviors are likely to have little or no influence on it.

To summarize, as reported in this and the previous section, the results of the data analyses show that Chinese employees expect their expatriate supervisors to demonstrate rather high levels of both task- and relations-oriented leadership behaviors. The results also show that the degree of Chinese employee satisfaction with their expatriate supervisors is higher when their expatriate supervisors demonstrate high levels of task- and relations-oriented leadership behaviors, thus matching their expectations.

The implication of these findings is clear: to enhance the positive emotional state Chinese employees feel toward their expatriate supervisors, it is necessary to meet their expectations of a leader. Thus, in their leadership roles, expatriate managers should, on the one hand, impose their authority over their Chinese subordinates and demand that they efficiently improve or accomplish their tasks and, on the other hand, provide their Chinese subordinates with care, support, and protection in order to establish trust and cooperation.

Overall, my findings indicate that leadership behaviors cannot be divorced from cultural contexts and follower expectations, thus suggesting that, when working in unfamiliar cultural settings, leaders should keep an open mind to new situations and be willing to change their own leadership behaviors and to conform to local societal expectations.

Summary

- Although traditional work values (e.g., collectivism, thrift, persistence, and relationship harmony) are still prevalent in contemporary Chinese society, the findings of recent research indicate that Chinese workers now value monetary work aspects much more than non-monetary ones.

- Many studies conducted in China have found that most Chinese workers expect their leaders to show strong authority, fatherly benevolence, and strong moral principles.

- The results of my research show that Chinese employees expect their expatriate supervisors to demonstrate authority and fatherly benevolence (i.e., high task- and relations-oriented leadership behaviors). My research also shows that the satisfaction of Chinese employees toward their expatriate supervisors is high when the latter's leadership behaviors match their expectations.

- Based on the research findings presented in this chapter, those expatriate managers who are currently or will be working in China should demonstrate authority and fatherly benevolence (i.e., high task- and relations-oriented leadership behaviors). In other words, when carrying out their leadership roles, expatriate managers should, on the one hand, impose their authority over their Chinese subordinates and demand that they efficiently improve or accomplish their tasks and, on the other hand, provide their Chinese subordinates with care, support, and protection in order to establish trust and cooperation. By doing so, expatriate managers would meet the expectation of their Chinese employees and enhance their positive emotional state in the workplace.

- When working in foreign cultural contexts—in which the expectations for leaders differ substantially from those found in their home countries—expatriate managers need to conform to local societal expectations in order to enhance their employee satisfaction with them.

References

Bond, M. H. (1996). Chinese values. In M. H. Bond (Ed.), *The Handbook of Chinese Psychology* (pp. 208–226). New York: Oxford University Press.

Bond, M. H., & Hwang, K. K. (1986). The social psychology of Chinese people. In M. H. Bond (Ed.), *The Psychology of the Chinese People* (pp. 213–266). New York: Oxford University Press.

Cao, M. L. (2009). Analysis of professional choice behavior: Survey of freshmen enrolled in 2008 of Nanjing Tech University. *Journal of Cultural and Educational Materials, 35,* 121–124.

Cheng, B. S., Huang, M. P., & Chou, L. F. (2002a). Paternalistic leadership and its effectiveness: Evidence from Chinese organizational teams. *Journal of Psychology in Chinese Societies, 3*(1), 85–112.

Cheng, B. S., Shieh, P. Y., & Chou, L. F. (2002b). The principal's leadership, leader-member exchange quality, and the teacher's extra-role behavior: The effects of transformational and paternalistic leadership. *Indigenous Psychological Research in Chinese Societies, 17,* 105–161.

Cheng, B. S., Chou, L. F., Wu, T. Y., Huang, M. P., & Farh, J. L. (2004). Paternalistic leadership and subordinate responses: Establishing a leadership model in Chinese organizations. *Asian Journal of Social Psychology, 7*(1), 89–117.

Chinese Culture Connection. (1987). Chinese values and the search for culture-free dimensions of culture. *Journal of Cross-cultural Psychology, 18*(2), 143–164.

Epitropaki, O., & Martin, R. (2005). From ideal to real: A longitudinal study of the role of implicit leadership theories on leader-member exchanges and employee outcomes. *Journal of Applied Psychology, 90*(4), 659.

Farh, J. L., & Cheng, B. S. (2000). A cultural analysis of paternalistic leadership in Chinese organizations. In *Management and Organizations in the Chinese Context* (pp. 84–127). London: Palgrave Macmillan.

Farh, J. L., Liang, J., Chou, L. F., & Cheng, B. S. (2008). Paternalistic leadership in Chinese organizations: Research progress and future research directions. In *Leadership and Management in China: Philosophies, Theories, and Practices* (pp. 171–205). London: Cambridge University Press.

Gelfand, M. J., Erez, M., & Aycan, Z. (2007). Cross-cultural organizational behavior. *Annual Review of Psychology, 58,* 479.

Henderson, D. J., Wayne, S. J., Shore, L. M., Bommer, W. H., & Tetrick, L. E. (2008). Leader-member exchange, differentiation, and psychological contract fulfillment: A multilevel examination. *Journal of Applied Psychology, 93,* 1208–1219.

Hofstede, G., & Bond, M. H. (1988). The Confucius connection: From cultural roots to economic growth. *Organizational Dynamics, 16*(4), 5–21.

House, R. (1971). A path goal theory of leader effectiveness. *Administrative Science Quarterly, 16*(3), 321–339.

House, R. J., Hanges, P.J., Javidan, M., Dorfman, P. W., & Gupta, V. (Eds). (2004) *Culture, Leadership, and Organizations: The GLOBE Study of 62 Societies.* Thousand Oaks, CA: Sage.

Hui, C. H., & Tan, C. K. (1996). Employee motivation and attitudes in the Chinese workforce. In M. H. Bond (Ed.), *The Handbook of Chinese Psychology* (pp. 364–378). New York: Oxford University Press.

Lambert, L. S., Tepper, B. J., Carr, J. C., Holt, D. T., & Barelka, A. J. (2012). Forgotten but not gone: An examination of fit between leader consideration and initiating structure needed and received. *Journal of Applied Psychology, 97*(5), 913.

Li, Y., & Sun, J. M. (2015). Traditional Chinese leadership and employee voice behavior: A cross-level examination. *The Leadership Quarterly, 26*(2), 172–189.

Lin, C. (2008). Demystifying the chameleonic nature of Chinese leadership. *Journal of Leadership & Organizational Studies, 14*(4), 303–321.

Littrell, R. F. (2002). Desirable leadership behaviors of multi-cultural managers in China. *Journal of Management Development, 21*(1), 5–74.

Lu, L., Kao, S. F., Siu, O. L., & Lu, C. Q. (2011). Work stress, Chinese work values, and work well-being in the greater China. *The Journal of Social Psychology, 151*(6), 767–783.

Locke, E. A. (1976). The nature and causes of job satisfaction. In M. D. Dunnette (Ed.), *Handbook of Industrial and Organizational Psychology* (pp. 1297–1349). Chicago: Rand McNally.

Lord, R. G., De Vader, C. L., & Alliger, G. M. (1986). A meta-analysis of the relation between personality traits and leadership perceptions: An application of validity generalization procedures. *Journal of Applied Psychology, 71*(3), 402.

Lord, R. G., & Brown, D. J. (2001). Leadership, values, and subordinate self-concepts. *The Leadership Quarterly, 12*, 133–152.

Marstand, A. F., Martin, R., & Epitropaki, O. (2017). Complementary person-supervisor fit: An investigation of supplies-values (SV) fit, leader-member exchange (LMX) and work outcomes. *The Leadership Quarterly, 28*(3), 418–437.

Masterson, S. S., & Lensges, M. (2015). Leader–member exchange and justice. In T. Bauer, & B. Erdogan (Eds.), *The Oxford Handbook of Leader-Member Exchange.* New York, NY: Oxford University Press.

Meglino, B. M., Ravlin, E. C., & Adkins, C. L. (1992). The measurement of work value congruence: A field study comparison. *Journal of Management, 18*(1), 33–43.

Nie, P., & Sousa-Poza, A. (2017). What Chinese Workers Value: An Analysis of Job Satisfaction, Job Expectations, and Labor Turnover in China. Institute of Labor Economics (IZA), Discussion Paper Series, IZA DP No. 10963.

Niu, C. P., Wang, A. C., & Cheng, B. S. (2009). Effectiveness of a moral and benevolent leader: Probing the interactions of the dimensions of paternalistic leadership. *Asian Journal of Social Psychology, 12*(1), 32–39.

Redding, S. G., Norman, A., & Schlander, A. (1994). The nature of individual attachment to the organization: A review of East Asian variations. *Handbook of Industrial and Organizational Psychology, 4,* 647–688.

Scott, D., Bishop, J. W., & Chen, X. (2003). An examination of the relationship of employee involvement with job satisfaction, employee cooperation, and intention to quit in US invested enterprise in China. *The International Journal of Organizational Analysis, 11*(1), 3–19.

Subramaniam, A., Othman, R., & Sambasivan, M. (2010). Implicit leadership theory among Malaysian managers: Impact of the leadership expectation gap on leader-member exchange quality. *Leadership & Organization Development Journal, 31*(4), 351–371.

Templer, K. J. (2010). Personal attributes of expatriate managers, subordinate ethnocentrism, and expatriate success: A host-country perspective. *The International Journal of Human Resource Management, 21*(10), 1754–1768.

Tsui, A. S., Wang, H. U. I., Xin, K., Zhang, L., & Fu, P. P. (2004). "Let a thousand flowers bloom": Variation of leadership styles among Chinese CEOs. *Organizational Dynamics, 33*(1), 5–20.

Varma, A., Budhwar, P., & Pichler, S. (2011). Chinese host country nationals' willingness to help expatriates: The role of social categorization. *Thunderbird International Business Review, 53*(3), 353–364.

Walder, A. G. (1988). *Communist Neo-traditionalism: Work and Authority in Chinese Industry*. California: University of California Press.

Wang, A. C., & Cheng, B. S. (2010). When does benevolent leadership lead to creativity? The moderating role of creative role identity and job autonomy. *Journal of Organizational Behavior, 31*(1), 106–121.

Wu, M., Huang, X., Li, C., & Liu, W. (2012). Perceived interactional justice and trust-in-supervisor as mediators for paternalistic leadership. *Management and Organization Review, 8*(1), 97–121.

Yukl, G. and Gardner, W. L. (2019). *Leadership in Organizations* (9th ed.) Harlow: Pearson.

Zhang, Y., Huai, M. Y., & Xie, Y. H. (2015). Paternalistic leadership and employee voice in China: A dual process model. *The Leadership Quarterly, 26*(1), 25–36.

Zhang, X., Kaiser, M., Nie, P., & Sousa-Poza, A. (2019). Why are Chinese workers so unhappy? A comparative cross-national analysis of job satisfaction, job expectations, and job attributes. *PLoS ONE, 14*(9), e0222715.

Bibliography

Bond, M. H. (1988). Finding universal dimensions of individual variation in multicultural studies of values: The Rokeach and Chinese value surveys. *Journal of Personality and Social Psychology, 55*(6), 1009.

He, G. (2004). What Do Workers Want in China's Industrial Workplace? *China: An International Journal, 2*(2), 323–329.

Pellegrini, E. K., & Scandura, T. A. (2008). Paternalistic leadership: A review and agenda for future research. *Journal of Management, 34*(3), 566–593.

Redding, G. (2002). The capitalist business system of China and its rationale. *Asia Pacific Journal of Management, 19*(2), 221–249.

Xu, L. C., Chen, L., Wong, D., & Xue, A. Y. (1985). The role of psychology in enterprise management. *Acta Psychologica Sinica, 17*, 339–345.

Part IV

Suggestions and Conclusions Drawn from the Expatriate Senior Managers' Experiences

Chapter 9

Insights and Suggestions for Effectively Managing and Leading Chinese Employees

In this chapter, I present the key insights conveyed and suggestions made by the expatriate senior managers for managing and leading Chinese employees. As in Chapters 6 and 7, direct quotes are used to enable readers to glean the expatriates' perspectives and experiences in detail and to formulate their own interpretations and judgments. Where appropriate, I add information drawn from the literature and views expressed by the interviewed Chinese employees.

The key insights and suggestions presented in this chapter are as follows:

(1) understand Chinese cultural values and be sensitive to cultural differences;
(2) avoid employee loss of face by providing indirect feedback in private settings;
(3) build personal *guanxi* (relationships) with Chinese employees;
(4) adjust one's own leadership approaches or fail;
(5) adopt a more paternalistic leadership approach;
(6) learn and master the Chinese language;
(7) break down tasks into small chunks and monitor progress;
(8) give clear instructions and check that they have been understood;
(9) build trusting relationships and create a safe environment conducive to open communication;

(10) encourage proactiveness and initiative by setting performance targets, communicating one's own expectations of initiative taking, rewarding employees, delegating responsibility, and training employees to work on their own;

(11) enhance accountability by setting and communicating responsibilities, providing training, giving rewards, accepting and encouraging mistakes, and using a checking system;

(12) overcome resistance to change by changing the group, not the individual.

Understand Chinese Cultural Values and be Sensitive to Cultural Differences

Cultural values can profoundly affect the attitudes, behaviors, and performance of workers. Chinese philosophy and its cultural values direct Chinese workers' attitudes, behaviors, and expectations for leadership (see Chapters 4 and 5). Many of the expatriates who took part in the research said that, in order to become effective business leaders in China, it is important to understand Chinese cultural values, be sensitive to cultural differences, and to adjust one's own leadership. They also said that the wholesale adoption of Western approaches within the Chinese context would be culturally insensitive.

They stated that expatriate managers need to take the time to get to know their Chinese staff, "learn more about the Chinese language and culture", "understand the Chinese culture and way of thinking", "show a sincere interest in local culture and customs", and "adapt their leadership style to the Chinese way of doing things", in order to exhibit culturally acceptable leadership behaviors and thus make their Chinese staff feel comfortable. By so doing, they would also make their Chinese employees feel that they care and that they are interested in them and in their country, which would lead to greater workforce motivation and contentment. The following quotes illustrate their experiences and suggestions:

> You cannot change a culture and I have witnessed other expatriate managers try and fail in their attempts to change this. The best expatriate managers in China are those who have taken the time to get to know their staff and learnt more about Chinese language and culture. Knowledge of this will make it easier for Chinese employees to feel you

are interested in them and their country which will lead to a more moti-
vated and happy workforce.

(British expatriate, 20–24 years old, Education)

Expats who are sensitive to cultural change are the ones that usually
stay longer in China and adapt better to the Chinese way of doing
things. On the other hand the ones who fail to change and adapt their
leadership style to the Chinese way of doing things are the ones that
leave disappointed, clash with employees daily and leave China perma-
nently with a bad experience and memories.

(New Zealander expatriate, 35–39 years old, Hospitality)

More than try to change them, I tried to understand them in order to be
able to make them feel comfortable and therefore obtain the best possi-
ble performance.

(Venezuelan expatriate, 25–29 years old, Architecture)

For China specifically it is important to show a sincere interest in local
culture and customs, more so than in many Western countries, where
business can be done with relatively little understanding. China has
been a closed economy, therefore has maintained a lot of its cultural
aspects, whereas many other countries have been more influenced by
global culture.

(Dutch expatriate, 35–39 years old, Design/Advertising)

Understanding Chinese culture and way of thinking helps. Encouragement
to share opinions and discuss freely, rather than agree with me. Giving
face, building trust and believing in someone's abilities—I find my
Chinese staff really show their competency and are very open under
these circumstances, and show great loyalty ... Understanding the
importance of food, the early lunchtime... Understanding relationships.

(No demographic information)

A good leader has to adjust his leadership style to each individual and
to her/his cultural background and belief system.

(No demographic information)

You must have patience, you must earn trust, you must be willing to learn some Mandarin and be willing to experience everything from eating, meeting, etc., differently.

(No demographic information)

You are being evaluated constantly, you need to show you understand, ACCEPT and respect the culture of the country you're working in. Sincerely accept it.

(No demographic information)

I do think a foreign leader in China has to remain aware of the differences at all times. Even in one's own country however, people are all different from each other, so this type of awareness is really in fact important everywhere. Perhaps one can afford to be more relaxed about it when one is working in a single cultural environment though.

(British expatriate, 35–39 years old, Government)

The expatriates affirmed that it is crucial to understand and respect Chinese cultural and societal norms, as failing to do so will lead to negative consequences, such as difficulties in maintaining relationships with Chinese staff, losing the respect of one's team, struggling to manage effectively, and facing drops in productivity and increased staff turnover.

Among the various Chinese cultural values, they emphasized the importance of understanding the concepts of face and *guanxi* (see Chapter 4 for a description of these concepts). The following two sections present their related suggestions.

Avoid Employee Loss of Face by Providing Indirect Feedback in Private Settings

"Face" is highly valued and carefully maintained by most Chinese because it reflects one's reputation, esteem, pride, social status, prestige, image, and respectability (see Chapter 4 for more details about the concept). Most Chinese employees will go to any length to avoid loss of face. For example, many Chinese employees will demonstrate behaviors such as not speaking in meetings or public to avoid saying something wrong, not taking initiatives to avoid making mistakes, and not admitting any lack of skills or knowledge in relation to a task (see the section on "the high value placed on face" in Chapter 6).

Many of the expatriates emphasized that it is vital to understand the concept of "face" and to avoid Chinese employees feeling its loss. The following quotes illustrate their views on the importance of understanding the concept of "face":

If you come as a foreigner you need to learn about the local and national culture, habits and traditions. Especially in terms of how to put someone on stage, giving face and respect in front of others. In other countries you can teach by being straightforward, in China it is more difficult as it might come across as an insult or "loosing (sic) face" in front of others.

(Australian expatriate, 35–39 years old, Hospitality)

There is always the issue of "face" as well, which comes up regularly in meetings. Generally, in China, staff do not want to ask questions during the meeting. Therefore as a leader you must learn that this is often the case and spend more individual time before and after meetings.

(Australian expatriate, 30–34 years old, Training and Development)

Face is an important part of the culture that needs to be at least partly understood by any leader in China.

(British expatriate, 50–54 years old, Education)

The expatriates suggested that, to avoid causing loss of face by Chinese employees, any provision of feedback to them (particularly if critical or negative) should be done in an indirect and non-confrontational fashion, in private, and on a one-to-one basis. The following quotes illustrate their suggestions and the approaches they had taken:

In China you have to give more indirect feedback and need to make sure that you don't make it too public in order to avoid that your employee is "loosing (sic) face".

(German expatriate, 25–29 years old, Marketing/Advertising)

I am mindful of "face" and always deal with performance issues on a one-to-one basis.

(British expatriate, 30–34 years old, Food and Beverage)

I have to keep in mind the Chinese culture of "face", which means that negative feedback needs to be tempered down and delivered in a non-confrontational manner.

(Indian expatriate, 30–34 years old, Media and Advertising)

Had to keep in mind that face is very important, so the rough and tumble construction activities/meetings need to be modified to accommodate that face-saving axiom.

(American expatriate, 55–59 years old, Nuclear energy)

The above approaches may be seen by some readers as passive responses to the issue of "face". A number of the expatriates said that they had actively tried to overcome their Chinese employees' fear of losing face by teaching them that it would be OK for them to make mistakes and to ask for help should they not know how to do something. However, it had been difficult to convince their Chinese employees. As an American expatriate said, the fear of losing face is so deeply rooted in Chinese employees that it would take a great amount of time and effort to eradicate it.

The challenge of the fear of loss of face due to failure is drummed into the Chinese employee since they could learn to walk and talk. It is not something you can teach in one sitting. . . it takes an investment of time, patience, persistence, and genuine sincere concern for the employee.

(American expatriate, 55–59 years old, Financial and other sections)

Build Personal *Guanxi* (Relationships) with Chinese Employees

Guanxi (i.e., relationships) plays a very important role in Chinese people's social and working lives (see Chapter 4 for more details). In order to do business in China, it is crucial to build and maintain good *guanxi* with employees, business contacts, and other stakeholders. In terms of employee relations, *guanxi* between managers and workers can have a great influence on the latter's engagement, commitment, and job satisfaction.

Chinese *guanxi* is always based on trust and built up from and on a "personal" level. Chinese individual's *guanxi* networks often include people they trust and have known personally for a long time, for example, extended family members, school friends, close friends, and others with whom they regularly come into contact. Chinese people interact and share information for commercial, social, work, and interpersonal purposes through these personal and trusted relationships. Please see the section entitled "Build trusting relationships and create a safe environment conducive to open communication" for the expatriates' views on the importance of building trust.

Many of the senior expatriate managers said that building and maintaining good "personal" relationships/*guanxi* with Chinese subordinates are important in relation to leading them. The following quotes illustrate their views and experiences:

> ...*interpersonal bonding with Chinese employees is more important than in the west.*

> (American expatriate, 40–44 years old, Advertising)

> *You will need to interact with Chinese staff on a more personal level if you want them to use their full potential.*

> (German expatriate, 25–29 years old, Consulting)

> *"Guanxi" and relationship management are key here and are a big challenge to those not familiar with China. You need to have an open mind and at the same time take a hard line to what you need. This attitude and approach needs to be maintained.*

> (No demographic information)

> *Due to the high competition in the labor market you have to lead on a much more personal level.*

> (Austrian expatriate, 35–39 years old, Automotive)

I need to be much more proactive in building relationships with the team at all levels...I need to ...reach out in a more personal way as well.

(American expatriate, 30–34 years old, Research/Consulting)

...need to establish a personal connection with employees as role model to motivate.

(Swiss expatriate, 45–49 years old, High-Tech Electronics and Materials)

For Chinese teams you need to adopt a "motherly/fatherly" approach. You also need to invest time in building a personal connection.

(Australian expatriate, 30–34 years old, Recruitment)

Getting close to your employees; establish good working and personal relationship.

(German expatriate, 25–29 years old, Retail)

...spend more time on building personal relationships. The boss is like the leader of a family.

(American expatriate, 40–44 years old, Wine & Spirits)

I make myself more available to my team to engender trust and understanding...I ask questions about their personal life and things completely unrelated to work...

(American expatriate, 40–44 years old, Advertising)

...the dynamics among people at the same level is different, more complex than in counter-part situations in, for example, the U.S. The dynamics of relationships here in China, are, in my experience, much more "personal"—and that is "personal" on many levels: your character; background and connections; and outside activities.

(American expatriate, 55–59 years old, IT)

I worked more on building personal relationships with colleagues, made sure I was well established in the Chinese organization. This created a specific authority in the Chinese workforce that helped also with leading my direct team: I felt that I had to embed myself into the Chinese organization to lead. Leadership was never perceived as something individual—a leader was somebody who could influence beyond the official area of responsibility. I had the impression that my reports were closely watching and deciding whether they follow or not. I have the suspicion that had I been an isolated expat who thinks facts and figures are everything I would not have moved a single stone.

(German expatriate, 35–39 years old, Chemical)

Some expatriates suggested that, when building personal relationships and socializing with employees, care needs to be paid to maintaining fairness and to avoiding favoritism.

I am much more careful about personal relationships and avoid putting myself in situations where I may appear to be favoring one group over another. Staff pay a lot more attention to who I socialize with and I have adjusted to this by how I go about things so as to avoid the appearance of creating a clique or inner-circle.

(British expatriate, 40–44 years old, Financial Services)

Getting the balance right is key, and you can very quickly get out of balance if you spend too much time with one person. Everything is watched…every interaction is more important that (sic) other places. It is fascinating.

(American expatriate, 45–49 years old, Financial Services)

A more conservative approach is required with most individuals. Humor use and the development of personal relationships have to be more carefully considered.

(British expatriate, 30–34 years old, Media)

A further issue is to watch very closely the dynamics between one's foreign staff and one's Chinese staff. The latter will be immediately aware if the leader appears to be favoring his/her own nationals over them, with immediate negative effects for team dynamics. This is also really a generic point though, since even in a single cultural environment, teams will often have different social or other groups of people, all of whom need to be treated fairly and equitably. A good leader will make it clear that he/she values the diversity of the team, so that staff feel their differences are a strength to be pleased about, not a weakness to be regretted.

(British expatriate, 35–39 years old, Government)

Adjust One's Own Leadership Approaches or Fail

Another key suggestion made by the expatriates in relation to effectively leading/managing Chinese employees was to adjust one's own leadership approaches to the Chinese environment. Some expatriates expressed the belief that making adjustments to one's own leadership is essential to avoid failure. The following quotes illustrate their views:

I think you have to understand as much as you can about how business and hierarchy work in the Chinese mindset. I find myself being far more strategically minded here, I have to remember the rules of business, etiquette and corporate culture differs from back in the UK. I have to adjust, no other way, adjust or fail.

(British expatriate, 25–29 years old, Recruitment)

If you don't adjust your leadership, you will fail. Firstly, as a leader, you need to fully adapt to the culture you are facing, then when you fully understand them, you show them a different way to proceed in your culture. Be an example and show the way. First adapt yourself, second make them evolve in a new mixed culture. There is no specific way to reach this adjustment, it will depend on your environment, the change will come from yourself and it is far more than a professional change, it's also a personal one.

(French expatriate, 20–24 years old, Cyber Security)

You will have to adjust as the "direct" European approach does not work in China.

(Dutch expatriate, 30–34 years old, Hospitality)

You have to adjust, otherwise it creates a losing proposition for both sides.

(American expatriate, 40–44 years old, Chemical)

You have to change your behavior while interacting with Chinese colleagues, which, to me, is like a tool to be effective with your leadership approach... adjustment is in the listening to people and pay more attention to the formalities. You need to adjust to be effective leading.

(Italian expatriate, 45–49 years old, Pharmaceuticals)

Personally I believe that you have to flex your style of management, depending on your environment, the employees you are working with and also depending on the audience. This is not only about China, as a good leader you have to be able to adjust according to the situation.

(Australian expatriate, 35–39 years old, Hospitality)

I tried to challenge the mindset of some Chinese staff so that they work more independently and are not afraid of making mistakes...To change the mindset in China, you need your staff to believe in you and your idea, you need to connect with them. This is only possible if you adjust yourself and try to understand China. Do not see China as a 3–4-year career station, then they will not follow you.

(German expatriate, 25–29 years old, Consulting)

Many expatriates said that making adjustments according to the culture, situations, and environments is important in relation to showing understanding and flexibility and to building credibility.

The adjustment is necessary to prove you are willing to listen, understand and be humble enough to cooperate with Chinese people in China. To show yourself as a flexible individual even when presented with situations that appear as "not for negotiation" at first (you are usually being tested to gauge your reaction, all the time).

(No demographic information)

You need to be adaptable & able to change your style based on the situation that you are presented with. You need to be culturally attuned, as it is important that you build credibility in the eyes of your local employees.

(Australian expatriate, 30–34 years old, Recruitment)

Showing understanding and will to adapt to the Chinese cultural environment is something anyone should do while working here.

(Italian expatriate, 25–29 years old, Consulting)

I lead a team made up 50% of westerners and 50% of Chinese. You cannot use one approach for the team. You have to differentiate your management style according to who you are managing. International managers often think that they can use an "international" style of management—a kind of global one-size-fits-all approach. Wrong. In China you need to understand the culture, the norms, the sensitivities of the Chinese staff, respect them for what and who they are and adjust your management style accordingly. There is no such thing as East meets West. These are tectonic plates which rub together across fault-lines. You have to manage across these tectonic plates, dealing with earth tremors and the occasional earthquake as part of the job. Interpersonal competencies, cultural understandings, respect, tolerance, and all the other attributes of EQ are therefore infinitely more important than any narrow business competency.

(British expatriate, 60 years old or over, Education)

The expatriates mentioned various aspects in relation to the aspects they had adjusted in their leadership approaches. For example, they said they had changed their ways of communicating, increased their monitoring frequency, given specific and detailed task instructions, become more directive and controlling, and engaged in greater micro-management. Please see Chapter 7 for the top 10 aspects the expatriate managers said they had adjusted.

Some respondent managers suggested that it would be beneficial for expatriates to adapt to the Chinese environment while, at the same time, maintaining some Western management approaches that they considered to be effective.

*A good balance of western tactics and understanding of the Chinese
work dynamics definitely helps.*

(Italian expatriate, 25–29 years old, Consulting)

*I have always recognized that in order to lead effectively in China, I
have to, to some extent, adapt my leadership and become more Chinese.
However, I am not Chinese and trying to do everything in a Chinese
fashion will put me in a distinct disadvantage. Even more so, there are
many excellent traits in Swedish management that promotes more efficient organizations and that would be stupid to leave out of your management style. For Chinese companies to become more efficient and
modern, as the economy grows more sophisticated, a shift toward this
end of management (less autocratic, more delegating of responsibilities
and decision power) will be necessary. I therefore balanced my leadership and my Chinese employees have no choice but to answer to this and
grow as professionals. My employees thus enjoy a higher degree of
independence and more responsibilities than the employees of a typical
Chinese company.*

(No demographic information)

Adopt a More Paternalistic Leadership Approach

Research shows that most Chinese employees expect their leaders to
engage in paternalistic leadership (see Chapter 8). In other words, most
Chinese employees expect their leaders not only to be capable of taking
decisive action, providing instructions for improvement, and reprimanding poor performance, but also to provide their subordinates with care,
support, and protection in both the work and non-work domains.

In Chapter 7, I reported the top 10 aspects in regard to which the
expatriate managers said they had adjusted themselves; among these, two
were to become more directive and to assume a more fatherly or brotherly
attitude. Relating to these two aspects of adjustment, some expatriates
suggested that, to cater to their Chinese employees' expectations of a
leader, expatriate managers should ideally adopt a paternalistic leadership
approach that combines high levels of authoritarianism and fatherly
benevolence; that is, on the one hand, leaders should impose their authority and demand good performance and, on the other hand, they should

show concern for individuals' familial and personal situations. The following quotes exemplify such suggestions and the adjustments the expatriate managers had made to act in a "bossy" or a "fatherly" fashion to meet the expectations of their Chinese employees:

> *For Chinese teams you need to adopt a "motherly/fatherly" approach. You also need to invest time in building a personal connection.*
>
> (Australian expatriate, 30–34 years old, Recruitment)

> *It's best to utilize a strong, more top-down managerial style in China. This is especially true when entering into a position with Chinese staff. Once this has been established, a more collaborative style can be slowly adopted. I have adjusted by being more authoritative in my interaction with staff. Needless to say that it is imperative to maintain respect, calmness, and a certain level of friendliness. I do not wish to alienate staff.*
>
> (American expatriate, 35–39 years old, Architecture)

> *...I sometimes need to act like a "boss" in the Chinese definition to get an appropriate response...I also find that positive reinforcement and incentives have more impact here than back home. There is also a slightly more paternal sense to leadership than back home, with more concern shown for the individual's family & personal situation.*
>
> (American expatriate, 45–49 old, Consulting/Technology Transfer)

> *As a senior figure I am regarded and attempt to be a "Father" figure to my team or Da Lao Ban. In that respect I have to tap into the softer drivers of the team such as what in the West we call "touch feely" side of relationships...lots of team dinners and respect building by reinforcing the cultural expectation.*
>
> (British expatriate, 55–59 years old, Domestic Appliances)

> *In Europe it's more about results than personal relationships. In China, a boss should be something like a father figure. Be stern, but also benevolent. Give instructions that are detailed and control and often get feedback.*
>
> (German expatriate, 45–49 years old, Consulting)

Chinese employees like strong and decisive leaders who make decisions by themselves; who act as a family-type figure who will protect their employees and take an interest in their personal lives; who will take responsibility when something goes wrong; who is efficient. A very traditional role model who gives orders. Flat management structures are not very welcome. So, Western managers must adapt to the above whilst also helping Chinese employees develop skills that we in the West find important. The key thing is to earn the trust of your Chinese employees and then they will be willing to follow you. Chinese employees are usually more loyal to their managers than to the wider company.

(British expatriate, 25–29 years old, Green Energy)

Chinese style is based on hierarchy and personal leadership: the boss decides and the rest follow the leader. There are no consultations and the decision making process is one person's decision (very quick process)— Chinese style understands that the best of employees rise under pressure and test, the leader helps employees to grow using pressure, rushing them beyond what a Western guy could accept in Europe.

(Spanish expatriate, 30–34 years old, Renewable Energies Technology)

The Chinese employees I interviewed generally agreed that the paternalistic leadership style is acceptable for many Chinese employees. However, they emphasized that the authoritative and top-down aspects of paternalistic leadership would not be appropriate for some employees; for example, those holding high management positions, those who are high performers, and those who believe in equal employee–manager relations. They said that those employees would prefer a more equal working relationship, expect a leader to meet employee needs, and require high job autonomy.

Learn and Master the Chinese Language

Language differences were perceived as one of the most challenging aspects by all the expatriates, regardless of their degree of command of the Chinese language (see the section on "the language spoken and an indirect communication style" in Chapter 6). Some of the expatriate managers strongly recommended that expatriates learn and master Chinese because the ability to communicate with their employees in their own language would yield various benefits, such as improving working relationships, helping overcome culture- and language-related challenges, helping better communicate, making employees feel comfortable, and creating a more motivated and happier workforce. The following quotes illustrate their views on the importance and benefits of being able to communicate in Chinese:

> *The main challenge is being able to communicate. A good knowledge in Chinese helps very, very much. I could not have run the companies that I ran (one was 30M USD and one was 300M USD in turnover) without speaking Chinese.*
>
> (Swedish expatriate, 30–34 years old, Heavy Manufacturing)

> *The culture and language are different so especially communication needs to take this into consideration. I have studied the language and culture for several years and would say that this has reduced the challenges.*
>
> (German expatriate, 30–34 years old, IT)

> *The best expatriate managers in China are those who have taken the time to get to know their staff and learnt more about Chinese language and culture. Knowledge of this will make it easier for Chinese employees to feel you are interested in them and their country which will lead to a more motivated and happy workforce.*
>
> (British expatriate, 40–44 years old, Education)

> *If you do not master the language you will probably get the wrong idea on how to lead Chinese employees.*
>
> (Danish expatriate, 45–49 years old, Medical Devices)

> *In China, it is better to speak or to understand the language to be a manager as Chinese consider people speaking Chinese as being smart.*
>
> (No demographic information)

Break Down Tasks into Small Chunks and Monitor Progress

As reported in Chapter 6, many of the expatriates said that a key challenging characteristic of their Chinese employees was their expectation to be given detailed instructions and clearly defined tasks, rather than being empowered and entrusted with responsibilities. They also said that, should no specific guidance and direction be given, their Chinese employees would get lost or fail to complete their tasks. Some expatriates thus suggested breaking down tasks into small chunks and constantly monitoring progress in order to ensure their completion.

> *Learn to split one task into many small ones to make it more understandable is a good practice. This is the only way you can get things done. It is a constant challenge, because it does not reflect the typical way of working in Western economies.*

(Italian expatriate, 25–29 years old, Consulting)

> *I try to be more patient and develop further our process into smaller sub-process. I create lots of checklists and formatted document to ensure method and process are respected. Adjustments are made everyday depending on how the tasks are successfully completed or not.*

(French expatriate, 30–34 years old, Consulting)

> *To our experience, and generally speaking, permanent supervision and control is necessary.*

(French expatriate, 40–44 years old, Service)

> *...of course regular checks on the status of the task are necessary to avoid missing the deadline without a warning from them.*

(Italian expatriate, 30–34 years old, Paratheatrical)

> *you have to...structure your demands and present them in "chewable portions".*

(Austrian expatriate, 35–39 years old, Automotive)

...you need to be more involved in what the employee is doing and monitoring them, because once they are done with a task, they may just wait for you to assign them a new one.

(American expatriate, 30–34 years old, Professional Services)

From the above quotes, it can be seen that breaking down tasks into small chunks and constant monitoring was seen by the expatriates as a necessary—albeit challenging and demanding—measure. Nevertheless, some expatriates stated that such efforts had paid off as the situation had improved once their employees had reached a certain level.

In China I need to teach my staff more basic things and it takes more time to get things done. ...Basically, it is necessary to explain more and give not only directions but clear instructions. But over time it gets better when the people have reached a certain level.

(German expatriate, 40–44 years old, Automotive)

I also had a number of employees that initially needed more supervision because they lacked skills but I learnt with delight that they were as capable as European employees to work independently in the end—but I had to train, coach and insist. I made sure they experience the consequence of their errors because I always asked them to "clean-up" afterwards.

(German expatriate, 40–44 years old, Chemical)

When I first came to China in 1996 I naively though (sic) *everything I said and heard was no different to a conversation at home. At that time I expected employees who did not understand my instruction to say something—this did not happen and resulted in considerable frustration. I found that I was having to spend time checking on results— something that happens considerably less at home. However once there was a clear understanding—an understanding of my subject, a familiarity with the syntax, vocabulary, usage, idioms, language functions, jargon of our business—then all went well.*

(Canadian expatriate, 60 years old or over, Education)

Give Clear Instructions and Check That They Have Been Understood

Another key suggestion made by the expatriates was to provide staff with clear task instructions and check whether they had understood them. They said that their Chinese employees were efficient when they had been given complete, clear, and specific instructions and explanations for the intended outcomes. They also said that it was necessary to check whether their Chinese employees had understood the instructions and explanations given because many of them would not seek clarification if they had not. The following quotes illustrate the expatriates' experiences and suggestions:

> *...you have to be very clear and strong. In the USA I tended to give direction but expect directs to fill in the gaps. You cannot do that in China, you have to be clear...In my experience the Chinese associates love to be clear about what needs to be done and will execute very efficiently.*

(British expatriate, 45–49 years old, Financial)

> *You have to be much more specific, much more clear and cannot expect too much initiative from the employee as many seem not to know by themselves what is expected and how to go about it.*

(Israeli expatriate, 40–44 years old, Consulting)

> *There is less independent initiative. You have to draw a very detailed roadmap for each task, even for excellent employees of high education. The same is true for other employees, who need a lot of supervision/ control because they otherwise tend to stray out of bounds (in many ways of varying seriousness).*

(No demographic information)

> *I would be more detailed and specific in my instructions to them, also you need to get feedback to ensure they clearly understand what is asked for.*

(Swiss expatriate, 45–49 years old, Manufacturing)

...with Chinese colleagues you have to be very specific with the request, spend a long time to explain the context and closely check the progress of the work.

(Italian expatriate, 45–49 years old, Pharmaceuticals)

In the west we give more freedom of actions to achieve goals, in China you have to be very specific about tasks and ultimately the employees expect the leader to be the final responsible party, it takes much more supervision in China than in the west.

(American expatriate, 55–59 years old, Engineering and Construction)

You have to have patience and willingness to invest the time to explain very thoroughly the "why" and specific desired outcomes.

(Australian expatriate, 35–39 years old, Building Products)

Chinese do not want lose face, so even if something is not clear they will not tell you. You have to check/normally they wait for a command...

(Italian expatriate, 45–49 years old, Telecommunication)

You must ALWAYS check for understanding, as what is said and what is heard are often 2 different things...

(British expatriate, 25–29 years old, Tech/Fashion Accessories)

...you have to learn not to make assumptions about requests and demands being fully understood. The key terms I believe are active listening and follow-up. Each act of communication needs to end with a confirmation of the understanding. Each process needs to have daily follow-up built into it. By internalizing these practices, many problems can be prevented.

(No demographic information)

Build Trusting Relationships and Create a Safe Environment Conducive to Open Communication

An employee's willingness to express opinions, make suggestions, and solve problems bestows various benefits on organizations, such as improving organizational functioning, enhancing the quality of managerial decisions, enhancing organizational adaptability, and providing developmental opportunities. Many expatriates, however, said that their Chinese employees tended to be reserved and inexpressive. As reported in Chapter 6, this was the fifth most mentioned characteristic of Chinese employees by the expatriates, who saw it as very challenging. For example, the expatriates said that they were unable to get feedback or viewpoints from their subordinates and that problems could not be addressed in a timely fashion because their Chinese employees did not proactively voice their concerns, rarely confronted people with problems, and showed unwillingness or fear of expressing their views in public forums (please see Chapter 6 for details).

Some expatriates said that the establishment of trusting relationships with Chinese employees is essential to make them feel confident enough to voice their concerns and make suggestions. The following quotes illustrate their views on the importance of building trust:

...you have to build a relationship with them, of trust and protection... losing your temper or being coercive, abusive or blindingly applying corporate rules will not get you far, soon or later they will leave or make you leave and you will not see it coming, they are very reserved in their attitude, difficult to see what they think.

(American expatriate, 55–59 years old, Engineering and Construction)

People don't follow you right away, but if you gain their trust they become very respectful and loyal...You must have patience, you must earn trust... arrogance and a brash approach will get you nowhere.

(No demographic information)

...creating a culture of trust so that they believe that they can make a difference without being told how.

(British expatriate, 40–44 years old, Automotive)

I created a trust relationship with them so that they feel free to voice out their opinion in a particular frame. It was my way to get the best out of people.

(French expatriate, 40–44 years old, Retail)

Chinese are very loyal and committed if they trust you. More time needs to be spent on gaining their trust, i.e., prove you are there to support them and protect the team. Communication and interaction need to take into account high context and low context, so care needs to be made to ensure that what I want to say is fully understood.

(No demographic information)

In the US on the whole, the work relationships are quite superficial and people like it that way, in China there is much more context with work relationships. You have to work at building trust in relationships...

(American expatriate, 45–49 years old, Financial Services)

Building trust, however, is not an easy task. Some expatriates said that it had taken them time and effort to develop trust in China.

It takes time to build trust in Chinese teams to open up and actively contribute to shaping opinions or solutions. Too often, they fear express-ing their opinion freely and possibly disagreeing with their superior.

(Finnish expatriate, 35–35 years old, Steel)

There is no question that trust takes longer to develop in China.

(Canadian expatriate, 55–59 years old, Education)

Great effort and time must be spent to overcome general issues of trust. Chinese employees are great but society maintains less trust of the world and organizations so to get local employees in China (whether Chinese or foreign) trust must be built.

(American expatriate, 40–44 years old, Advertising)

Challenges are to build trust & respect.

(British expatriate, 45–49 years old, Retail)

Although building trust in China does take longer than in other coun-tries, it is true not only in relation to foreigners but also between the Chinese themselves, as *guanxi* networks often include only close and extended family members and people who have known each other person-ally for a long time (see Chapter 4). Nevertheless, lasting trusting relationships can be developed between expatriate managers and Chinese employees. The following quotes illustrate the experience of some expatriates:

> *You have to spend a lot of time investing in the relationship with your peers in order for them to trust you. However, once the trust is established it stays strong for quite a long time.*

> (American expatriate, 30–34 years old, Media)

> *In China I lead by supporting the team personally and professionally for as long as it takes to build trust. Once trust is built and the team is aware that I am there to support them and help them grow they will perform.*

> (American expatriate, 40–44 years old, Retail Sales)

> *I must make much time to ensure people feel trust in talking and working independently. The people have much to offer but the traditional Chinese boss does not listen or respect...I adjust by listening more and taking every idea very seriously and talking about what we should do. It takes a little extra time in the beginning but by gaining the people's trust it works well in getting much done.*

> (American expatriate, 50–54 years old, Manufacturing)

From the expatriates' approaches and suggestions presented above, it can be seen that the establishment of trusting relationships with Chinese employees can not only help overcome their reservedness in communication but also help them to perform. This is because employees are more likely to voice any concerns and make suggestions when they feel it is safe or worthwhile to do so. For how to build such relationships, see the section on *guanxi* in Chapter 4.

Some expatriates said that, to motivate Chinese employees to voice their concerns and make suggestions, it is important to create a safe environment in which they feel safe and comfortable to do so.

> *Creating an environment in which Chinese staff feel completely secure to offer ideas and feedback is the biggest challenge here, but it is vitally important to do so.*

> (British expatriate, 20–24 years old, Education)

Chinese staff are much less vocal, and afraid to have an opinion...We very much encourage the team to become more independent, think for themselves and speak up. This is a long-term process that is not quick or easy—and it requires a "safe environment" where they feel they can share their opinions.

(Dutch expatriate, 40–44 years old, Consulting)

One common approach that some of the expatriates had taken to create a safe environment for their Chinese employees to share ideas had involved private or one-to-one sessions/communications.

I favor one-to-one discussions rather than group ones to ensure I got proper inputs and feedbacks from my employees.

(Spanish expatriate, 45–49 years old, Energy)

I take more time to talk to stakeholders one-on-one and in private. I find that using instant messaging can sometimes give Chinese staff the freedom to express themselves openly.

(American expatriate, 25–29 years old, Publishing)

I have tried encouraging my Chinese team members to be more vocal in their opinions in public forums. I realized that they have some good ideas and thoughts, when I discuss with them in private, but are unable to bring it out in front of clients or senior bosses, due to two reasons. 1. Culturally, it's not good for employees to disagree/voice out their opinion without knowing what the boss says 2. Most of them are not very comfortable with fluent spoken English.

(Indian expatriate, 30–34 years old, Media and Advertising)

Use meetings as formal forums to give info, use informal meetings one-on-one sessions to get input.

(Danish expatriate, 45–49 years old, Consulting)

Meetings had to be extensively prepared in one to one or small groups meeting where decision are more openly discussed and the general meeting has the sole function to sanction and make official the decisions taken in the private sessions.

(Italian expatriate, 30–34 years old, Energy)

Valuable feedback of individual employee on issues at hand in one-to-one session and not in team sessions necessary, need to establish a personal connection with employees as role model to motivate.

(Swiss expatriate, 45–49 years old, High-Tech Electronics and Materials)

Constructive criticism in a group environment is hard to get, use of WeChat or other tools is much more efficient to collect information.

(Swiss expatriate, 30–34 years old, Automotive Services)

In addition to building trusting relationships and creating a safe environment, the expatriates suggested various other approaches suited to encourage their Chinese employees to express their views and to share ideas. For example, a British expatriate suggested asking employees to express their viewpoints on a situation first to make them feel open to talk. He said the following:

Ask for people's viewpoints on a situation before defining the challenge. This ensures people feel open to talk things through rather than feel judged to have a solution.

(British expatriate, 40–44 years old, Advertising)

Another British expatriate had made his Chinese staff open up about their work problems by breaking down the barriers between boss and employee. He said the following:

...the adjustment I had to make was to initially breakdown the boss employee barrier, by taking time once a week to get out of my office and walk and talk to each team member. This initially was frowned upon by the staff as they thought I was a crazy westerner trying to make friends, but after a while and many portions of silence I began to understand my staff from a professional and personal level while they began to open up about what they felt frustrated with within their working day and disclose some of the problems they encountered which would have normally been hidden or they would deal with on their own.

(British expatriate, 45–49 years old, Trading/ Recruitment)

An American expatriate said that he had been successful in making his Chinese subordinates talk to him and each other by holding daily meetings. He explained his approach in the following quote:

I try hard to get my Chinese people to open up and feel comfortable. To do so I cannot be harsh or short with answers. I am usually very quick with a response but now I wait longer to gauge reactions and see how the people feel... I had daily meeting with my staff to get them to talk to each other and me with problems. It took time but after a month or two the people started to discuss problems and it was successful as they started to find ways to help themselves and other team members.

(American expatriate, 55–59 years old, Manufacturing)

A British expatriate said that a communication forum had succeeded in making their Chinese employees communicate with each other and with their managers. He said the following:

Direct questioning to solve an issue was often perceived as confrontation...We developed a communication forum where the managers would explain the problems they were facing—then the mistakes they had made—and then the steps they took to resolve the mistake. Then we would encourage the team members to contribute in the same format. 2 things happened, the teams started to communicate with each other and with management—and we identified issues we were not aware of in the operations—the positive affect was that issue identification and owner-ship were embraced—and then we were able to coach the teams to put effective resolution in place.

(British expatriate, 40–44 years old, Financial Services)

The communication forum and the daily meeting used by the British and American expatriates had given their Chinese employees the confidence to start to discuss and communicate their problems by providing opportunities to "learn and practice" how to share ideas and voice concerns, thus going a step further than merely conveying to Chinese employees the importance of doing so, which is likely to be less effective, as most of them are not accustomed to being vocal in sharing their viewpoints and thus do not feel comfortable in doing so.

Encourage Proactiveness and Initiative by Setting Performance Targets, Communicating One's Own Expectations of Initiative Taking, Rewarding Employees, Delegating Responsibility, and Training Employees to Work on Their Own

As reported in Chapter 6, the second most mentioned challenging characteristic of Chinese employees was their low degree of proactiveness and initiative. Many expatriates stated that most of their Chinese employees rarely took initiatives or acted proactively to deal with tasks, issues, and problems; instead, they expected to be given instructions as to how to complete a task. To encourage proactiveness and initiative, the expatriates had used and suggested various approaches, the main of which are reported in the following:

Setting performance targets. Some expatriates said that they had found setting and agreeing on performance targets to be one of the best ways to foster proactiveness and initiative in their employees, as they would find ways to meet such targets. An American expatriate said the following:

> *I found the best way is to list all the targets or "success criteria" for a project or task. Once we get everyone to agree on targets, then it is easier to allow people to find their own solution that meets those targets. Nevertheless, micro-management of teams is still necessary to make sure everyone is proceeding properly.*
>
> (American expatriate, 55–59 years old, Automotive and Energy)

Clearly communicating one's expectations in regard to initiative

As mentioned at the beginning of this section, many expatriates said that most of their Chinese employees rarely took initiative; instead, they expected to be given instructions as to how to complete a task. Some expatriates suggested that, to remedy this situation, it would be necessary to convey to the employees the management's expectation of them taking initiatives. They said the following:

Managers are suggested to clearly communicate that they expect employees to take initiatives.

(No demographic information)

In China I have had to make certain expectations that we assume are normal in western office environments clear. Below I've described two main areas I try and work with my Chinese directs on... 1. Be proactive. It's a complex lesson, but there are two parts. One, There's no need to grin and bear a fundamentally flawed work situation. If there is something wrong, they should let someone know as soon as possible. Two, employees are expected to assess whether they actually need someone's help to fix a work problem. If there is a problem (or opportunity) that they can make forward progress on, then they have a responsibility to try and tackle that challenge...

(American expatriate, 25–29 years old, Business Intelligence)

Rewarding employees who take initiatives

Some expatriates had engaged in and suggested rewarding employees for taking initiatives by means of, for example, financial rewards and flexible working hours. They said the following:

Most of the time they see no benefit to making improvements and only a chance to make a mistake. You must reward the employees that take initiative and stand behind them to take responsibility if something goes wrong. I develop self-motivated employees especially the ones that are able to grasp the company direction and make cross functional process changes. Non-self-motivated employees are given tasks and monitored yet are encouraged to participate in the change process and being team members for various projects.

(American expatriate, 50–54 years old, Music Equipment Manufacturing)

I give people the opportunity to learn and make mistakes, show that you care for them and reward them for speaking out, providing input. It doesn't happen overnight. Then again, I also need to learn and adjust to be effective so it is a two-way street approach to tackle this challenge.

(Dutch expatriate, 50–54 years old, Computer and Machinery)

Try to change so employees can try to think more for themselves by empowering them. It helped although there have been errors along the way but we've been patient and this has paid off in time. One way has been to give stock options to key employees within the organization as well as give them free flexibility in the working hours with the hope to get better productivity.

(Venezuelan expatriate, 40–44 years old, Marketing)

Delegating responsibility and training employees to work on their own

Many expatriates said that, in order to develop their Chinese employees' proactiveness and initiative, they had invested them with responsibilities and asked them to make decisions and solve problems themselves, while providing training or coaching along the way. They stated the following:

...the biggest change has to be to allow them to work on their own volition. Teaching to work more independently without the need to refer back for decisions...coaching the personnel in what they are responsible for, why this was their responsibility and instituting a system where the direct managers did not point blame in the case of a wrong decision, instead coached personnel why they thought this was a bad or wrong decision.

(British expatriate, 40–44 years old, Metal)

Tried to give more responsibility and decision-making by themselves and implement open feedback.

(German expatriate, 30–33 years old, Executive Search/HR Consulting)

I always delegate as much as it is safe to do so. I let them work the problem and don't micro-manage them. I want the result to be in a certain range—the rest is up to them. Some people are not comfortable with this kind of "freedom"—but only by letting them make mistakes employees will have a greater understanding of the impact of their actions (or no actions for that matter). Some people like this creative atmosphere and grow—not quickly—but sustainably—then you can have people working for you 10–15 years (and of course you have to pay fair).

(Austrian expatriate, 45–49 years old, Trade)

I give staff freedom, but they have to be able to deal with this freedom. To a certain extent I try to coach them, this takes more time and effort in China than in my home country.

(Dutch expatriate, 40–44 years old, Architecture/Construction)

I put more and more responsibilities on them. Otherwise I would have to make all decisions by myself. Now they decide on daily business by themselves and only report the results to me. In the beginning they were not used to taking responsibilities at all but now it works very well.

(German expatriate, 55–59 years old, Automotive)

Main change was giving employees enough space and confidence to make their own opinions, devise their own solutions, and have a comfortable and non-critical environment in which to err safely.

(No demographic information)

Instead of giving a direct action and solution and I guide my team to find the solution on their own. I do so by asking questions.

(Brazilian expatriate, 25–29 years old, Chemicals)

I have tried to make my Chinese staff more autonomous and give them the power and flexibility to achieve goals using their own methods. I have also encouraged staff to look further than the immediate goal and try to "think like a boss" and figure out what the next step would be. This is often met with mixed results and generally the Chinese staff prefer a step-by-step guide to how to do their job.

(Australian expatriate, 35–39 years old, Entertainment)

Enhance Accountability by Setting and Communicating Responsibilities, Providing Training, Giving Rewards, Accepting and Encouraging Mistakes, and Using a Checking System

As reported in Chapter 6, the ninth most challenging characteristic of Chinese employees mentioned by the expatriate managers was their lower accountability when compared with their counterparts in their own home countries. They said that most of their Chinese employees were unwilling to take, or afraid of taking, responsibility and that they did not seem to understand that they were accountable for any tasks delegated to them, and thus were not prepared to take responsibility. To enhance their accountability, the expatriates had taken and suggested several approaches. This section reports the main ones.

Setting and communicating responsibilities

An approach that had been taken and suggested to enhance the employees' sense of ownership and accountability was setting and communicating responsibilities. Some expatriates suggested that responsibilities needed to be set and communicated clearly to ensure that their employees would understand them. Some expatriates said that they had had to clearly and explicitly communicate any responsibilities to make employees understand what was expected of them. The following quotes illustrate their suggestions and experiences:

> *Sense of ownership and accountability are lower. Responsibilities need to be set clearly. If they are not set, some employees will just wait without asking.*

> (Italian expatriate, 40–44 years old, Manufacturing)

> *Talk to them clearly about importance of each task and their job responsibility in the company. Make them understand that the company can only be successful if everybody does his work well and works together.*

> (Swiss expatriate, 45–49 years old, Manufacturing)

We shifted from having "Job Descriptions" to "Employee Accountability Statements". The idea is to have each employee understand what are the desired "end result" opposed to assigning specific tasks.

(Canadian expatriate, 45–49 years old, Food and Beverage)

I had to clarify much more explicitly the boundaries of responsibility I expect each position to cover and act upon.

(Italian expatriate, 30–34 years old, Energy)

We have consciously tried to change the organization to utilize the inherent strengths and skills of our Chinese team. We have been explicit about the manner and specifically what the US organization needs to do differently, or not at all, to allow the Chinese team to take the leadership and responsibility.

(Australian expatriate, 40–44 years old, Building Products)

One thing that I have very much worked on to change is "responsibility" as a team and owning problems in the office...Too often I have heard "meiyoubanfa" (Chinese for "No way possible"). Building a cohesive team who mutually trust, from my experience, has been a real challenge. How I went about changing things—spent more time individually with members to understand how they feel about responsibility, while also explaining that us, as a company, a small one, we need to take ownership and make decisions by our own sometimes. Getting the team to understand that they can make a decision (within boundaries) was a big step in them owning their position in our company.

(Australian expatriate, 30–34 years old, Training and Development)

Providing training and coaching

Another approach that had been taken and suggested to enhance the employees' sense of ownership and accountability had involved providing them with training, coaching, and/or mentoring. The following quotes illustrate some of the expatriates' approaches:

I gave my employees responsibility and trained them to take pride in their own projects. I would sometimes not help them in times where I felt it was better for them to learn by making mistakes.

(American expatriate, 30–34 years old, Hospitality)

I have and I am changing the work practice within my organization... The efficiency and accountability in the organization were not at the level I expected. I have been changing by delegating responsibility and coaching the managers.

(Finnish expatriate, 40–44 years old, Industrial Automation)

Changing the responsibilities to allow ownership is a challenge, but supporting the employees in their decisions, even if sometimes their decisions may not be the right ones, but coaching rather than telling usually results in the correct decision.

(British expatriate, 40–44 years old, Metals)

...to encourage the employee to take over responsibility for planning and clearly define goals for the work to do. The need for this change was initiated by increasing the efficiency. I achieved this change by daily training to develop an independent working style. The challenge is to do it continuously over a long period of time.

(Dutch expatriate, 40–44 years old, Industry and Engineering)

...try to get them to plan and take more responsibility. Provide project management templates, starting with small projects for them to complete. Find they need a lot more hand holding to get the hang of it. Of course, give them a bit of a break since they have to do this in foreign language. Also give them room to make mistakes and learn from them.

(American expatriate, 45–59 years old,
Consulting/Technology Transfer)

I've tried to encourage them to challenge more, and I've tried to encourage them to feel more ownership and sense of personal responsibility for the overall team and its objectives, rather than just their individual objectives. There are many ways to do this, including personal mentoring, group events, providing encouragement and criticism of individuals and the whole team in equal measure. And being very careful to model behaviors myself that I want team members to display.

(British expatriate, 35–39 years old, Government)

Rewarding and encouraging employees to take responsibility

Some expatriates had engaged in and suggested motivating employees to take responsibility by presenting them with the possibility of, for example, promotions and/or pay rises. They said the following:

Chinese company culture has a tendency to try to upwards delegate all decisions if possible—the boss decides...It takes effort to counter this by building trust in employees to take responsibility and reward them for independent and proactive work.

(Finnish expatriate, 35–39 years old, Steel)

The most important thing for me to change was to get the managers below me to take responsibility for their work and to readily lead projects...At first I tried to understand better why they didn't want to take responsibility. Once this was done I had to work on two aspects to get them to develop: Practical and Mental. The practical side meant giving them a career development road map to show that I was interested in helping them develop and not just giving them more work to do; so if they met targets they could expect a promotion and pay rise. It also meant working closely with them to go through their workload, and then give them clear responsibilities, while moving some tasks to other people. Mental was creating the right atmosphere for them to take responsibility and be willing to lead. This meant that they had to feel safe in making decisions in the knowledge that I would support them if they failed and not throw them down a hole; also that they should get achievement for their efforts.

(British expatriate, 25–29 years old, Green Energy)

Accepting and valuing mistakes

Some expatriates stated that, in order to overcome their Chinese employees' fear of failure or of making mistakes when taking responsibility, they would suggest, or had engaged in, conveying to them that mistakes were acceptable and even valued as learning opportunities. They said the following:

Making mistakes needs to be made acceptable and even encouraged.

(Finnish expatriate, 35–39 years old, Steel)

Deploy tasks to the teams to allow autonomy and development of solutions by teams...do not punish failure! Prompt it to learn by it without consequences.

(British expatriate, 55–59 years old, Domestic Appliances)

Chinese employees are afraid of making mistakes. I always tell them that I would be disappointed if they don't make mistakes, because that means they haven't tried something new.

(German expatriate, 45–49 years old, Consulting)

I wouldn't say I managed to change them, but they gained in confidence and took more responsibilities. I had to reassure them that a mistake is not a big deal, it is also the way to learn.

(French expatriate, 25–29 years old, Architecture)

I have embraced a number of things...Reward risk and—if done for the right reason—don't criticize failure.

(British expatriate, 35–39 years old, Advertising)

Using a checking system

Some expatriates said that they had used a checking system or process to enable their employees to identify any problems themselves and to help build a sense of responsibility. They described their approaches in the following statements:

I am trying to get people to take more responsibility for their work and the mistakes. Sometimes there was an attitude of I'll do the work and it is someone else's job to see if there are any mistakes. If you design the work so that the mistakes are clearly obvious and the person realizes that mistakes will be caught and that they will be held responsible then things get better. It takes a lot of time to design a good process so that mistakes are easily recognizable. Also I believe putting in checklists for people to follow and sign off builds responsibility. If you say you went through the checklist, but the error still got through, it is fairly obvious you lied about following the checklist and should be held accountable.

(American expatriate, 40–44 years old, Furniture Trading/
Manufacturing)

We built tools for and a weekly system to review tasks, update status and assign responsibility. We first showed the tools, how to use them and explained why this was important. Challenges included our leaders not accepting it at first, and not using it. If they didn't use it, others didn't follow. Over time, they saw more problems without the system, and we encouraged them to use the system, suggesting it could help their current time and project management challenges.

(American expatriate, 25–29 years old, Education)

Overcome Resistance to Change by Changing the Group, Not the Individual

The implementation and management of change are among the items found on a business leader's list of key tasks. Like their Western counterparts, most Chinese employees dislike change. As reported in Chapter 6, a great number of the expatriates conveyed the challenges linked to trying to change their Chinese employees in terms of their characteristics, such as their high respect for hierarchy and authority, lower initiative, reservedness and inexpressiveness in communication, and lower propensity toward accountability. The expatriates had taken various approaches to try to do so. For example, as reported in the last section, they had tried to enhance their Chinese employees' accountability by taking approaches such as setting and communicating responsibilities, providing training, and giving rewards.

Some expatriates suggested that, when implementing changes, as a general rule, it would be more effective to do so at the group level, rather than at the individual one. This can be explained by the Chinese collectivist culture, which emphasizes interdependence, conformity, belongingness, and obedience. This culture tends to make most Chinese people behave in socially and collectively accepted ways and to feel more comfortable and more willing to accept and make changes when they see their peers also doing so. Any change falling out of the comfort zone of Chinese employees would be difficult to implement. Two expatriates shared their experiences of implementing changes at the group level:

> *I have found that changes are more successful if they are carried out in group sessions rather than individual. The reason is simple. Chinese people thrive more in group participation where success is shared and celebrated as a team. Targeting individuals in my experience came across as the boss isolating the abilities and performance of one individual which lead to a loss of face value.*

> (New Zealander expatriate, 35–39 years old, Hospitality)

> *I have run a number of change initiatives in our China firm, including introducing new technology, and cultural changes…It is not easy in China, as I find there is a general resistance to change. People watch what their peers are doing very carefully, and often do not want to be the first to change. Therefore, you have to persuade a few people of the benefits at first, and then start to communicate these benefits to a wider community. Also, sometimes you have to take a very draconian approach by saying everybody must do something differently immediately, no exceptions. If you can get everyone to move at the same time then people feel more comfortable as they feel they are following orders and also following the group.*

> (British expatriate, 40–44 years old, Financial/Accounting)

Summary

This chapter presented the key insights and suggestions provided by the expatriate business leaders for effectively managing and leading Chinese employees. Their suggestions were as follows:

- **Understand Chinese cultural values and be sensitive to cultural differences.** Many of the expatriate managers affirmed that Western management methods rarely work in China if unmodified. They highlighted the critical importance of understanding Chinese cultural values, being sensitive to cultural differences, and adjusting one's own leadership. This would help expatriate managers exhibit culturally acceptable behaviors and make their Chinese staff feel comfortable and that their expatriate managers were interested in them and their country. Among the various Chinese cultural values, the importance of understanding the concepts of face and *guanxi* was emphasized.

- **Avoid employee loss of face by providing indirect feedback in private settings.** Many of the expatriates observed that their Chinese employees saw upholding "face" as being extremely important; thus, they suggested avoiding any situations that might lead to staff losing face. In particular, they suggested that any critical or negative feedback should be conveyed to Chinese employees in a highly indirect and nonconfrontational way, in private, and on a one-to-one basis.

- **Build personal *guanxi* (relationships) with Chinese employees.** *Guanxi* (i.e., relationships) plays a very important role in Chinese people's social and working lives; Chinese *guanxi* is always based on trust and built up from and on a "personal" level. Many of the expatriate senior managers said that building and maintaining good "personal" relationships/*guanxi* with Chinese subordinates is important for leading them. Some expatriates suggested the careful maintenance of fairness and avoidance of favoritism to be necessary when building personal relationships and socializing with employees.

- **Adjust one's own leadership or fail.** Many expatriates said that adjusting one's own leadership approach according to Chinese culture and environment is crucial when leading/managing Chinese employees. This is because such an adjustment will show understanding and flexibility and help to build credibility. Some respondent managers suggested that it would be beneficial for expatriates to adjust to the Chinese environment while, at the same time, maintaining some Western management approaches that they considered to be effective. Most (79.8%) of the expatriates who took part in my research had simultaneously adjusted their own leadership approach and changed (or tried to change) their Chinese employees, as reported in Chapter 7.

- **Adopt a more paternalistic leadership approach.** Given that most Chinese employees expect their leaders not only to take decisive action, provide instructions for improvement, and reprimand for poor performance but also to provide their subordinates with care, support, and protection in both the work and non-work domains, some respondent managers suggested that expatriate leaders should ideally adopt a paternalistic leadership style, which combines strong authority and fatherly benevolence. Several expatriates said that they had adjusted their leadership style to act as a father/mother (or elder brother/sister) figure. The Chinese employees I interviewed generally agreed that the paternalistic leadership is a style that is acceptable for many Chinese employees, but they said that the authoritative and top-down aspect of paternalistic leadership would not be appropriate for some employees such as those holding high management positions, those who are high-performers, and those who believe in equal employee–manager relations.

- **Learn and master the Chinese language.** Several expatriates suggested that learning to speak Chinese would yield various benefits— e.g., improve working relationships and overall business operations, help overcome culture- and language-related challenges, help better communicate, make employees feel comfortable, and create a more motivated and happier workforce.

- **Break down tasks into small chunks and monitor progress.** Instead of empowering and delegating responsibilities, some expatriates suggested breaking down tasks into small chunks, giving employees complete and clear instructions, and regularly following up on the work progress in order to ensure task completion. Although this had been seen as a challenge, some expatriates stated that their efforts in this direction had paid off, as the situation had taken a turn for the better once their employees had reached a certain level.

- **Give clear instructions and check that they have been understood.**
  Many of the expatriates suggested giving Chinese employees complete and specific instructions and explaining the intended outcomes. They did so because they had observed that their Chinese employees were efficient when given such information. In addition, they highlighted the importance of checking whether all instructions had been correctly understood because many of their Chinese employees would not ask for clarification if they had not.

- **Build trusting relationships and create a safe environment conducive to open communication.** Several expatriates stated that gaining the trust of their Chinese employees and providing a safe environment had been the two key conditions for them to feel comfortable in sharing their views and voice their concerns. The expatriates said that, although gaining the trust of their Chinese employees had been a long and on-going process, once a trusting relationship had been established, many good things had followed (e.g., loyalty and commitment). A common method whereby some expatriates had created a safe environment for their Chinese employees to share their ideas had involved private or one-to-one sessions. The expatriates had taken and suggested various other approaches to encourage their Chinese employees to express their views and share ideas, such as removing the barriers between boss and employee and setting up communication forums and daily meetings.

- **Encourage proactiveness and initiative by setting performance targets, communicating expectations of initiative taking, rewarding employees, delegating responsibility, and training employees to work on their own.** To encourage proactiveness and initiative, the expatriates had taken and suggested various approaches. The main ones had included setting and agreeing on performance targets and letting their employees find their own ways to meet them; clearly making their employees aware that they were expected to take initiatives when performing their tasks; rewarding those employees who had taken initiatives; and allocating responsibilities to their employees and asking them to make decisions and solve problems on their own while, at the same time, providing training or coaching along the way.

- **Enhance accountability by setting and communicating responsibilities, providing training, rewarding, accepting and encouraging mistakes, and using a checking system.** The expatriates had taken several approaches to enhance their employees' sense of ownership and accountability, including setting and clearly communicating their responsibilities; providing them with training, coaching, and/or mentoring; rewarding them for taking responsibilities; conveying the acceptability of mistakes and even their valorization as learning opportunities to overcome their fear of failure; and using a checking system to help develop a sense of responsibility.

- **Overcome resistance to change by changing the group, not the individual.** Like their Western counterparts, most Chinese employees dislike change. Some expatriates suggested that the implementation of changes, as a general rule, would be more effective at the group level, rather than at the individual one. This can be explained by the collectivist Chinese culture, in which interdependence, conformity, belongingness, and obedience are emphasized. Their collectivist culture tends to make most Chinese people behave in socially and collectively accepted ways and to feel more comfortable and be more willing to accept and make changes when their peers are also doing so.

Chapter 10

Conclusion

Effective cross-cultural leadership is crucial for the operation of international businesses. Many Western expatriate managers assigned to work in China may have found it challenging to lead and manage Chinese employees, who hold cultural values, beliefs, and work attitudes that are rather different from their own and from those of employees in their home country and/or in other countries in which they had previously worked. Such differences make it important for expatriate business leaders to understand Chinese cultural values and employee work behaviors and expectations of leaders, and to ensure that their own management and leadership approaches are compatible with local culture and practices.

In this book, I have presented theories, concepts, research findings, and the views, experiences, and suggestions conveyed by 391 expatriate senior managers directly involved in leading and managing Chinese employees. I hope that readers will find the information and analyses presented in this book to be useful. I hope that this book will help those expatriate managers who are currently leading or working with Chinese employees understand the latter's unique values and attitudes and that the practical insights given by the expatriate senior managers will provide them with some corroboration of their own thoughts and approaches, give them some new perspectives, and/or inspire them to lead their Chinese employees in new, different, or more effective ways. I further hope this book will provide researchers and management consultants with useful information regarding the work attitudes and behaviors of Chinese employees and issues related to cross-cultural leadership and leadership behavior adjustment, and on how the fit between observed and demonstrated leadership behaviors is associated with employee satisfaction. I finally hope that this book will inspire more researchers to conduct cross-cultural leadership research aimed at uncovering further insights into this important area of international management.

In this conclusion chapter, I highlight three key themes stemming from the research findings reported in this book and discuss their significance for leading and managing Chinese employees:

(1) the need to understand Chinese cultural values, social relations, and exchange rules;
(2) paternalistic leadership as the style expected by most Chinese employees; and
(3) the need for cross-cultural leadership adjustment.

The Need to Understand Chinese Cultural Values, Social Relations, and Exchange Rules

As cross-cultural business leadership involves influencing and leading host country employees, a key to effectively lead in cross-cultural contexts is to understand the drivers of host country employee attitudes, behaviors, and expectations. Traditional Chinese philosophy and cultural values/characteristics (e.g., strong collectivism, high acceptance of hierarchy, high power distance between managers and employees, and the high value placed on harmonious relationships) have influenced the work attitudes and behaviors of Chinese workers and their expectation of leadership (see Chapters 4 and 8). To be effective leaders in China, expatriate business managers thus need to gain a good understanding of Chinese cultural values, social relations, and exchange rules. The more expatriate managers succeed in doing so, the more competent they will be in their working relationships with their Chinese employees. Without a proper understanding, expatriate managers are likely to make embarrassing mistakes, behave in socially unacceptable ways, and cause misunderstandings when leading and managing Chinese employees.

The four doctrines of Confucianism (i.e., *xiao, wu lun, ren,* and *li*) and the three key Chinese cultural values (i.e., *guanxi, mianzi, and renqing*) discussed in Chapter 4 wield a strong influence on traditional Chinese leadership, employees' expectations of leaders, Chinese social relations and exchange rules, and the work attitudes and behaviors of Chinese employees. A good understanding of Chinese doctrines and cultural values should thus help expatriate managers develop effective strategies to lead and manage their Chinese employees.

As reported in Chapter 9, one of the key suggestions made by the 391 expatriate senior managers to effectively lead in China was **learning Chinese cultural values and being sensitive to cultural differences**. They highlighted the critical importance of understanding and respecting Chinese cultural and societal norms and of being sensitive to cultural differences. They said that, by doing so, expatriate managers would be better able to exhibit culturally acceptable behaviors, make their Chinese staff feel comfortable, and show that they have an interest in them and their country, all of which would lead to a more motivated and happier workforce. They also said that failing to do so would lead to negative consequences, such as difficulties in maintaining relationships with Chinese staff, losing the respect of one's team, struggling to manage effectively, and facing reductions in productivity and increases in staff turnover.

Paternalistic Leadership as the Style Expected by most Chinese Employees

In Chapter 5, I explained that Chinese cultural values and traditions have given rise to a paternalistic leadership style and discussed how the key reason for the long acceptance and practice of this style in China is its alignment with the Chinese cultural characteristics of high collectivism, high-power distance, and high value attributed to strong family bonds. As described in Chapter 5, the paternalistic leadership style combines the strong imposition of discipline and authority with fatherly benevolence and moral integrity; in other words, it is a paternal style in which strong authority is combined with concern and consideration for subordinates' personal well-being. Research shows that the paternalistic leadership style is the one most prevalently used in China and that most Chinese employees expect and even prefer their leaders to demonstrate it; that is, they expect their leaders to be both benevolent and authoritarian, showing not only consideration for their followers, but also the ability to take decisive action (see Chapters 4, 5, and 8).

In Chapter 5, I discussed that, although the paternalistic leadership style has been the subject of various negative criticisms from Western scholars (e.g., for issues related to control over subordinates, the intent behind benevolent behaviors, and the unequal power relationship between leaders and their subordinates), research has shown it to be directly related to numerous positive employee work outcomes (e.g., loyalty, commitment, and job satisfaction), particularly when employees have a high respect for hierarchy and a high reliance on leaders for resources. The findings of such research suggest that it would be advantageous for expatriate business leaders to adopt the paternalistic leadership style when leading and managing Chinese employees because high collectivism and high acceptance of hierarchy are features of the local culture and Chinese employees tend to see the organization for which they work as a family and thus expect their employers to be invested in their welfare.

Accordingly, a key suggestion made by the 391 expatriate senior managers for effectively leading in China did indeed point at the **adoption of a more paternalistic leadership approach** (see Chapter 9). This was due to their observation that most of their Chinese employees expected their leaders not only to be capable of taking decisive action, providing instructions for improvement, and reprimanding for poor performance but also to provide them with care, support, and protection in both the work and non-work domains. Their suggestion was thus aimed at meeting their employees' expectations of a leader, which is key to gaining employee cooperation, loyalty, and satisfaction.

In Chapter 8, I reported that those Chinese employees who took part in my research expected their expatriate supervisors to demonstrate authority and fatherly benevolence (i.e., high task- and relations-oriented leadership behaviors) and that their satisfaction with their expatriate supervisors was high when the latter's leadership behaviors matched their expectations. The implication of this finding is clear: to enhance the positive emotional state felt by Chinese employees toward their expatriate supervisors, the latter need to meet their expectations of a leader.

The Chinese employees I interviewed agreed that the paternalistic leadership style is acceptable for many Chinese employees; nevertheless, they pointed out that the authoritative and top-down aspects of the paternalistic leadership style would not be appropriate for some employees, for example, those holding high management positions, those who are high-performers, and those who believe in equal employee–manager relations (see Chapter 9).

The above jointly suggest that a paternalistic leadership approach would help expatriate managers meet the expectations of "most" of their Chinese employees and enhance the positive emotions felt by the latter towards them. However, expatriate managers would need to minimize the top-down and authoritarian aspects of such an approach for some employees, for example, those who are highly self-motivated, those who want high job autonomy, and those who believe in equal employee-manager relations.

The Need for Cross-Cultural Leadership Adjustment (Leadership Adjustment & Subordinate Change)

In Chapter 7, I reported my research findings pertaining to the degree and pattern whereby the 391 expatriate senior managers had adjusted in response to Chinese culture, the characteristics of their Chinese employees, and their own standards and perceptions. I analyzed two dimensions of their adjustment: (i) the extent to which they had changed their own leadership approaches (leadership adjustment) and (ii) the extent to which they had changed (or had attempted to change) the work values and behaviors of their Chinese subordinates (subordinate change). The related findings are inspiring, as they show that the sample expatriate senior managers had *significantly* adjusted their leadership behaviors when leading/managing Chinese employees and that an overriding majority of them (79.1%) had simultaneously adjusted their own leadership approach *and* changed (or tried to change) their Chinese employees, thus displaying the *exploration* pattern of adjustment.

The *exploration* pattern of adjustment had been exhibited by such a high proportion of the expatriate senior managers due to their need to respond to various internal and external demands relating to the following: (1) their own standards and perceptions (e.g., their standards of work quality; their perceptions of the best way to lead, and the need to adapt to local culture and to meet the expectations of Chinese employees); (2) local culture and employee characteristics (e.g., reservedness in communication, high dependence, and low proactiveness); and (3) the need to improve employee and organizational performance (see Chapter 7).

The results of the statistical analyses reported in Chapter 8 show that the satisfaction of Chinese employees toward their expatriate supervisors is high when the latter's leadership behaviors match their expectations. The result suggests the need to adjust leadership behaviors to match employee expectations. When working in China, where the expectations of leaders may differ substantially from those found in their home countries, expatriate managers should thus adjust their own leadership approaches in order to meet the expectations of their Chinese employees and to enhance the positive emotional state the latter feel toward them.

As reported in Chapter 9, one of the key suggestions made by the 391 expatriate senior managers to lead/manage Chinese employees effectively was **adjusting one's own leadership behaviors** to fit the Chinese environment. Some of the expatriates expressed the belief that such adjustment is essential to avoid failure. Many of them said that adjusting to the Chinese culture, situation, and environment is important in order to show understanding and flexibility and build credibility. Some of the expatriates suggested that it would be beneficial for expatriates to adjust to the Chinese environment while maintaining some Western management approaches that they considered to be effective, which is in consistent with what most (79.8%) of them had actually done—they had adjusted their own leadership approach and, at the same time, had changed (or had tried to change) their Chinese employees in relation to accepting and adopting Western work ideas and practices, as reported in Chapter 7.

The need for cross-cultural leadership adjustment is supported by both empirical research and leadership theories. As discussed above, the research findings reported in Chapters 7, 8, and 9 underline the importance of making leadership adjustments, making changes to Chinese subordinates, and adapting one's leadership style to that expected by Chinese employees in order to enhance their satisfaction toward their expatriate supervisors and improve individual and organizational efficiency. The leadership theories discussed in Chapter 2—such as the Situational Leadership Theories (SLTs), Implicit Leadership Theory (ILT), and Culturally Endorsed Implicit Theories of Leadership (CLTs)—suggest that leaders should be adaptable/flexible and demonstrate leadership in ways that match employees' cultural expectations in order to effectively manage and lead people in unfamiliar cultural settings.

The following statements help highlight the need for cross-cultural adjustment.

The achievement of business goals *will be determined by the role, strength, quality, and adaptability of the leadership demonstrated by their senior managers, whose key task is to deliver results by leading people* (Tsai, 2018: 108).

Leaders must be flexible, responsive, and adaptive in order to *balance competing demands and reconcile tradeoffs among different performance determinants* (Yukl & Lepsinger, 2004: 203).

Final Words

As an overall conclusion, the research findings and practical insights presented in this book show that, to lead and manage Chinese employees effectively, it is necessary to have a good understanding of Chinese cultural values, of the work attitudes and values of Chinese employees, and of their expectations of leaders, and to adjust one's own leadership approaches to cater for the expectations of Chinese employees and to conform to local societal norms. This indicates that effective cross-cultural leadership cannot be divorced from cultural contexts and follower expectations, suggesting that a mindset of openness to new situations, a readiness to change one's own leadership behaviors, and a conformation to local societal expectations are necessary to work in China. Indeed, international management research has shown that leadership behaviors are interpreted and evaluated differently in different cultural environments, depending on variations in people's ideas of the ideal leader, with some leadership styles being preferred over others. Deviating from local practices and societal expectations may cause employees to exhibit low satisfaction, high resistance, diminished respect, and high turnover, and cause leaders to be ineffective.

The following quotes from my research participants provide some positive notes for leading and managing Chinese employees. I hope that those expatriate managers who are currently working or who will be working in China will find them encouraging.

If you are open to the culture of China and adjust yourself, surprisingly it can be quite enjoyable and easy to lead Chinese staff.

(Germany expatriate, 25–29 years old, Consulting)

It is pleasant working with Chinese employees as they are always eager to learn.

(Belgian expatriate, 50–54 years old, Pharmaceuticals)

Chinese employees are hard working, very good at following instructions, and very efficient in completing tasks if instructions are clear. These have been contributed directly to organisational efficiency.

(No demographic information)

Compared to my home country Chinese employees are willing to go to greater length to succeed and are much more flexible with regard to work hours to accomplish tasks.

(Danish expatriate, 55–59 years old, Management Consulting)

... I have learned to adapt to and have enjoyed the steep learning curve ...

(South African expatriate, 30–34 years old, Water Filtration)

With nearly 30 years of expatriate management under my belt, my leadership approach is most likely classified as paternalistic and autocratic. I enjoy the coaching, counselling and training of my teams and have always prided myself on this ...

(Dutch expatriate, 40–44 years old, Hospitality)

References

Tsai, C.-J. (2018). *Cross-Cultural Business Leadership in Thailand: Insights from 178 Expatriate Senior Managers*. CreateSpace Independent Publishing (available in paperback and on Amazon).

Yukl, G. A., & Lepsinger, R. (2004). *Flexible Leadership: Creating Value by Balancing Multiple Challenges and Choices*. San Francisco: Jossey-Bass.

Appendix A

Expatriate Leader Survey (ELS)

Cross-Cultural Leadership

Expatriate Manager Survey

Dear Sir/Madam,

We would like to thank you in advance for taking the time to complete this questionnaire, which is part of the research project, "Cross-cultural leadership". Your responses will help us understand your leadership approach and your experience in leading Chinese subordinates.

Please be assured that your responses will be treated in the strictest confidence and used solely for research purposes. At no point will your name and the name of the company be revealed. The questionnaire should take about 10–15 minutes to complete.

----

(1) **Is leading Chinese employees different from leading employees in your home country? What are the similarities and differences? What are the challenges?**

(2) **Have you had to adjust your leadership approach while working in China at all? If so, what have you had to adjust? What led to the need for adjustment? How have you adjusted?**

(3) Have you changed (or tried to change) your Chinese employees and/or the subsidiary's work practices? If so, what have you changed (or tried to change)? What led to the need for change? How did you go about changing it? What challenges have you faced?

(4) Please indicate to what extent (1) you currently use the following leadership behaviors, (2) you used the behavior before working in China, and (3) you perceive each behavior should be used when leading Chinese subordinates. Please write a number in each box, based on the following scale:

1 Extremely Small Extent	2 Very Small Extent	3 Small Extent	4 Moderate Extent	5 Large Extent	6 Very Large Extent	7 Extremely Large Extent	Currently in use	Used prior working in China	Should be used
Plan how to use personnel and resources to accomplish a task efficiently							□	□	□
Clarify what results are expected for a task....................							□	□	□
Explain priorities for different task objectives....................							□	□	□
Monitor operations and performance of subordinates............							□	□	□
Provide support and encouragement to subordinates..............							□	□	□
Provide recognition for achievements and contributions.........							□	□	□
Provide coaching and mentoring when appropriate..............							□	□	□
Consult with people on decisions affecting them.................							□	□	□
Empower people to take initiative in problem solving...........							□	□	□

(5) Please indicate the degree to which you agree or disagree with the following statements.

Please write a number for each statement, based on the following scale:

1	2	3	4	5	6	7
Strongly disagree	Moderately disagree	Slightly disagree	Neither agree nor disagree	Slightly agree	Moderately agree	Strongly agree

- I feel comfortable when I interact with people from different cultures.   □
  ....

- Meeting and getting to know people from different cultures is interesting   □
  and enjoyable.........

- I like to meet people from different cultures and become friends.   □
  ....

- I wish I had more friends from different cultures.   □
  ....

- People from different cultures have little understanding of my culture and way   □
  of thinking

- People from different cultures have very little to teach us about   □
  business.......................

- I can laugh at myself when I make a cultural faux   □
  pas...

- I like being with all kinds of people.   □
  ....

- I like to try new things.   □
  ....

- I could live anywhere and enjoy life.   □
  ....

- People who know me would describe me as a person who is intolerant of others'   □
  differences...

- When I meet people who are different from me, I tend to feel judgmental about   □
  their differences...

- When I meet people who are different from me, I am interested in learning more   □
  about them...

- As a foreigner/expatriate, it is important to adjust my behavior to the local   □
  norms...............

- In a different culture setting, leadership behavior should be changed to match   □
  the expectation of local employees. ....

- Leaders should adjust their leadership approach/behavior according   □
  to the characteristics of their followers. ....
- Business leaders should adopt a more authoritarian approach when working   □
  in a hierarchical society..
- Business leaders should adopt a more directive approach when working   □
  in a masculine culture. ....
- The greater the cultural difference between my home country and the host   □
  country, the greater the need to adjust my leadership behavior.
  ....
- I adapt well to China's business customs and norms..................................   □
- I interact well with Chinese coworkers...   □
- I have established good relationships with key Chinese business contacts.........   □

(6) Compared with the country where you grew up, to what extent is China similar in the following aspects?

(Tick one box in each row)	Not at all similar			Somewhat similar			Very similar
Everyday customs that must be followed……..............	□	□	□	□	□	□	□
Cultural values about what people can do and cannot do...	□	□	□	□	□	□	□
Cultural values about what is right or wrong……………..	□	□	□	□	□	□	□
The way people behave in the workplace………………...	□	□	□	□	□	□	□
Types of foods…………………………….	□	□	□	□	□	□	□
Clothes…………………………………….	□	□	□	□	□	□	□
Architecture……………………………….	□	□	□	□	□	□	□

(7) Please indicate the extent to which you have tried to influence *your Chinese subordinates* in the following aspects since working in this subsidiary:

(Tick one box in each row)	Extremely Small Extent	Very Small Extent	Small Extent	Moderate Extent	Large Extent	Very Large Extent	Extremely Large Extent
• Values—what is important to them in life……	□	□	□	□	□	□	□
• Attitudes—the things they like and dislike…...	□	□	□	□	□	□	□
• Career goals—their plans about their future….	□	□	□	□	□	□	□
• Personality—what sort of people they are……	□	□	□	□	□	□	□

(8) Please indicate the extent to which you have changed *your subordinates' work* in the following aspects since working in this subsidiary:

(Tick one box in each row)	Extremely Small Extent	Very Small Extent	Small Extent	Moderate Extent	Large Extent	Very Large Extent	Extremely Large Extent
• Work targets/objectives	□	□	□	□	□	□	□
• The methods used to achieve work targets/objectives	□	□	□	□	□	□	□
• The order in which different parts of the job are done	□	□	□	□	□	□	□
• With whom they deal with in order to carry out their work duties	□	□	□	□	□	□	□

(9) For each pair of characteristics, please circle the number which is the most accurate description of how your Chinese subordinates behave when interacting with you. (For example, if you feel they are friendly most of the time you might circle the number 6.)

Unfriendly	1 --- 2--- 3--- 4 --- 5 --- 6 --- 7	Friendly
Hostile	1 --- 2--- 3--- 4 --- 5 --- 6 --- 7	Supportive
Rejecting	1 --- 2--- 3--- 4 --- 5 --- 6 --- 7	Accepting
Frustrating	1 --- 2--- 3--- 4 --- 5 --- 6 --- 7	Satisfying
Unenthusiastic	1 --- 2--- 3--- 4 --- 5 --- 6 --- 7	Enthusiastic

(10) Please tell us something about your company and yourself. (The information given is anonymous and will only be used for interpreting the results of this survey.)

Are you male or female?
Male
Female

How old are you?

20–29	40–44	55–59
30–34	45–49	60 or over
35–39	50–54	

What is your nationality?

What is your job title?

How many Chinese subordinates report directly to you?

In what industry sector does your company operate?

How long have you worked in this company/subsidiary? (month/year)

How long have you worked in this country? (month/year)

How well do you speak Chinese?

Not at all	Conversational	Very fluent/bilingual
A small amount	Fluent	

Interested in knowing the views of your Chinese direct report subordinates on your leadership approach?

We are able to send you a statistical report!

All you need to do is leave your name and email address here (we will then send you a link to the Chinese Manager Survey with your name on it) and ask your subordinates to complete an online survey. The Chinese Manager Survey asks your subordinates a number of questions about their job, their views on your leadership approach, and their perceived relationship with you.

Your name:
Your email address:

If there are any comments that you would like to make on any of the above issues, please write them here.

Thank you very much for your help!

Appendix B

Chinese Manager Survey (CMS)

Survey of Cross-Cultural Leadership

Dear Sir/Madam,

We would like to thank you in advance for taking the time to complete this questionnaire, which is part of the research project, "Cross-cultural Leadership". We are researching senior expatriate managers' leadership behavior and would like to know your views on the leadership approach of your expatriate manager/supervisor — Mr./Ms. XXXXX.

Please be assured that your responses will be treated in the strictest confidence and used solely for research purposes. At no point will your name and the name of the company be revealed. The questionnaire should take about 10–15 minutes to complete.

A. You and the expatriate manager(see his/her name on the previous page)

A1. How long have you known the expatriate manager? _____
    months _____year(s)
A2. How long have you worked with him/her?_____ months
    _____year(s)

A3. Please indicate the extent to which you interact with him/her.
Please write a number for each statement, based on the following scale:

1	2	3	4	5	6	7
Hardly Ever	Rarely	Once in a While	Sometimes	Often	Very Often	Almost Always

- How often do you and he/she talk about work? ☐
- How often does he/she initiate a work-related interaction with you? ☐
- How often do you initiate a work-related interaction with him/her? ☐
- **How often do you interact with him/her informally or socially at work?** ☐

A4. For each pair of characteristics, please circle the number which is the most accurate description of how the expatriate manager behaves when interacting with you. (For example, if you feel the expatriate manager is friendly most of the time you might circle the number 6.)

Unfriendly	1 ----- 2----- 3----- 4 ----- 5 ----- 6 ----- 7	Friendly
Hostile	1 ----- 2----- 3----- 4 ----- 5 ----- 6 ----- 7	Supportive
Rejecting	1 ----- 2----- 3----- 4 ----- 5 ----- 6 ----- 7	Accepting
Frustrating	1 ----- 2----- 3----- 4 ----- 5 ----- 6 ----- 7	Satisfying
Unenthusiastic	1 ----- 2----- 3----- 4 ----- 5 ----- 6 ----- 7	Enthusiastic

A5. How far do you agree or disagree with the following statements?
Please write a number for each statement, based on the following scale:

1	2	3	4	5	6	7
Strongly disagree	Moderately disagree	Slightly disagree	Neither agree nor disagree	Slightly agree	Moderately agree	Strongly agree

- I always know how satisfied the expatriate manager is with what I do. ☐
- He/she completely understands my problems and needs. ☐
- He/she fully recognizes my potential. ☐
- He/she would certainly be personally inclined to help me solve problems in my work. ☐
- I can count on him/her to "bail me out" at his or her expense when I really need it. ☐

- I have enough confidence in him/her that I would certainly defend and justify ☐ his or her decisions if he or she were not present to do so.
- My working relationship with him/her is very effective. ☐
- The expatriate manager has adapted well to China's business customs ☐ and norms.
- The expatriate manager has established good relationships with key Chinese ☐ business contacts.
- The expatriate manager interacts well with Chinese coworkers. ☐

A6. Please indicate the extent to which the expatriate manager has influenced *you* in the following aspects:

(Tick one box in each row)	Extremely Small Extent	Very Small Extent	Small Extent	Moderate Extent	Large Extent	Very Large Extent	Extremely Large Extent
• Values—what is important to me in life	☐	☐	☐	☐	☐	☐	☐
• Attitudes—the things I like and dislike	☐	☐	☐	☐	☐	☐	☐
• Career goals—my plans about my future	☐	☐	☐	☐	☐	☐	☐
• Personality—what sort of person I am	☐	☐	☐	☐	☐	☐	☐

A7. Please indicate the extent to which the expatriate manager has changed the following aspects of *your work*.

(Tick one box in each row)	Extremely Small Extent	Very Small Extent	Small Extent	Moderate Extent	Large Extent	Very Large Extent	Extremely Large Extent
• Work targets/objectives	☐	☐	☐	☐	☐	☐	☐
• The methods used to achieve work targets/objectives	☐	☐	☐	☐	☐	☐	☐
• The order in which different parts of the job are done	☐	☐	☐	☐	☐	☐	☐
• With whom you deal with in order to carry out your work duties	☐	☐	☐	☐	☐	☐	☐

A8. Please indicate how satisfied you are with the following aspects of the way in which the expatriate manager works.

Please write a number for each statement, based on the following scale:

1	2	3	4	5	6	7
Very Dissatisfied	Dissatisfied	Slightly Dissatisfied	Neither Satisfied nor Dissatisfied	Slightly Satisfied	Satisfied	Very Satisfied

- The amount of respect and fair treatment I receive from him/her ☐
- The amount of support and guidance I receive from him/her ☐
- The overall quality of the supervision I receive from him/her ☐

A9. Please indicate the extent to which your expectations of the expatriate manager's leadership are being fulfilled.

Please write a number in each box, based on the following scale:

1	2	3	4	5	6	7
Extremely Small Extent	Very Small Extent	Small Extent	Moderate Extent	Large Extent	Very Large Extent	Extremely Large Extent

- Overall, to what extent do you feel the expatriate manager is performing his/her job the way you would like it to be performed? ☐
- To what extent has the expatriate manager met your expectations in his/her managerial roles and responsibilities? ☐
- If you had your way, to what extent would you change the way in which the expatriate manager is doing the job? ☐

B. *Your view about the expatriate manager's leadership behavior*
B1. Please indicate to what extent the expatriate manager <u>currently uses</u> each of the following leadership behaviors.

Please write a number in each box, based on the following scale:

1	2	3	4	5	6	7
Extremely Small Extent	Very Small Extent	Small Extent	Moderate Extent	Large Extent	Very Large Extent	Extremely Large Extent

- Plan how to use personnel and resources to accomplish a task efficiently ☐
- Clarify what results are expected for a task ☐
- Explain priorities for different task objectives ☐

- Monitor operations and performance of subordinates ☐
- Provide support and encouragement to subordinates ☐
- Provide recognition for achievements and contributions ☐
- Provide coaching and mentoring when appropriate ☐
- Consult with people on decisions affecting them ☐
- Empower people to take initiative in problem solving ☐

B2. Please indicate to what extent the expatriate <u>used each behavior in the first three months</u> working in this subsidiary.

Please write a number in each box, based on the following scale:

0	1	2	3	4	5	6	7
Don't know	Extremely Small Extent	Very Small Extent	Small Extent	Moderate Extent	Large Extent	Very Large Extent	Extremely Large Extent

- Plan how to use personnel and resources to accomplish a task efficiently ☐
- Clarify what results are expected for a task ☐
- Explain priorities for different task objectives ☐
- Monitor operations and performance of subordinates. ☐
- Provide support and encouragement to subordinates ☐
- Provide recognition for achievements and contributions ☐
- Provide coaching and mentoring when appropriate ☐
- Consult with people on decisions affecting them ☐
- Empower people to take initiative in problem solving ☐

B3. Please indicate extent to which you perceive he/she <u>should use</u> each behavior.

Please write a number in each box, based on the following scale:

0	1	2	3	4	5	6	7
Don't know	Extremely Small Extent	Very Small Extent	Small Extent	Moderate Extent	Large Extent	Very Large Extent	Extremely Large Extent

- Plan how to use personnel and resources to accomplish a task efficiently ☐
- Clarify what results are expected for a task ☐
- Explain priorities for different task objectives ☐
- Monitor operations and performance of subordinates. ☐

- Provide support and encouragement to subordinates ☐
- Provide recognition for achievements and contributions ☐
- Provide coaching and mentoring when appropriate ☐
- Consult with people on decisions affecting them ☐
- Empower people to take initiative in problem solving ☐

C. *You and your job*

C1. Please indicate the extent to which you feel the following statements accurately describe your job and your own behavior when you are at work. Remember: There are no right or wrong answers. Your responses will be held in strict confidence.

Please write a number for each statement, based on the following scale:

1	2	3	4	5	6	7
Very inaccurate	Mostly inaccurate	Slightly inaccurate	Uncertain	Slightly accurate	Mostly accurate	Very accurate

- My job requires me to use a specific set of steps. ☐
- There is a specific way my job has to be done. ☐
- There are different kinds of work for me to do every day in my job. ☐
- I do the same tasks all the time. ☐
- Every day I have something different to do. ☐
- The job denies me any chance to use my personal initiative or judgment in carrying out the work. ☐
- The job gives me considerable opportunity for independence and freedom in how I do the work. ☐
- The job gives me almost complete responsibility for deciding how and when the work is done. ☐
- I do my best work when my job assignments are fairly difficult. ☐
- I try very hard to improve on my past performance at work. ☐
- I take moderate risks to get ahead at work. ☐
- I try to avoid any added responsibilities in my job. ☐
- I try to perform better than my co-workers. ☐
- In my work assignments, I try to be my own boss. ☐
- I go my own way at work, regardless of the opinions of others. ☐
- I disregard rules and regulations that hamper my personal freedom. ☐

- I consider myself a "team player" at work.   □
- I try my best to work alone on a job.   □

C2. Please indicate the degree to which you agree or disagree with each of the following statement.

Please write a number for each statement, based on the following scale:

1	2	3	4	5	6	7
Strongly disagree	Moderately disagree	Slightly disagree	Neither agree nor disagree	Slightly agree	Moderately agree	Strongly agree

- I am quite proud to be able to tell people who it is I work for.   □
- I feel myself to be part of the organization.   □
- In my work I like to feel I am making some effort, not just for myself but for the organization as well.   □
- I like to know that my own work makes a contribution to the good of the organization.   □
- Even if the firm were not doing well financially, I would be reluctant to change to another employer.   □
- The offer of a bit more money with another employer would not seriously make me think of changing my job.   □
- Generally speaking, I am very satisfied with the kind of work I have to do on my job.   □
- I frequently think of quitting my job.   □
- Generally speaking, I am very satisfied with my job.   □
- Children should be taught to obey authority.   □
- In this complicated world, the only way to know what to do is to rely on leaders and experts.   □
- Any good leader should be strict with people under him in order to gain their respect.   □
- One should always show respect to those in authority.   □
- You should obey your superiors whether or not you think they're right.   □

D. Please tell us something about yourself

*The information given is *anonymous* and will only be used for interpreting the results of this survey.*

D1. Are you male or female?

Male ☐

Female ☐

D2. How old are you?

20–24 ☐ 35–39 ☐ 50–54 ☐

25–29 ☐ 40–44 ☐ 55–59 ☐

30–34 ☐ 45–49 ☐ 60 or over ☐

D3. What is the highest educational qualification you hold?

Junior high school ☐

High school ☐

College ☐

University ☐

Masters ☐

PhD ☐

Other (please specify):_____

D4. How long have you worked at this organization?

Less than 1 year ☐

Between one and two years ☐

Between two and five years ☐

Between five and ten years ☐

Ten years or more ☐

D5. What is your job function area?

(please tick all that apply)

Finance or Accounting ☐

Sales and Marketing ☐

Production ☐

Human Resources ☐

Information Technology ☐

Operations ☐

Research and Development ☐

Administration ☐

Other (please specify) _____ ☐

D6. If there are any comments that you would like to make on any of the above issues, please write them here.

Thank you very much for your help!

Name Index

Subject Index